To Lou and Marcia,
If you laugh every day
for the next 80 years, you'll
live a long time and never
grow old! Lynne
Alpern

HUMOR AT WORK

HUMOR AT WORK

The Guaranteed, Bottom-Line, Low-Cost, High-Efficiency Guide to Success Through Humor

Esther Blumenfeld and Lynne Alpern

PEACHTREE PUBLISHERS, LTD.
ATLANTA

Published by
PEACHTREE PUBLISHERS, LTD.
494 Armour Circle, NE
Atlanta, Georgia 30324

Cover design by **janteldesign, *Atlanta***
Interior design by **Twin Studios, *Atlanta***

Manufactured in the United States of America

10 9 8 7 6 5 4 3 2 1

This book is an expanded, updated, and revised edition of *The Smile Connection* (Prentice-Hall, Inc., 1986).

Library of Congress Cataloging-in-Publication Data
Blumenfeld, Esther.
Humor at work : the guaranteed, bottom-line, low-cost, high-efficiency guide to success through humor / Esther Blumenfeld and Lynne Alpern.
p. cm.
Rev. ed. of: The smile connection : how to use humor in dealing with people / Esther Blumenfeld and Lynne Alpern. c1986.
Includes index.
ISBN 1-56145-085-5 (pbk.)
1. Interpersonal relations. 2. Wit and humor—Social aspects. 3. Wit and humor—Psychological aspects. I. Alpern, Lynne. II. Blumenfeld, Esther. Smile connection. III. Title.
HM132.B58 1994
152.4—dc20 93-43081
CIP

DEDICATION

For Warren and Joshua, with whom
I've shared love and the richest laughter.
And for Aunt Ruth.

Esther

For my own fountain of youth — Bob, Ken, and Eve.

Lynne

ACKNOWLEDGMENTS

Laughing with other people creates a strong bond, and we enjoyed the laughs we shared with those who contributed their own special blend of encouragement and humor to this book.

Our additional thanks to Linda Agro, JoDale Brodnax, Max Cleland, Jack Duncan, Douglas Fletcher, William F. Fry Jr., Nancy Goldberg, Joel Goodman, Mark Johnson, Marsha Londe, Harry Maziar, Mike Mescon, Karen Nussbaum, Robert Orben, June Ray, Karl Richter, Vera Robinson, Bob Rozakis, Ruth Shapiro, Ina Slutsky, Saul Sutel, and Erwin Zaban. Our appreciation also to attorney Mary Ann Oakley, for her professional opinion concerning sexual harassment.

For our chapter on teaching we especially thank the following teachers for graciously sharing their experiences: David Anderson, Gary Engler, Gloria Winger, David Hegner, Stephanie Radke, Rick Owens, and Ronald Lee Rubin. And a special thanks to Karyn Buxman, R.N., M.S., for her listing of hospital humor rooms in *The Professional Nurse's Role in Developing a Humor Room in a Health Care Setting,* her 1990 thesis at the University of Missouri-Columbia.

And finally, we also want to thank Margaret Quinlin, Emily Wright, Bruce Covey, Vicky Holifield, Kathy Landwehr, Loraine Balscik, and their hard-working colleagues at Peachtree Publishers, Ltd. If we have inadvertently omitted anyone's name, please forgive us. If you're Esther's friend, it is Lynne's fault. If you're Lynne's friend, it is Esther's fault. And if you're a friend of both, it is our editor's fault.

TABLE OF

PART THREE
COMMUNICATION

PART FOUR
SPECIFIC PROFESSIONS

PART FIVE
PARENTING

PART SIX
GETTING FUNNY

PREFACE

Let's suppose that your job includes picking up a twenty-pound rock every day and walking around town for thirteen miles. Each hour the rock feels heavier and heavier, until you feel you can't take another step. If you do make it down the home stretch, you'll be exhausted, your muscles will be sore, and you'll have no energy, mental or physical, to cope with anything at home. Not only that, how heavy will your rock feel tomorrow? Will you even be able to pick it up again?

But imagine, as you're hiking through town, that you stop every hour, set your rock aside for a few minutes, and rest. You'll have time to forget your burden and relax your muscles. Then, when you do pick that load up again, it won't feel any heavier than the first time you lifted it. Your muscles won't be overtaxed, and you'll be able to cope, reach your goal, and begin again tomorrow.

Laughter can accomplish the same thing. Taking a humor break, scheduling time for fun, and looking at situations from a humorous perspective can recharge the physical and emotional energies necessary to keep stress manageable. Humor allows you to set aside your troubles and responsibilities. Not to ignore them, but to set them aside briefly, while you renew yourself.

So *caveat emptor!* Let the buyer beware, because this book is going to show you how to open yourself up to laughter. Once you've increased your humor awareness, it's likely to change the way you look at life. But that's not so bad—maybe it's time for a change.

This book about using humor effectively is an outgrowth of the humor workshops we conduct throughout the country and the course we teach in the Community Educational Services Department at Emory University, "Adding Humor to Your Life: The Salt-Free, Low-Calorie, Polyunsaturated, All-Natural Guide to Feeling Good."

But now it's time to zero in on humor and the workplace. We incorporate important resources in Chapter 14, add information about the relationship between humor and productivity and creativity, and provide great detail in the applications of humor at work, which we define as individual or cooperative efforts to achieve a goal, whether as salaried members of the work force or volunteers on committees, in neighborhood associations, or in charities.

Something is out of whack when humor becomes a luxury. As a positive attitude toward people and circumstances, humor is a life-giving force. Besides being fun, laughter bridges gaps in age, background, and experience—a skill vital to anyone who has to come out from behind the desk every once in a while.

HUMOR OFTEN SUCCEEDS AS A COMMUNICATION TOOL WHEN OTHER METHODS FAIL

Although laughter cannot make problems magically disappear, it is possible to take yourself lightly while still being serious about work. A humorous approach can help you face the enormous challenges and daily disappointments of the nine to five world and provides the resilience to begin again.

The suggestions, warm-up exercises, and examples throughout the book will stretch your funny bone and improve your own humor fitness as you pump up your humor skills. Like any other communication technique, humor takes time and practice to develop its full potential. We hope you will use our ideas as a springboard for finding what works best for you.

WHAT'S IN IT FOR YOU?

Rarely has attention been paid to why women have trouble using humor. Chapter 8 explores not only the sources of this problem, but also the ramifications and solutions for contemporary women. Men and women can learn to recognize the negative uses of humor, gauge its effects, and discover how and when it is used to disguise aggression and anger, and how to deal with those who manipulate it. Other chapters explore the beneficial uses of humor in the health professions, in the classroom, in sales and training, and for secretaries and other unsung heroes who every day are caught on the firing line between the customer and the boss. We focused on these professions for several reasons:

1. The suggestions and examples for using humor in these four professions have wide-ranging possibilities in other fields.
2. The health professions are breaking new ground in the use of humor as a potent ally in healing.
3. The material on humor in teaching addresses one of America's most pressing concerns—improving the educational environment.
4. Most people recognize that the sales profession often uses humor to establish rapport with customers.
5. Millions of secretaries who survive the daily crunch with their sense of humor intact can teach us all a lesson or two.

Other chapters demonstrate applications of humor in public speaking and conducting meetings. You will learn how humor can reduce stress when you are the boss, how you can create a more cooperative atmosphere when dealing with difficult people, and how a laugh can grease the wheel of friendship with new business contacts.

Since the pressures and tensions you carry home from work affect everyone in your family, Chapter 13 will help you communicate more effectively at home when the workday is over. With the increase in two-career families, controlling these stresses is even more important in keeping your balance and fostering cooperation, fun, and realistic expectations with family. And you will pick up practical pointers on why and how humor is helpful in dealing with children.

Chapter 14 is a compilation of recommended reading along with a detailed listing of professional humor consultants, organizations, hospital humor programs, courses, and subscription materials.

AND THE PUNCH LINE IS...

Laughter is instantaneous and brief, yet its effects can be positive and lasting. It is far from frivolous if it can reduce stress, enhance communication, and improve the quality of your life. And that's why there's no business that isn't funny business. Humor is accessible. It adds zest to life, and it is absolutely free.

People consciously pursue education, a brighter future, a better job. Why not, for the pleasure of your company, also pursue a happier, healthier, and more humorous perspective to help you cope with the complexities of the workplace? If, after reading this book, you recall, overhear, or experience an interchange at work or after hours in which humor played a part, we encourage you to write us, especially on Mondays, the toughest day of any work week:

Esther Blumenfeld and Lynne Alpern , PO Box 421461, Atlanta, GA 30342

PART

The Foundation

Humor on the Job: The Pleasure of Your Company

LAYING THE FOUNDATION FOR HUMOR AT WORK

"I never mix business with pleasure."

That may be your first mistake! Increasingly, on-the-job studies and interviews with business leaders indicate that for many top executives, humor is an integral part of their management style. Properly used, humor can help resolve conflicts, open communication, relieve office tensions, and promote teamwork, whether you work as president of IBM or as a volunteer for a charity or neighborhood association.

In the past, humor has been neglected by researchers because it doesn't lend itself easily to experimental procedures. It is difficult to control and measure. But because humor plays an important role in human relations, and human relations deal with the ways people in organizations behave toward each other, researchers are increasingly interested in learning how to describe, predict, and control humor at work.

A survey of leading business executives and business school deans conducted by Richard J. Cronin for his executive search firm in Rosemont, Illinois, shows that sixty-two percent of the deans responding believe that humor and executive success are related. And, "significantly, the corporate

CEOs (chief executive officers), almost to a man agreed that humor in business is healthy and important to the conduct of business; executives should develop a greater sense of humor in conducting business activities, and all other qualifications being equal, they would hire the job applicant with a better sense of humor."

GOOD HUMAN RELATIONS CAN BE TRANSLATED INTO DOLLARS

People working for the same organization all depend on the same business for their livelihood. Thus, avoiding strife as much as possible is cost-effective for everyone. But life-styles, backgrounds, and interests outside the office are often drastically different.

So how do you get along with people with whom you have to work every day but don't necessarily have much else in common?

For the humor to be used constructively, first there has to be a regard for individual differences and at least some basic feeling of respect and trust among people who are carrying their fair work load. Only then can a mutually supportive relationship, including humor, be developed.

Humor is not a cure-all, but it can be an effective bonding agent to help create a new sense of rapport. Used effectively, it can help reinforce feelings of "we are all in this together."

WHERE TO BEGIN

Dealing with reality is what humor is all about—making the imperfections more bearable and taking the bad with the good. Before you can lay the foundation for humor at work, you need to ask yourself some questions to evaluate the existing humor atmosphere in your office.

1. How many hours do you spend at work? How many enjoyable hours do you spend at work?

2. You need to take your work seriously, but are you taking yourself too seriously? How do you feel your professional image would change if you lightened up a bit?

3. Is your office atmosphere comfortable? Are you and your co-workers secure enough to poke fun at yourselves while creating climate for reciprocal humor?

4. Does anyone in your workplace use humor to make mistakes more bearable and the pressures more tolerable, and does it ease the bad days?

5. Is most of the humor used at work stress-reducing or stress-producing? That is, does it make people comfortable or uncomfortable?

6. Is humor being used as a break from the tedium or as a motivator to increase productivity?

7. Are the lines of communication open for cooperation and friendship?

8. Is humor being used to train employees and help sell ideas and products? Does anyone use it effectively to reinforce the recall of those ideas?

9. Does anyone in your office use humor as a tool for defusing anger, easing criticism, or facilitating negotiations?

10. Is humor being used to stimulate creativity?

By answering these questions, you will find that some people's approach to humor is not as haphazard as you might have thought. There are people around you who know how to use humor deliberately and constructively as a tool to get the job done in the best way possible. It is part of their style.

However, everyone's style is different. No two people are alike, nor should they be. No one can teach you to be humorous, but as you become more aware of the untapped resources in humor you will be able to adapt them to your particular personality and individual style.

For instance, a low-keyed personality may be more comfortable with understated humor, like the hospital supervisor who was scheduled for minor surgery:

The young admissions clerk was quite nervous when she discovered she had been chosen to fill out her boss's admission papers. As soon as her supervisor arrived, he was ushered into her office. Without so much as a hello, trying to be as efficient as possible, she immediately began asking him the questions on the form. Without looking up from her paperwork she recorded as he fired back the answers. When she got to the question, "Church preference?" without hesitating he murmured, "Gothic." Startled, the clerk then laughed heartily.

The young admissions clerk was quite nervous when she discovered she had been chosen to fill out her boss's admission papers. As soon as her supervisor arrived, he was ushered into her office. Without so much as a hello, trying to be as efficient as possible, she immediately began asking him the questions on the form. Without looking up from her paperwork she recorded as he fired back the answers. When she got to the question, "Church preference?" without hesitating he murmured, "Gothic." Startled, the clerk then laughed heartily.

This simple use of understated humor by a boss eased the stress and made the situation more comfortable. At the same time it set an atmosphere for easier communication in the future. As you become more secure in your position at work, and if the boss is open to humor, you can use it the other way around, too.

At a twenty-fifth anniversary celebration of a Fortune 500 company, a division president went up to the microphone and said, "On this special occasion, I feel it's time to be very honest with the chairman of the board. When I applied for this job twenty years ago, he asked me how much money I was making, and I told him $125 a week. I guess now it won't hurt to admit that at the time I was really only making one hundred dollars week." After the laughter subsided, the chairman of the board responded, "I appreciate your confession, but actually I was prepared to pay you $150."

This flamboyant banter, in contrast to the previous example, was more in keeping with the personalities and style of both highly successful executives. This exchange in front of an audience combined all the elements of stress-reducing humor. Here's another example of constructive humor, this time between co-workers in a midwestern high school.

A school nurse and the attendance counselor shared adjacent offices. Twice during the week, the nurse visited another school. In her absence the counselor, through necessity, had taken care of a few minor health emergencies. The nurse felt guilty because she knew this wasn't her co-worker's job. But on the other hand, if a student fainted over her desk, the counselor couldn't ignore the girl until the nurse returned.

One day, agitated because she had been unnecessarily detained at the other school, the flustered nurse rushed back.

Arriving much later than expected, she found a boy lying on the cot in her office with a large bandage on his nose. When she questioned him, he told her he had been bitten by a rat in biology lab. She dreaded facing an upset co-worker, but

A school nurse and the attendance counselor shared adjacent offices. Twice during the week, the nurse visited another school. In her absence the counselor, through necessity, had taken care of a few minor health emergencies. The nurse felt guilty because she knew this wasn't her co-worker's job. But on the other hand, if a student fainted over her desk, the counselor couldn't ignore the girl until the nurse returned.

One day, agitated because she had been unnecessarily detained at the other school, the flustered nurse rushed back.

Arriving much later than expected, she found a boy lying on the cot in her office with a large bandage on his nose. When she questioned him, he told her he had been bitten by a rat in biology lab. She dreaded facing an upset co-worker, but knew she'd have to get the details immediately. Timidly she knocked on the door and entered the counselor's office, but before she could say anything, the woman greeted her with, "Don't worry, I isolated the rat. He's all yours!"

knew she'd have to get the details immediately. Timidly she knocked on the door and entered the counselor's office, but before she could say anything, the woman greeted her with, "Don't worry, I isolated the rat. He's all yours!"

The counselor could have responded angrily to the nurse's late arrival, but instead chose a humorous quip to defuse a potentially volatile situation. Although these co-workers shared little in common outside the workplace, humor created a foundation of positive feelings on which to build a later discussion on solving their work-related problems.

These are only three examples of thousands of humorous exchanges that go on at work every day. So how do you build a humor foundation for your own particular situations? Start slowly—finish fast.

1. *Start slowly.* Observe and listen for funny work-related anecdotes or incidents. Write down those you want to remember and which can be told at an appropriate occasion in the future (see humor journal, Chapter 2).

2. *Begin reading books of humor collections* and write down those quotes, stories, or jokes that apply to you or your work situation.

3. *Take one anecdote and experiment with it.* Personalize it by surrounding it with true details from your work situation and then try it out on a few co-workers.

EXAMPLE: "I have two brothers, one in the_______business and one sentenced to the electric chair. My problem is, if I want to impress the man I'm going to marry, should I tell him about my brother in the_______business?"

4. *Be prepared.* Think of some humorous "wish I had said" responses and change them to "next time it happens, I'm going to say" responses.

   EXAMPLE: An editor tells her reporter to "put the article through the typewriter one more time."

   RESPONSE: "I took your suggestion and put the article through the typewriter one more time, but that didn't work. I still had to sit down and rewrite it."

5. *Focus your humor on yourself and your work situation,* not on other people (particularly if you don't know them well). "I've been sitting at this desk so long I don't know where my back leaves off and the chair begins." And finally,

6. *If you think of an appropriate funny response,* don't hesitate—use it!

WHY HUMOR?

Unlike fairy tales, laughter cannot make all our beastly problems magically disappear. However, coupled with an ability to think and reason, a humorous approach to life can help you recast those troubles in a different light and cope with an imperfect world. Humor is more than the mere ability to tell funny jokes and stories. Laughter not only helps you face your disappointments but provides the resilience to begin again. Yet laughter is more than a coping mechanism.

At a twenty-fifth anniversary celebration of a Fortune 500 company, a division president went up to the microphone and said, "On this special occasion, I feel it's time to be very honest with the chairman of the board. When I applied for this job twenty years ago, he asked me how much money I was making, and I told him $125 a week. I guess now it won't hurt to admit that at the time I was really only making one hundred dollars week." After the laughter subsided, the chairman of the board responded, "I appreciate your confession, but actually I was prepared to pay you $150."

Think about someone you consider young at heart. What makes that person seem ageless? Along with mental alertness and an upbeat attitude in general, a large part of your answer will lie in good humor and a sense of playfulness. The *real* fountain of youth is humor, and its sound is bubbling laughter.

YOU DON'T NEED A LICENSE TO LAUGH

In *Iacocca: An Autobiography,* Lee Iacocca expresses amazement that executives boast they worked so hard they didn't take any vacation. To Iacocca, it's nothing to be proud of. "I always feel like responding, 'You dummy. You mean to tell me that you can take responsibility for an eighty million dollar project and you can't plan two weeks out of the year to go off with your family and have some fun?'"

Laughter makes life fun, and regular doses of humor, especially at work, are a healthy tonic. Laughter is good for us, both mentally and physically, and no one is too old or too young to enjoy the benefits of hearty laughter.

When we laugh, we feel alive. "It felt so good to laugh." "I needed a good laugh." "I laughed until I cried." Laughter is a positive emotion. And as long as we choose to laugh, it means we affirm life—no matter how burdensome it might become.

It is sometimes difficult for aware, thinking people to deal with their own vulnerabilities, the imperfections of others, or unexpected troublesome events. Without a sense of humor, too often the chosen alternative is to withdraw or become the pessimist whom John Galsworthy described as "always building dungeons in the air."

A Russian negotiator joked with an American: "Do you know the difference between a communist and a capitalist? In capitalism, man exploited man. In communism, it was the other way around."

No matter how carefully we map the path of our future, there are times when each of us has to cross a rickety bridge, face an unexpected beast, or climb back out of a dark depression along the way. Nothing's fun all the time, but if you *never* have any fun, something is wrong.

Tactics differ for dealing with various problems. But approaching aggravations with a tinge of humor results in fewer harmful side effects than anger or aggression and de-beastifies the problem by tempering a wide range of annoyances.

The rules of society can constrict, and humor offers a temporary escape. With a hint of playfulness, laughter can release feelings of hostility, veil aggression, or cloak anger and, at the same time, provide an acceptable means of expressing and decompressing these feelings.

Even in repressive societies, where jokes are often censored and humor is suspect, people have always managed to find humorous expression. A Russian negotiator joked with an American: "Do you know the difference between a communist and a capitalist? In capitalism, man exploited man. In communism, it was the other way around."

Humor requires a measure of both truth and distortion. What seems logical is often illogical, and humorous expression springs from the ability to view these incongruities through a mental fun-house mirror.

A humorous approach offers more than frivolous pleasure. It gives us balance and adds color to the human condition.

LAUGHTER, THE UNIVERSAL LANGUAGE

Humor can be found in every culture, and laughter has been with us since the beginning of the recorded history of civilization. As King Solomon exhorts in the Bible, "A merry heart doth good like medicine." Finely honed wit exists in every form of literature as playwrights, essayists, novelists, and poets sharpen their quills with ingenious puns and dissect the truth with humorous paradox.

Renowned artists and musicians have also used humorous expression as a means of communication. Social satire can be found in the lithographs of Daumier, and Haydn's trick of waking dozers with an unexpected bombastic chord in a serene passage of his *Surprise* Symphony is probably music's most famous practical joke.

Humor also bridges cultural gaps and language barriers. This is beautifully demonstrated in pictures of laughing children in countries around the world reacting to the clowning antics of the Sesame Street Muppets.

The surprising power of humor is that the laugh is so short-lived, but its effects so lasting.

THE HUMOR EQUATION

Sigmund Freud, the founder of psychoanalysis, said, "Joking activity should not, after all, be described as pointless or aimless, since it has the unmistakable aim of evoking pleasure in its hearers." [1]

> "Joking activity should not, after all, be described as pointless or aimless, since it has the unmistakable aim of evoking pleasure in its hearers."
>
> Sigmund Freud

If television's Comedy Channel were playing in an empty room, would the impact be the same as if you were watching? Obviously not, because creating humor is only half of the equation. No one can create humor in a vacuum. Without an audience Roseanne Arnold would just be a boisterous, disheveled, put-upon mother muttering to herself about her kids. Comedians base their livelihood on making a person-to-person connection, and the one who reacts with laughter is just as important to the equation as the person who initiates the joke.

Humor, therefore, requires a stimulus and a response. And although one person can produce both by himself, it is the shared experience that makes an impact and gives so much pleasure. So why humor?

1. Humor makes work fun.
2. Humor can help us cope with problems.
3. Humor with a hint of playfulness is a safety valve for aggression and an acceptable means to express anger.
4. Humor offers perspective and balance.
5. Humor isn't fattening.

6. Humor is a means of communication and creative expression.
7. Humor provides temporary relief from society's restrictive regulations.
8. Humor is a way to express the truth even when truth is feared and repressed.
9. Humor is mentally and physically good for you.
10. Laughter affirms life and brings people together.
11. Humor often succeeds where other methods have failed.
12. It beats all the alternatives.

Laying the Cornerstone: Who, What, When, Where, and How Funny Is It?

INCREASING YOUR HUMOR AWARENESS

If a burly man crept down the street wearing black leather pants, a floppy black hat, a black satin cape, with a pink sack slung over his shoulder filled with clanking silverware, the ordinary citizen probably wouldn't even notice him. On the other hand, a police officer, because of his specialized training and heightened sensitivity to people and daily events, might become a bit suspicious. (At least he would wonder why the sack wasn't more in keeping with the rest of the outfit.)

Although the example may be a bit extreme, the point is not. As we become more absorbed in ourselves, we become less aware of life around us in general and certainly less aware of the humor in every quarter, ready for the taking. Humor is accessible. It adds spice to life, and it is absolutely free!

Every day you get up, brush your teeth, get dressed, have breakfast, and get ready to begin your day. Do you look up to make sure the sky is still there? Doubtful. If you're like most people, you rarely notice the sky at all, unless the weatherman has forecast locusts. But whether you notice it or not, it's there.

So is humor. It's there whether you notice it or not. All you have to do is look for it. That sounds simple enough, yet how many of us take the time to thaw out our long-frozen humor skills to warm up our life for a moment? Awareness means sticking up your humor antenna, tuning in to different vibrations, and interpreting what's going on around you in a new way.

Children are naturally sensitive to funny things because they view life with a peripheral humorous vision. As we get older, however, parents and teachers tell us to "grow up" or "get serious." And in the process, many of us stifle spontaneous humorous expression. The more serious we become, the more our awareness of humor diminishes and in many cases becomes completely dormant.

With many people the childlike quality that created easy laughter when you were ten years old is now buried. But you are still the same person. That ten-year-old child is in there somewhere, only the facade has changed. Being childlike does not mean being childish. It means opening yourself up once more to spontaneity, imagination, creativity, and fun.

So now is the time to *really* get serious—serious about nurturing your sense of humor. Here's how to begin.

OPEN YOUR CIRCLE OF AWARENESS

Start Doing Things Differently

Try varying your daily routine, doing something a little different each day. Whether it's merely altering your pre-breakfast ritual or driving a different route to work, the very act of altering your set patterns will make you more conscious of details in your surroundings and will help you begin changing customary thought patterns.

Tomorrow when you get dressed, put your left sock on first and imagine the humorous consequences of doing so. Your boss will notice you are walking with a jaunty gait, and this self-assured attitude will stimulate him to give you that raise you've been wanting. Your raise will be so astonishing it will be reported on the six o'clock evening news. And anyone who can get a raise mentioned on television is definitely suitable to run for public office. The opportunities for the future become unlimited.

Tomorrow when you get dressed, put your left sock on first and imagine the humorous consequences of doing so. Your boss will notice you are walking with a jaunty gait, and this self-assured attitude will stimulate him to give you that raise you've been wanting. Your raise will be so astonishing it will be reported on the six o'clock evening news. And anyone who can get a raise mentioned on television is definitely suitable to run for public office. The opportunities for the future become unlimited.

In reality, changing your sock ritual won't change your life, but altering your daily routine will force you to think about what you're doing, provide fodder for your imagination, and open viewpoints for expanded humor awareness.

Lighten Up With New Assumptions

Stop old assumptions about what's going on around you. Other people's viewpoints need not be yours. Nor, for that matter, does your old way of looking at things need to be the only way you can see them. As soon as you break old patterns, almost anything can be viewed from a humorous angle. Let's say that it is early in the morning, and you are driving your teenaged son to school. He begins to cough.

You have two choices: ask him if he's feeling all right and go to the drugstore for cough drops, or compliment him on having a terrific cough for a sixteen-year-old boy who doesn't smoke. Then you can point out that with such a juicy cough, he has an ideal vehicle for impressing his friends. First of all, instruct him to cough and tell his friends, "I've got to cut down." Then tell him not to brush his teeth for a few days so they will become stained. Furthermore, he can rub yellow food coloring on the top knuckle of his index finger as a mark of distinction and sprinkle ashes on his clothes to achieve the appropriate aroma. That way, you finally point out, he can be a "rebel" without killing himself. New assumptions can be both fun and illuminating. As an exercise in stimulating creativity and perspective at our humor workshops we ask participants to find new uses for ordinary objects.

- A bowling ball became a balloon for pessimists or a new method of birth control (place it between the two people).
- A paper clip, straightened out, became a lightning rod for a tiny house.
- A saltine cracker became a placemat for a roach.
- A tennis ball sliced in half became a shell to hold to your ear and listen to the roar of John McEnroe.

Try it yourself to expand your view of everyday objects and rev up your creative juices.

Start Paying Attention to What's Going On Around You

All of us get caught up in our own concerns and our *circle of awareness* tightens around us. Look up from your own navel (it isn't going anywhere) and take note of the people and happenings around you.

Be Adventurous

Try approaching people with humor, and you'll find most people will respond favorably.

A nursing instructor, on her way to teach a CPR class, put a life-sized infant mannequin in the trunk of her car. The trunk wouldn't accommodate Resusci-Annie, the adult mannequin, so she tossed Annie into the front seat, belting her in to keep her from flopping around. As she pulled out, the mannequin slumped over into an unnatural position.

For the next ten blocks, each time the nurse stopped at a red light she received frightened glances from passengers in the cars next to her. Suddenly she saw the blue flashing light of a police car. The police had received reports of a woman with a dead body in her car.

As the patrolman walked over, the nurse realized what had happened, rolled down her window and said, "If you think this looks suspicious, officer, wait till you see what I've got in the trunk!"

A nursing instructor, on her way to teach a CPR class, put a life-sized infant mannequin in the trunk of her car. The trunk wouldn't accommodate Resusci-Annie, the adult mannequin, so she tossed Annie into the front seat, belting her in to keep her from flopping around. As she pulled out, the mannequin slumped over into an unnatural position.

For the next ten blocks, each time the nurse stopped at a red light she received frightened glances from passengers in the cars next to her. Suddenly she saw the blue flashing light of a police car. The police had received reports of a woman with a dead body in her car.

As the patrolman walked over, the nurse realized what had happened, rolled down her window and said, "If you think this looks suspicious, officer, wait till you see what I've got in the trunk!"

She could have responded in anger, berating the policeman for making her late to class, in turn making him angry. But instead she approached the problem with humor and turned what could have been an unpleasant incident into a good story for her class.

INCREASE YOUR LISTENING SKILLS

After you begin changing your primary level of awareness, it is time to start listening. Hearing the melody is easy. The real trick is listening for the counterpoint and the dissonance that hold the key to humor both at work and after hours with your family.

Listen to Your Inner Voice

Mama always told us to think before we speak, and there are times when that advice is appropriate. But constant hesitation kills the spontaneity so vital to humor. So even if you aren't ready to voice your reaction aloud, take note of your first, uncensored response.

A college student attended a lecture in a large, crowded auditorium. Afterward he thought to himself, "That speaker really underwhelmed me with his logic." He was too shy to say it, and the stranger next to him never heard it. However, his mental response turned an unpleasant situation into a humorous one for him, and that was a beginning.

If your first reaction seems funny to you, but you're reluctant to say it aloud, test it with friends. Later you'll get the courage to be more spontaneous among strangers.

Listen to What Makes Your Friends AND Co-workers Laugh and Decide if Their Brand of Humor Is Acceptable to You

Is everyone included? Is the result constructive? If the humor is appropriate, it should make you comfortable and happy, and you should be able to build on it. You can increase your sensitivity to what kind of humor is acceptable by becoming aware of what hurts people. If even one person in the group is uncomfortable with the type of humor being used, then it is a pretty good bet that the humor is inappropriate and will serve no positive purpose. In fact, in the workplace it can be detrimental. In this way you can match the humor to a particular individual and group.

If something isn't funny to you, however, it doesn't necessarily mean it isn't funny to someone else. And what's funny in one situation may not be appropriate in another. Don Rickles's style of humor may be a laugh riot in a club setting, but it can be devastating in an office.

Listen to Other People

Eavesdropping in public places is fun. We don't expect you to be up against a wall with a glass to your ear, but anyone talking loudly in public asks to be heard. There's a gaggle of incredible conversations going on out there, so pay attention in restaurants, department stores, or office building elevators. It can even make waiting in line worthwhile. It will more than likely be your *observation* that creates the humor. On the other hand, you might overhear, as comedy writers Bonnie and Terry Turner did in a Chinese restaurant, a snatch of conversation funny enough to inspire an entire skit: "It's not the egg roll, Harold, it's our whole life." Or this comment overheard on a Caribbean cruise ship, "My allergy is so much better since we sailed. What is the altitude here?"

Listen for Incongruities

People engrossed in conversation often don't listen to what comes out of their own mouths. Sometimes, what we try to say and what we really say are entirely different.

- "In Florida we drove across a bridge that is seven miles long, with water on both sides of it."
- Driving back to Texas from Florida, a bus passenger exclaimed, "Oh, I-10 goes west? I always thought it went east."

Listen for Malaprops, the Misuse of Words

If you've ever heard comedian Don Novello doing his character, Father Guido Sarducci, you know there's enough humor in the English language to sustain a career. Here is a sampling from our "pride of lines":

- "In small European towns, markets were the hublub of activity."
- "The Bible forbids fortification."
- She: "We had some wonderful soup in France called Beelzebub." He: "No, dear. It's named after one of the fish in it and it's called Billy bass."
- "The only activity our grandchildren are interested in at the circus is going on the cannibal rides."

Listen for Funny Stories and Jokes

This anecdote was overheard on an airplane:

A grandmother was sitting on the beach with her young grandson. He had on his little hat, his little sunsuit, and was playing with his little bucket and shovel. Suddenly a big wave came and swept the child out to sea. The grandmother fell to her knees and prayed. "Oh, God, please return my grandchild. He is such a sweet boy, such a good boy, such a wonderful child." Miraculously another big wave returned the child exactly to the spot where he had been before, unhurt, wearing his little sunsuit, carrying his little bucket and shovel. The grandmother looked to the heavens, threw up her arms, and cried out, "He had a hat!"

Listen for the Intentionally Funny Remark

Listen for the play on words that turns an ordinary phrase into a thing of beauty worth remembering and recording (and reusing):

> "He's very vitriolic." "You mean he's still using that greasy kid stuff in his hair?"

A grandmother was sitting on the beach with her young grandson. He had on his little hat, his little sunsuit, and was playing with his little bucket and shovel. Suddenly a big wave came and swept the child out to sea. The grandmother fell to her knees and prayed. "Oh, God, please return my grandchild. He is such a sweet boy, such a good boy, such a wonderful child." Miraculously another big wave returned the child exactly to the spot where he had been before, unhurt, wearing his little sunsuit, carrying his little bucket and shovel. The grandmother looked to the heavens, threw up her arms, and cried out, "He had a hat!"

"If God had intended us to see the sun rise,
He would have created it later in the day."

"Esprit d'rancorps"
. . . and it goes on and on.

KEEPING A HUMOR JOURNAL

As you increase your humor awareness, it is time to begin keeping a humor journal. Why have a humor collection? Well, most humorous observations and snatches of conversations flash through your consciousness briefly and then vanish. So unless you have a photographic memory, it is essential to write them down. Get in the habit of carrying a pen and paper or three-by-five cards with you and keep a small notebook or tape recorder in your car.

Record humorous anecdotes and unusual situations, as well as funny remarks and jokes. These can later form a base of relevant humor to use in particular situations (you will find specific examples throughout the book).

It is up to you how well organized you want your collection to be. Your humor journal can be any notebook, scrapbook, index card file, desk drawer, closet, or garage. No matter what you use, collecting and writing down humor regularly is a basic building block of humor at work. At first it takes a conscious effort to build your file, but keep at it until recording humorous events becomes a habit.

The owners of a hardware store enter the funny customer requests or comments into their computer at the end of each day. ("I found exactly what I'm looking for, but it isn't what I wanted.") It helps them keep their cool while dealing with the most outrageous customer, and ends their day with a laugh.

What to include? The following items are merely suggestions. Be creative and add any categories that appeal to your sense of humor. If you have a specific goal in mind (for instance, to use in presentations or meetings), you can tailor your collection accordingly.

1. Written humor is the easiest way to begin.

   Bumper stickers that tickle your fancy. Here's one seen on the Santa Monica Freeway—"Do schizophrenics pay double indemnity?"

   Odd newspaper headlines. We put this one on our classroom door—"No one spits on a smiling face."

Billboards. A true and enticing, "Myrtle Beach has 700 restaurants. There goes your diet."

Signs. Outside a church in Tampa, Florida, "We fitly pray."

Cartoons. Always fun, particularly those relating to your family, hobbies, and occupation.

2. Next, write down observations, funny comments, and especially anecdotes that appeal to you. Later you can adapt them to fit a particular situation or personalize them to suit your personality and lifestyle. These anecdotes are great sources for presentations, speeches, or correspondence.

When Gert's grandchildren came for a visit, they always worked in her restaurant. When Gert retired, her grandson fondly remembers, "Grandma was the only employer we ever had who made us do two hours of work for ten hours of pay."

We have collected anecdotes on a wide variety of subjects, from eating French onion soup at a power lunch to carpooling with a motivational tape fanatic. Here's one about mixing business with family:

When Gert's grandchildren came for a visit, they always worked in her restaurant. When Gert retired, her grandson fondly remembers,"Grandma was the only employer we ever had who made us do two hours of work for ten hours of pay."

3. Humor shared is doubled, so look for a kindred spirit in your office or business, someone with whom you can share a laugh. You will also find as you bring more humor into your life, you will naturally attract other people with a sense of humor.

   In the humor business it is definitely a something-for-something world—not only will you attract people who are funny themselves, but you will also attract those who just like to laugh. Laugh takers are attracted to laugh makers.

DEVELOPING A HUMOROUS PERSPECTIVE

Goodman Ace, the talented comedy writer, once said, "You can't overestimate the unimportance of practically everything." It was his way of encouraging us to put some balance back into our lives, to take a step back and give the everyday minor frustrations that confront us their appropriate value and rank in life. One of the best ways to do this is to develop a humorous outlook.

WIPE THAT SMILE BACK ON YOUR FACE

As we get older, society encourages us to bury our natural humorous impulses deeper and deeper. As we conform to customs and behavioral norms, we tend to overlook using humor even when it might be appropriate. So how can we recapture that humorous perspective? The first step is to understand and accept the imperfections and frailties in each of us.

HUMOR PERSPECTIVE AND SELF: IF YOU CAN LAUGH AT YOURSELF, YOU'RE A GROWN-UP

Having a good sense of humor is compensation for not being the fastest runner on the track team, the prettiest girl in the class, or the president of the company. If you don't like who you are, perhaps you have been too rigid about focusing on your own real or perceived imperfections. It's time to *lighten up on yourself.*

Severely disabled people, for instance, will often use humor to diminish the impact of their disability and help others concentrate on what is really important. Max Cleland, Georgia's Secretary of State and former director of the U.S. Veteran's Administration, uses humor to keep himself on an even keel. A Vietnam veteran and triple amputee, Cleland's matter-of-fact attitude and humorous perspective about his disability immediately put people at ease. Cleland, however, has not always used humor. "In the beginning I was a very humorless person, still caught up in dealing with the war and my disability. I was a very serious, cause-oriented, boring, ineffectual pain in the rear!" With time and insight, however, his style has changed both in public and private.

> "In the beginning I was a very humorless person, still caught up in dealing with the war and my disability. I was a very serious, cause-oriented, boring, ineffectual pain in the rear!"
>
> Max Cleland

When he went before the Congressional hearings to gain approval of his appointment at the Veteran's Administration, the mood was already positive. After the basics were covered, Senator Matsunaga from Hawaii, a World War II veteran, sensed the light-hearted nature of the moment and said, "Mr. Cleland, we look forward to your coming to Hawaii as the head of the Veteran's Administration. I make the trip so often the jet lag never goes away. When it's time to feel sexy, I feel hungry, and when it's time to be hungry, I feel sexy." And Cleland replied, "Well, Senator, I don't believe that comes within the province of the Veteran's Administration."

On a more personal note, Cleland took a date to a movie. When they arrived at the theater, he rolled his chair next to the only empty aisle seat, swung over into it and left the wheelchair for her.

So take heart. If you don't yet have a humorous perspective, it can be developed. Before you can view others from a humorous perspective, you first need to lighten up on yourself. Here's how:

1. Acknowledge that you are not perfect and never will be. Try to begin by laughing and gently poking fun at yourself and your imperfections.
2. Set realistic goals for yourself. Maybe that proposal can't possibly be finished by six PM. Then learn to recognize and joke about the times you still try to be SuperPerson.
3. In your daily routine of sleep, good nutrition, and exercise, find time for a humor break (maybe you enjoy pumping iron, but you'll never get a hernia from humor). Read the daily comics. Smile at yourself in the mirror and try to look at minor frustrations with a "This isn't so bad. I'm lucky I didn't . . ." attitude. Or, take the situation and exaggerate it to its humorous extreme.

When a bus drove into Kate's Mystery Books in Cambridge, Massachusetts, it ruptured a gas line, burst water pipes, and made a horrible mess. Owner Kate Mattes closed the store and draped a tarpaulin over the storefront with a sign, "Kate's Bus Stop."

When a bus drove into Kate's Mystery Books in Cambridge, Massachusetts, it ruptured a gas line, burst water pipes, and made a horrible mess. Owner Kate Mattes closed the store and draped a tarpaulin over the storefront with a sign, "Kate's Bus Stop."

HUMOROUS PERSPECTIVE AND OTHERS

Time, then, to settle down and get funny. Forgiving yourself for your own imperfections is the first step to gaining a humorous perspective. Next you must be able to forgive others for not being perfect, and humor provides the tool to make this alteration.

One of our workshop participants told us about the day she mistakenly scheduled a dental appointment for her son at the same time he had a soccer game. Instead of getting angry, he humorously pointed out her mistake with this note—"I'd be happy to get my teeth cleaned at three o'clock on Friday. But Dr. Adkins is going to have to run fast and kick straight in the process."

Admittedly, changing old mental outlooks to new viewpoints is not easy, but it is also not impossible. Try to position yourself at a different angle and look at situations within a new humorous framework.

A customer standing at a counter in an elegant jewelry store overheard an obnoxious patron bemoaning his financial state to the saleslady. He loudly disparaged his three ex-wives, blamed them for his predicament, and bragged about "dumping them." He finally complained that he was driving the station wagon because his last wife got the Mercedes. At that, the customer nearly blurted out, "She earned it."

She didn't say it, and the obnoxious man never heard it. But her thinking changed an unpleasant encounter into a funny memory.

PUTTING REALITY UP FOR HUMOR GRABS

Psychologically, seeing the funny side of life and work helps you maintain your balance while trying to cope with daily irritations. Humor allows you to state your disgust, anger, or impatience in a socially acceptable way, and at the same time it defuses those feelings. We presented to our humor awareness class this example that occurred at a fast-food restaurant in the lobby of an office building.

Hungry customers were lined up at all four registers, and for some unexplained reason not one hamburger was in the bin, nor were there any forthcoming. Standing at the front of the line, I could feel the anger of the impatient office workers and could hear their complaints growing louder. Finally I turned around and said loudly, "All right, who ordered the lobster?"

Hungry customers were lined up at all four registers, and for some unexplained reason not one hamburger was in the bin, nor were there any forthcoming. Standing at the front of the line, I could feel the anger of the impatient office workers and could hear their complaints growing louder. Finally I turned around and said loudly, "All right, who ordered the lobster?" Humor brought this minor irritation into perspective for everyone.

The next step, then, is to *follow your intuition.* Don't be afraid to follow a humorous impulse. It's OK to be spontaneous. As a colleague's mother once advised, "Go ahead and try it. The worst thing you can do is make a fool of yourself in front of all your friends." Actually, the worst that can happen is that no one will laugh. So what? The best thing that can happen is that tension is relieved and they all end up with smiles on their faces and you to thank.

THE HUMOR LINK

Humor links you to other people. With a humorous approach, you can establish a small oasis of stability in the midst of an unpleasant or chaotic situation.

Consider a large convention of computer salespeople housed in a small hotel with only one functioning elevator. A conventioneer waited fifteen minutes for the elevator. When it finally arrived, jammed with disgruntled hotel guests, she barely managed to squeeze in.

As the doors closed, sensing the tense atmosphere, she announced, "Now that we are all here, the meeting can begin." And a voice from the rear replied, "In your absence you were voted chairman." By the time the elevator reached the lobby, one individual's humorous perspective had changed a disgruntled crowd into a congenial group, linked together by humor.

Consider a large convention of computer salespeople housed in a small hotel with only one functioning elevator. A conventioneer waited fifteen minutes for the elevator. When it finally arrived, jammed with disgruntled hotel guests, she barely managed to squeeze in.

As the doors closed, sensing the tense atmosphere, she announced, "Now that we are all here, the meeting can begin." And a voice from the rear replied, "In your absence you were voted chairman."

GO WITH THE FLOW

Don't be afraid to take a different approach. Humor is more than a momentary tension reliever. It offers a healthy means of accepting life's complexities.

A high school class wanted to test the mettle of a new teacher on her first day at school. At ten o'clock, as she wrote on the blackboard with her back to the class, all twenty-four students, as planned, simultaneously dropped their books onto the floor. The teacher turned, walked to her desk, knocked a book onto the floor, and said, "Sorry I'm late." She kept her composure, created rapport with the students, and gained their cooperation.

So *be versatile, be flexible, and adapt*. In other words, be a fun-making person. Life is short, and you might as well have your share of merriness. As Satchel Paige once said, "How old would you be if you didn't know how old you was?"

A high school class wanted to test the mettle of a new teacher on her first day at school. At ten o'clock, as she wrote on the blackboard with her back to the class, all twenty-four students, as planned, simultaneously dropped their books onto the floor. The teacher turned, walked to her desk, knocked a book onto the floor, and said, "Sorry I'm late."

I'LL NEVER LAUGH AGAIN

According to the *New York Times,* William Saroyan called the Associated Press five days before his death to leave a posthumous statement: "Everybody has got to die, but I have always believed an exception would be made in my case. Now what?"

Tragedy touches everyone's life. And as you read this book perhaps you have recently experienced a traumatic event in your own life. If this is true, you may feel that you will never be able to laugh again. But with time and perspective, humor can be a life-giving force. We cannot control all of the things that happen to us, but we do have a certain degree of control over our reactions to them. Once you are able to regain perspective, you will find that humor is a survival tool which can help you face your problems.

A woman was finally able to joke after a painful divorce, "He left me because he wanted to find himself. Now he doesn't like what he found." Another woman whose young husband died after an unexpected illness was eventually able to appreciate his humor and indomitable spirit when she recalled his reaction in the hospital to being told he was hooked up to a machine. "I am not," he replied, "the machine is hooked up to me."

A Japanese gentleman met a rabbi from Indiana on a street in Paris. The Japanese man pointed at a map in his hand, obviously wanting directions. The rabbi tried to explain in halting French that he was a tourist and wasn't familiar with the streets. And the Japanese gentleman said, "I'm sorry, I'm an American and don't speak French. Do you speak English?"

Crisis is real and often not immediately compatible with laughter. But with time and distance, humor can be an important step toward healing. Being able to laugh at the frustrations and painful things in life means we are on our way to overcoming them.

REFOCUS WITH HUMOR

Humor can refocus your vision of a situation, redirect your thinking, and even provide creative means of problem solving. The momentary use of humor distances you from the situation temporarily, giving you the opportunity to view it in a different light.

A man's twelve-year-old son brought home his report card, sporting a C in English. "How could you get a C in English?" asked the father. "You were born in this country!"

After you have increased your awareness and perspective, remember that perception is not everything, because reality is not always what it seems.

A Japanese gentleman met a rabbi from Indiana on a street in Paris. The Japanese man pointed at a map in his hand, obviously wanting directions. The rabbi tried to explain in halting French that he was a tourist and wasn't familiar with the streets. And the Japanese gentleman said, "I'm sorry, I'm an American and don't speak French. Do you speak English?"

HUMOR AND STRESS

WHAT IS STRESS?

We are all subject to mental tension, strain, and pressure. It is part of the price we pay in a fast-moving society. Stress is not the incident itself, but rather our reaction to that incident, producing physical responses to the nonspecific demands placed upon us.

Stress is not necessarily negative. Without it, the football team wouldn't have the competitive edge, the computer program wouldn't get developed, and the student wouldn't get to school on time. Stress can give you the energy you need in your work. It only becomes harmful when it causes more anxiety, hostility, anger, or frustration than you can comfortably manage.

A large audience had eagerly anticipated a lecture by a prominent professor. The organizers of the meeting were upset because their hotel conference room had mistakenly been given to another group. They were placed in a makeshift area with a hastily constructed podium for the lecturer and a temporary sound system placed behind a folding screen.

The professor began his lecture, but after five minutes the microphone gave out a piercing squeal, the lights dimmed, and a loud thud erupted behind the screen. Aware of his audience's discomfort, the speaker stopped, looked heavenward and said, "I think I'm having a religious experience."

SO WHERE DOES HUMOR FIT IN?

There are many ways to deal positively with stress. Some people meditate, others exercise. Humor, however, has decided advantages as a stress reliever. First, it is immediate. Humor can be applied at the moment of discomfort, wherever problems arise. During a confrontation with a colleague, you can't very well say, "Excuse me while I run my three miles." But you can take a humor break immediately by taking a mental step back from the arena and finding, *if only for yourself,* some humor in the situation.

Second, humor is relaxing. It can be used as a positive means to change your perceptions and attitudes. Approaching a stress-producing circumstance with humor can trigger the relaxation response needed to reduce the stress right then and there, for others as well as for yourself.

A large audience had eagerly anticipated a lecture by a prominent professor. The organizers of the meeting were upset because their hotel conference room had mistakenly been given to another group. They were placed in a makeshift area with a hastily constructed podium for the lecturer and a temporary sound system placed behind a folding screen.

The professor began his lecture, but after five minutes the microphone gave out a piercing squeal, the lights dimmed, and a loud thud erupted behind the screen. Aware of his audience's discomfort, the speaker stopped, looked heavenward and said, "I think I'm having a religious experience." By the time the laughter had subsided, the sound system was fixed and the professor could proceed. His humor elicited a relaxation response from the audience, and he had turned a stress-producing incident into a stress-reducing one.

RECOGNIZING STRESS-PRODUCING HUMOR

The first step in avoiding stress-producing humor is learning its danger signals. Here are some of the ways humor can be misused and abused to evoke stress.

STRESS-PRODUCING HUMOR

P okes fun at other people's individual shortcomings.

R eflects anger.

O ffends with inappropriate use of sexual references or profanity.

D ivides a group by put-downs.

U ses stereotypes to denigrate a person or group.

C reates a cruel, abusive, and offensive atmosphere.

I s insensitive to what causes others real pain.

N egates self-confidence.

G ives license to hurt someone.

Malpractice, or the Humor Quack

Just as people can misuse other skills, they can misuse humor in any of those nine ways. When they do, they misdirect or pervert humor, producing stress rather than reducing it.

As times change, so does the concept of what type of humor is socially acceptable. For instance, it is no longer considered funny to torture animals, nor is it fashionable to make fun of people with mental disabilities. So the tasteless "moron jokes" of the past have become disguised as "ethnic jokes." Both types reinforce negative stereotypes. The jokes are the same, only the group maligned has changed.

Ethnic, religious, or racial jokes can embody all the qualities of stress-producing humor. Because prejudice is at the core of much of this type of humor, it can be destructive and especially hazardous at work. But you will find that humor has no hard and fast rules. Even with ethnic, religious, and racial jokes, there is an exception.

The exception involves ethnic pride. One person who can get away with telling an ethnic joke effectively without offending is a cherished member of that group. A prominent Irish Catholic can tell an ethnic Catholic joke at a meeting of the Knights of Columbus that wouldn't be appropriate for a Baptist to tell at a Baptist church picnic.

> At lunchtime a man orders a salad and his colleague orders pie a la mode. He snickers, "I see you are still on your diet." She retorts, "I see we suffer from the same problem—we both have trouble keeping our mouths shut."

If you are part of a group, you share a historical, religious, or cultural background, as well as the burden of society's prejudices against that group. You can poke fun at your own people because you are also poking fun at yourself. Everyone is included and no slur is intended.

When an outsider tells the same joke, at best it falls flat. At worst it is hurtful because it is exclusionary and implies that the joke-teller feels superior over the group he ridicules. Using this kind of humor damages your work environment as surely as walking through a minefield with a push broom.

We tested this concept with a class of teenagers. One youngster wanted to tell the latest Polish joke. Our response was, "OK, go ahead and tell the joke, but you must substitute your own ethnic group for the word 'Polack.'" After the boy told the joke he moaned, "But it's not funny that way." And why not? Because suddenly he was the butt of the joke.

Test it yourself. Tell this joke, using your own group in the blank: How many_______does it take to change a light bulb? Three. One to hold the bulb and two to turn the ladder.

When telling these jokes, try substituting the word elephant for the ethnic group. The chance of someone laughing is greater, and the risk of getting trampled by an irate elephant is small.

Onedownsmanship

Because hostility is at the root of put-downs, getting caught in a cycle of onedownsmanship is stress-producing and creates a tense atmosphere. Put-downs, even humorous ones, not only hurt others but also can backfire, leaving the user unsatisfied and even more hostile.

At lunchtime a man orders a salad and his colleague orders pie a la mode. He snickers, "I see you are still on your diet." She retorts, "I see we suffer from the same problem—we both have trouble keeping our mouths shut."

Perhaps he hadn't intended the insult. Perhaps she didn't realize the impact of her sarcastic retort. But the humor backfired just the same.

As with ethnic humor, there are appropriate occasions for using put-downs. Notably, a humorous put-down (her answer) can be an effective way to handle an insult without a direct confrontation. Also, within a relationship based on respect and trust (among family, friends or business colleagues), people often give tacit approval for joking about faults and shortcomings. Call it *humor between consenting adults*. The trick is to recognize the boundaries of acceptable humor and not to go beyond them. And it is tricky! Approach this type of humor with extreme caution.

Dealing With Stress-Producing Humor

Assuming that you will not intentionally employ stress-producing humor, you can take four effective steps when someone directs stress-producing humor toward you. Let's say, for instance, that you're at an office party and someone tells an inappropriate joke.

1. Don't laugh.
2. Reply, "I don't think that's funny."
3. If you're feeling brave and feel the insult was intentional, ask the offender, "Why would you say something that obviously ridicules people's shortcomings?" (Or substitute the appropriate phrase from the stress-producing list.)
4. If you want to allow room for the offender to save face, try saying something like, "I'm sure you're not aware of how cruel that joke makes you sound, but many people find that type of humor offensive, and I would appreciate your not repeating it."

If a person constantly uses stress-producing humor in a group, you could use any of these methods in front of everyone. Or, you may prefer to discuss your feelings privately. The advantage of letting your opinion be known in front of a group, in addition to a measure of satisfaction in venting your own feelings, is that peer pressure may prevent the individual from repeating that particular brand of humor. At least, in your presence.

USING HUMOR TO REDUCE STRESS

As we did with stress-producing humor, we need to recognize the qualities of stress-reducing humor.

STRESS-REDUCING HUMOR

R educes tension by joking about universal human frustrations and faults.

E ncourages people to relax and laugh.

D elights in poking fun at oneself.

U nites people by building rapport.

C reates a supportive atmosphere of fun and caring.

I ncludes everyone in the good time.

N otes the positive aspects of human relationships.

G ives everyone a chance to participate.

These stress-reducing characteristics are pretty clear-cut. The positive forces of humor can help you reduce the stress involved in both your personal and business relationships with other people. And less stress means more energy to maximize your effectiveness, increase your level of enjoyment, and minimize the chances of burnout.

"Humor disappears with burnout, the result of persistent, unrelieved pressure. Burnout is characterized by exhaustion, dulled mental awareness, and a constriction of feeling and thought. If there were more humor in every exchange, perhaps there would be less burnout. Humor produces the opposite physiological response to stress. With stress you have a rapid pulse, muscles are tight, blood pressure is up. After laughing, all these signs are down."

Dr. Mel Udel

Dr. Mel Udel, a psychiatrist who has counseled executives suffering from burnout, notes, "Humor disappears with burnout, the result of persistent, unrelieved pressure. Burnout is characterized by exhaustion, dulled mental awareness, and a constriction of feeling and thought. If there were more humor in every exchange, perhaps there would be less burnout. Humor produces the opposite physiological response to stress. With stress you have a rapid pulse, muscles are tight, blood pressure is up. After laughing, all these signs are down."

PROGRAMMING YOURSELF FOR HUMOR

An actor combines memory, imagination, and concentration to get into a role as quickly as possible. He trains himself to recall a past reaction to an event, and reeducates his emotions so he can evoke that emotional response at any given time. The actor becomes an instrument who in turn communicates these feelings to his audience.

You, too, can train yourself to use the tools of concentration, memory, and imagination to hone only one skill—humorous recall. If you can once make a funny connection with a particularly tough situation, then the next time you encounter a similar situation, you will be able to recall the humorous reaction and become an instrument to ease the stress not only for yourself but for those around you.

One evening a physician came home exhausted and told his wife he had exchanged harsh words with the hospital administrator during a meeting. "I know tomorrow the very sight of him will get me furious all over again."

She replied, "Well, when you see him tomorrow, imagine that he is wearing a black lace bra and panties under his three-piece suit."

Walking down the hall the next day, a baffled hospital administrator encountered a smiling doctor. The problem hadn't changed, but the smile de-escalated the hostilities and opened the door to further discussion. And after that, the doctor never saw the administrator in quite the same light. Silly? Perhaps, but if it momentarily reduced the physician's level of stress, humor served a healthy purpose.

One evening a physician came home exhausted and told his wife he had exchanged harsh words with the hospital administrator during a meeting. "I know tomorrow the very sight of him will get me furious all over again."

She replied, "Well, when you see him tomorrow, imagine that he is wearing a black lace bra and panties under his three-piece suit."

Walking down the hall the next day, a baffled hospital administrator encountered a smiling doctor. The problem hadn't changed, but the smile de-escalated the hostilities and opened the door to further discussion. And after that, the doctor never saw the administrator in quite the same light. Silly? Perhaps, but if it momentarily reduced the physician's level of stress, humor served a healthy purpose.

Imagine yourself sitting in a traffic jam on the way to see a client. What humorous reactions could you develop to this common stressful situation?

1. Try completing this sentence: "I knew this was going to be a traffic-stopping day when . . . " (add whatever off-the-wall idea that pops into your head.)

2. Pretend you are writing an article about the aggravation, and come up with a funny headline or title for the situation *while you are experiencing it*. For instance, "Twenty-Seven-Year-Old Man Grows Ten-Foot Beard During Rush Hour," or, "The Frugal Gourmet's Secret Recipe for Perfect Traffic Jams."

3. Think of a funny billboard to fit the situation: "Fly Qantas because you sure aren't going anywhere this way."

4. Keep a notebook or tape recorder in your car so you can record your humorous responses. This serves three purposes. It will distract you temporarily, bring a chuckle of recognition when you reread your comments, and expand your humor file.

LAUGHTER, THE SAFETY VALVE

An extraordinary quality of a humorous response is that it is instantaneous and brief, and yet its effects are positive and in some cases permanent.

Although you can't avoid stress, you can respond in one of three ways:

1. Respond passively, then quietly stew about the problem and let your innards boil.
2. Respond in anger. This lets off steam, but may just compound the problem.
3. Respond with wit.

Like anger, humor can release some of your frustration and give you momentary relief. But unlike anger, humor will relax you, ease the tension, and consequently help open new doors to creative solutions.

> "That's terrible. That's awful. Boy, am I glad I didn't do it!"
> "I'm sorry you had to go through all that, because you're going to have to do it all over again when you find the person responsible."
> "If you find the person responsible, I'll help you beat him up."

A young woman in one of our convention workshops worked in a high-pressure advertising agency. Although she liked and respected her boss, he could at times become quite volatile. She would then become the target of his unfair criticism, taking the blame for something she didn't do.

In the past she had quietly stewed about the unfairness of his criticism. Now she wanted to know how she could handle it with humor the next time it occurred. These were some of the responses the group developed for her. Perhaps you can come up with some others.

After his tirade, say:

1. "I'm sorry you had to go through all that, because you're going to have to do it all over again when you find the person responsible."
2. (With deep empathy) "That's terrible. That's awful. Boy, am I glad I didn't do it!"
3. "If I were you, I'd find the person responsible and really let her have it."
4. "If you find the person responsible, I'll help you beat him up."

IF THERE'S NOTHING TO WORRY ABOUT, DON'T WORRY, I'LL FIND SOMETHING

Some people are natural worriers, and the stress they suffer is self-induced. With humor you can learn to sidetrack this brand of worry before it escalates to unmanageable proportions.

Sitting in the front row at the circus, you watch the clowns splash each other with water from a bucket. You worry that they will decide to throw water on you. All of a sudden, right in front of you, one clown turns toward the audience, picks up the bucket, and begins to swing it back and forth. He counts, "One, two, three." You close your eyes and wince as he throws, and you end up with a lap full of confetti.

Sitting in the front row at the circus, you watch the clowns splash each other with water from a bucket. You worry that they will decide to throw water on you. All of a sudden, right in front of you, one clown turns toward the audience, picks up the bucket, and begins to swing it back and forth. He counts, "One, two, three." You close your eyes and wince as he throws, and you end up with a lap full of confetti.

It was all make-believe. Why didn't you anticipate the switch? Too many of us try too hard to anticipate hurts, disappointments, and problems, as if worrying will in some way lessen the impact. Anxiety over problems is real, but self-induced worry about what hasn't happened is fabricated. It is confetti. Many of the bad things we worry about never come to be.

Get out of the self-induced worry trap! Self-induced worry is an exercise in futility, draining your energy and leaving you fewer emotional resources to cope with real concerns at work and at home. In order to temper the self-induced worry, you must first learn to accept three things:

1. You can't control everything.
2. You can only live your own life, not someone else's.
3. Everything changes.

Most "what-ifs" occur when you are alone, so if you find yourself in this stress trap, get out among people. If you can't change your physical setting, change your mental one with humor by answering your own "what-ifs" with humorous solutions. People who worry excessively have usually done so for many years. Breaking this habit won't be easy, but humor can help if you let it.

1. Instead of magnifying a problem, turn your mental binoculars around and shrink the scope of your worry. For instance, if you are worried that bad weather will delay your business trip, flip over the worry and expand it with your imagination.

So what if?

—what if my deodorant fails me?

—what if my nose is stuffy?

—what if I have an age spot?

"This is going to be the best day since the city began keeping records. It will be so clear I will see San Francisco from here without ever leaving Sioux City." "The weather will be so good I'll get a suntan on my way to the airport."

2. *Exaggerate the good results of bad weather.* What if the weather is so bad next week that I won't be able to get out of town for my vacation? "Scientists say people can live for thirty days on stored fat. Yea! So I'll be able to get rid of all the grease in my oven."

3. *Substitute your "what-ifs" with those provided for you on your television set.* Force yours out and let the silly ones in by focusing your attention on the worry-producing ads, and add the word so. So what if?

   a. So what if my deodorant fails me? (Answer: I'll get a seat on the bus.)

   b. So what if my nose is stuffy? (I'll open my mouth for a change.)

   c. So what if I have an age spot? (I'm entitled.)

By opening your circle of awareness, refocusing, and gaining new perspectives on yourself and the world around you, your new-found humor will enrich your relationships with other people both at work and at home.

EXERCISES FOR INCREASING YOUR HUMOR AWARENESS

1. *Take liberties with Ben Franklin.* This exercise involves altering Ben Franklin's famous words of wisdom. Leave the first half of the saying alone, such as "Early to bed and early to rise," and add a funny ending—"will give my boss a big surprise."

2. *Add to your humor collection at least twice a week,* focusing on a different category and tailoring it to your needs.

3. *Play with commercial slogans,* changing the ending with a humorous twist that individualizes them. This activity creates humor from nothing. "Have it your way . . . but not today."

4. *Choose a pet peeve* of yours and come up with four or five humorous ways of dealing with it.

EXAMPLE: how to cope with annoying junk mail by:

a) Sending other junk mail back to them in their self-addressed envelope.

b) Writing a funny letter: "I really have no use for lingerie here at the monastery."

c) Sending them the addresses of other junk mail folks so they can write to each other.

5. *Take cartoons and come up with different captions.* Then see if you can refine those captions further to personalize them for your friends, co-workers, or job.

6. *Put funny captions in your family photo album.* This can be a fun project for the whole family.

7. *Turn movie titles into funny double features:* "Who's Afraid of Virginia Woolf?" and "Conan the Barbarian" or, "In Praise of Older Women" and "Playing for Time."

8. *Play with names of streets and subdivisions,* looking for the reason behind the choice (you often won't find it, and therein lies the humor). For instance, in Atlanta, Georgia, there are no peach trees on any of its twenty-seven Peachtree Streets. Driftwood Court has no wood, no stream, and no judge. Look for funny names of businesses, or make up your own. We have found Chow Goldstein's Restaurant and The Potbelly Deli.

"I'd be happy to subscribe to your magazine if you would sign up for the lake front property I sell."

"I have my dog in the oven, and the roast needs to go out for a walk."

"No thank you, but would you like a free kitten?"

9. *Come up with several humorous (but not sarcastic) answers* for phone solicitors (they have to make a living too): "I'd be happy to subscribe to your magazine if you would sign up for the lake front property I sell." Or, "I have my dog in the oven, and the roast needs to go out for a walk." Or, "No thank you, but would you like a free kitten?"

10. *Read the paper for absurd headlines and premises for humor.* Newspaper item: Chinese zoologists find a species of mouse that survived through the Ice Age more than eleven thousand years ago. Idea: Imagine what an interview with the mouse

would be like. Newspaper item: What out-of-power Congressmen are doing now. Idea: Imagine an employment agency's analysis of the qualifications of a former senator and the bizarre jobs he is suited for.

11. *Keep a paper and pen with you,* and when something funny occurs in your head or in reality, write it down:

    Sitting on the horns of a dilemma can be very painful.

    A mother of twin toddlers' main ambition in life is to shave her legs and underarms on the same day.

    New sport: aerobic arguing.

    My new brother-in-law is a pureed-pea brain.

12. *Look at an old subject hind side first, upside down, and inside out.* You can come up with a funny idea by thinking about the ordinary in extraordinary circumstances, or vice versa. This technique sparks zany, off-the-wall humor. For example, how does Queen Elizabeth shop for a girdle?

Many of these exercises may not at first seem to relate directly to using humor with other people. But if it is just a veneer slapped on the surface of your personality, humor will not ring true. You have to build it on a solid foundation. And experimenting with some of these exercises will help you enlarge and strengthen that foundation.

HOW YOUR HUMOR CAN HELP OTHER PEOPLE

A man was running for political office. Whenever he saw small group of people assembled, he would saunter over, start telling stories, and presently get in his political pitch. It worked pretty well most of the time, but one particular group didn't warm up at all. "What's the matter with you folks?" the politician asked plaintively. "You act like you were at a funeral." "Brother," said a spokesman severely, "this *is* a funeral." [2]

A man was running for political office. Whenever he saw small group of people assembled, he would saunter over, start telling stories, and presently get in his political pitch. It worked pretty well most of the time, but one particular group didn't warm up at all. "What's the matter with you folks?" the politician asked plaintively. "You act like you were at a funeral." "Brother," said a spokesman severely, "this is a funeral."

In exploring the possibilities of humor for improving person-to-person relationships, you should heed this warning: no one can sally forth strewing humor indiscriminately and expect to accomplish very much. Using appropriate humor constructively requires a degree of perceptiveness about other people and a good sense of timing, for without them you will surely trip yourself on your own quips.

At a time of real tragedy, for instance, when a friend has just lost a loved one, efforts at humor will likely be interpreted as insensitive and uncaring. When someone comes to you for help, he or she will not appreciate your joking about the situation rather than offering a solution or at least a sympathetic ear (even if the crisis is less than a crisis to you). The slight, even if unintentional, is very real.

Also, if you are making a decision that will affect a person's future, this is not the time for levity. Hold the humor until after letting her know she has gotten the job, been accepted to the college of choice, or will get that raise in salary.

However, keep your goals realistic. As you exercise your funny bone and improve your own humor fitness, you can expand your skills beyond your present humor level. Like any other communication skill, humor takes time and practice to develop to its full potential for use with other people. Many occasions ripe for humor will be detailed in the following chapters. However, it might help to begin thinking about some general situations you find every day in which you could use humor to deal constructively, productively, and mirthfully with other people.

Examine these hypothetical situations and see if you can imagine additional humorous responses.

1. *When a person is too close to a problem.* Sometimes people get so caught up with familiar methods of solving problems that, when those methods fail, they see no alternative. Humor can remove their blinders, restate the problem, and break the cycle of unproductive thinking.

   A thirty-five-year-old woman prepared a dinner for company while a neighbor watched her as she cut off and threw away two inches of perfectly good—and expensive—ham. "You feed your garbage disposal better than I feed my husband," said the neighbor.

A thirty-five-year-old woman prepared a dinner for company while a neighbor watched her as she cut off and threw away two inches of perfectly good—and expensive—ham. "You feed your garbage disposal better than I feed my husband," said the neighbor.

"That's the way my mother always fixes it," replied the woman. "Isn't that the way everybody cooks a ham?"

A phone call revealed the truth. "I never had the right size pan," admitted her mother, "so I just cut off the end."

"That's the way my mother always fixes it," replied the woman. "Isn't that the way everybody cooks a ham?"

A phone call revealed the truth. "I never had the right size pan," admitted her mother, "so I just cut off the end."

Twelve-year-old Paula is visiting her grandparents in Florida. She would like to wade in the ocean but is afraid because she has just seen a movie about a killer shark.

Her grandfather holds her hand as they approach the surf together and tells her gently, "I know you're worried, but remember: in this world there are more people eating fish than fish eating people."

2. *When stress and pressure of unrelieved work and deadlines make people tense and irritable.* Six college students have been up all night studying for final exams. Scott walks in at three AM and kids, "OK, who's the joker who tacked my notes to the wall of the girls' locker room?" The six students laugh hysterically.

   Have you ever noticed how punchy people become after long hours of unrelieved work, particularly under a deadline? The students' laughter was certainly out of proportion to the amount of real humor in Scott's remark. But because pressure had built up, the first giggle poked a hole in their wall of tension, and the released frustration poured out in torrents. This pressure valve effect of humor is important, for often the tension is otherwise unbearable.

3. *When a person's fears are exaggerated.* Twelve-year-old Paula is visiting her grandparents in Florida. She would like to wade in the ocean but is afraid because she has just seen a movie about a killer shark.

   Her grandfather holds her hand as they approach the surf together and tells her gently, "I know you're worried, but remember: in this world there are more people eating fish than fish eating people." By making her laugh, he cut her fear down to manageable size.

Maxine feels miserable about not resolving a silly argument she had with her husband last night. She opens her refrigerator, reaches for the juice, and notices a pencil with a note on it stuck in the mound of leftover mashed potatoes. Her husband had written, "This is the way I feel. Please call me at the office when you wake up."

4. *When people are stalemated in conflict.* Maxine feels miserable about not resolving a silly argument she had with her husband last night. She opens her refrigerator, reaches for the juice, and notices a pencil with a note on it stuck in the mound of leftover mashed potatoes.

Her husband had written, "This is the way I feel. Please call me at the office when you wake up."

During confrontations, humor can break the tension, defuse some of the angry feelings, and move people a little bit off their entrenched positions, opening the way for communication.

5. *When the truth hurts.* A beginning golfer is disgusted that his game hasn't improved. His secretary cushions the truth by saying, "Don't get discouraged. At least today you *hit* the ball in one!"

6. *When people ignore reminders, written or spoken.* Here's a memo from Michael H. Mescon, former Department of Management Chairman at Georgia State University. "Dear Faculty: Permit me to remind you of that old academic caveat, 'If you plan to drink the punch, don't relieve yourself in the punch bowl.' In essence, please let the staff person at the reception desk know where you can be reached. Most of us do this routinely. Unfortunately, we have a few faculty members who seem to evaporate. Understandably, students and other taxpayers resent this. In short, don't be one of the 'relievers.' We've all worked too diligently in preparing the punch!" [3]

Here's a memo from Michael H. Mescon, former Department of Management Chairman at Georgia State University. "Dear Faculty: Permit me to remind you of that old academic caveat, 'If you plan to drink the punch, don't relieve yourself in the punch bowl.' In essence, please let the staff person at the reception desk know where you can be reached. Most of us do this routinely. Unfortunately, we have a few faculty members who seem to evaporate. Understandably, students and other taxpayers resent this. In short, don't be one of the 'relievers.' We've all worked too diligently in preparing the punch!"

7. *When a person is a stranger in a group of people.* One manager introduces her new employees to co-workers by way of joking. "This is Frank. He makes the best cup of coffee in the office." When everyone laughs, it becomes evident that Frank's talents lie elsewhere, and the new employee becomes privy to the "in" joke, making him feel part of the group.

Warm, non-hostile humor is a common denominator that cuts across barriers of age, background, and interests; it is equally effective at work, school, or social gatherings.

Laughter has added a positive note to each of these scenarios. But before you can run with it, you need to start your training and get on the humor track.

> "Whatever else an American believes or disbelieves about himself, he is absolutely sure he has a sense of humor."
>
> E. B. White

CAN YOU LEARN TO BE FUNNY?

E. B. White said, "Whatever else an American believes or disbelieves about himself, he is absolutely sure he has a sense of humor." It is not true, however, that everyone believes he or she has what it takes to initiate humor.

Any person can learn to be funny who's willing to become a different kind of person. You can learn to use humor if you:

1. Change the way you view people and events.
2. Improve your style and build on what's already there.
3. Take a few risks.

It's too much to expect someone who is not naturally funny suddenly to turn into a successful stand-up comedian. But then, neither would you expect the beginning piano student to master Beethoven's *Moonlight* Sonata in one easy lesson. As with any other skill, using humor takes practice, and the more you study and practice, the better you will become.

CHANGING THE WAY YOU VIEW PEOPLE AND EVENTS

Age is a great advantage in using humor with other people, because as you get older, you have more of life's experiences to draw from as material for funny stories and jokes. But experience is not enough. You must also be well-informed and aware of what's going on around you. Your humor growth can become stunted if it is not properly nourished. Humor sprouts from the seeds of truth. The more you learn from newspapers, magazines, books, radio, and television, the more raw material you will have for your humor. You can begin by picking up a newspaper and quickly scanning the headlines for funny possibilities, as Jay Leno frequently does. You might come up with such items as these, which appeared in a large city newspaper:

"GOOD SAMARITANS MAY GET STUN GUNS"

"MAN, 76, LOOKING FOR 27TH BRIDE"

"FINGERS ON DISABLED LIST"

"WE HAVE IMMEDIATE OPENING FOR TRUSS BUILDERS"

"FOR SALE: PUBLIC PHONE BOOTH, ALL WOOD, GOOD CONDITION"

Or, consider the classified ad description for houses. What do they really mean? "Nature lover's delight" might really mean, "the first thing you do is call the exterminator." If you turn your humor perspective loose, the opportunities for humor will multiply. And each time you do it, it will become easier.

If you want to incorporate more humor in your contact with others, you must also be aware of social change; learn what is acceptable and what isn't. It is amazing that the same people who are aware of changes in lapel widths, hemlines, or computer models and data bases are surprised when jokes about "the little woman" or "old folks" offend many in today's society.

To use humor with others, you must be tuned in to their sensibilities. If a young comedian does a routine of "mother-in-law" jokes for an audience of older women and doesn't get any laughs, he shouldn't be surprised.

IMPROVE YOUR STYLE AND BUILD ON WHAT'S ALREADY THERE

"But I can't tell a joke or a funny story." Wrong! You can if you add details from your own life, add local references, or attribute the story to a member of the group. Adapt it to your personality and style and then practice, telling it first to yourself and then to a friend. It's a lot harder to change the way you think than to change your hair style. But it's not impossible.

The first step is to *map your humor.* Begin by finding a role model. It could be a professional comic or a friend whose humor you admire. Ask yourself, "Why do I like that kind of humor, and what kind is it?" If you can recognize what makes you laugh, then you will begin with a frame of reference.

"But I can't tell a joke or a funny story." **WRONG!**

The next step is to *read joke books.* Select one-liners or stories that you can apply to your own life. Whether you spend your time as a dental technician, a homemaker, or a service station attendant, the same story can be adapted by adding your own details to make your version plausible.

For instance, the homemaker might tell a friend, "The person who said 'you can't take it with you' never saw my family pack for a trip." The service station attendant might change it to, "The person who said 'you can't take it with you' never saw this guy's windshield." And the dental technician might remark to the dentist, "The person who said 'you can't take it with you' never cleaned that kid's teeth."

You can also localize your story. Professionals do it all the time. People like to hear recognizable places mentioned in jokes. "I went to Philadelphia to forget my troubles. Then I came here to______to forget Philadelphia." Or, "I won't say that the_______Hotel is dull, but I called room service to bring me another Bible."

You can do the same thing. "I went to a party at Kathy's house last week. She really knows how to spoil her guests. She served prime cuts of beef, homegrown vegetables, Belgian chocolates. And when I wanted a glass of water, she asked, 'What year?'" This joke could just as easily apply to a fancy restaurant, a gourmet market, or a restaurant you visited on a recent business trip. Give a member of the group credit for the story. "As your president was telling me right before the meeting . . ."

Humor should fit your personality, and you need to be comfortable with your humor before you can use it effectively with other people. Begin by setting some humor standards for yourself. Analyze what's funny and what's not funny to you.

Even if everyone else is telling dirty jokes, if they make you uncomfortable, don't feel pressured to tell them. The truly professional comedians who use off-color material, like Eddie Murphy, George Carlin, and Joan Rivers, can also make people laugh with a clean version of their act when they appear on network television.

> "I went to a party at Kathy's house last week. She really knows how to spoil her guests. She served prime cuts of beef, homegrown vegetables, Belgian chocolates. And when I wanted a glass of water, she asked, 'What year?'"

People will often laugh at an obscenity because of the shock at hearing the unmentionable mentioned, rather than at the innate humor of the joke itself. Off-color jokes are likely to offend someone. Not being a professional comedian, you need to decide if you want to risk offending other people, and how you want others to view you. If you offend them, they may not like you or want to do business with you. And if that happens, your humor has misfired in the worst way. On the other hand, you may decide that doesn't matter.

But perhaps jokes and stories aren't your style anyway. You want to use spontaneous funny quips. How can you do this?

Again, learn from your role model. If you have ever seen your favorite comedian in a nightclub, you may be amazed at the humor of his or her spontaneous remarks, perhaps to a heckler or a waiter serving drinks during the act. If you observe this same comedian the next night, many of the "spontaneous" remarks will be the same.

Although people adept with humor can often invent funny off-the-cuff remarks on the spot, much of the spontaneous humor is preplanned for a specific situation. There is no reason you can't do the same thing.

Begin by selecting a situation that occurs frequently, such as not being seated immediately at a restaurant, and prepare an aside for your friends the next time it happens. "When I told the maître d' I had reservations, he must have thought I had doubts about wanting to be seated."

A lost tourist in New York stops a stranger on the street corner. "Excuse me, how do I get to Carnegie Hall?"

"Practice, practice, practice."

Another technique cleverly used by Will Rogers, among others, involves steering the conversation to the subjects for which you have prepared "spontaneous" humor. As George Burns bemusedly notes, "It's easy to ad-lib if you've got it written down." And if you do want to master the art of truly spontaneous humor, observe Steve Allen's style and respond to the unintentional meanings in someone's words.

EXAMPLE: A lost tourist in New York stops a stranger on the street corner. "Excuse me, how do I get to Carnegie Hall?"

"Practice, practice, practice."

TAKE A FEW RISKS: "I LAUGH IN THE FACE OF DANGER"

Once you think of a joke or funny remark, you need to courageously go ahead and try it. The worst that can happen is that no one will laugh. Even professional comedians don't know if their humor will work until they try it, and sometimes it falls flat. So what?

PART

Specific Groups

Humor With Employees: If Everyone Laughs and Your Joke Isn't Funny, You Must Be the Boss

I am convinced that a majority of good leaders have an above average sense of humor. Making light of life helps them to survive the pressure of the leadership role.

—*David P. Campbell, Senior Fellow, Center for Creative Leadership* [4]

TRUE OR FALSE?

 Using humor with your employees diminishes your authority.

 Laughing with co-workers is inappropriate at work.

 There is no correlation between humor and success as an executive.

If you answered true to any of these statements, you may be one of countless managers overlooking a powerful tool for improving your people-handling skills. Used appropriately, humor can help you motivate, relax, and inspire employees to top achievement. It can help make the burdens of organized life more bearable.

Successful executives realize that constructive humor can help create a positive office atmosphere, and they often use humor to spice up memos, illustrate points, and add color to their meetings.

As a boss, you control the thermostat for a healthy work atmosphere. You regulate the climate for acceptable behavior, and people in your organization will in turn adapt to your style. Being an executive takes talent and a lot of hard work. But do you enjoy what you do? And do your employees enjoy working for you?

True or false?

Using humor with your employees diminishes your authority.

Laughing with co-workers is inappropriate at work.

There is no correlation between humor and success as an executive.

Harry Maziar, president of Zep Chemical Company, reflects, "Going through the mechanical operations of a business—buying low, selling high, and maintaining what you have—that's all business is, and it is extremely vanilla. There are many more flavors to business, if you can relax and enjoy yourself. Too many executives place an inflated importance on what they do far beyond its real merit, and imagine they're having a great impact on society. These people take themselves far too seriously, and it keeps them at the vanilla stand."

If you feel you've been at the vanilla stand too long, maybe it's time to sit back and enjoy the environment you're in. React to your employees positively with humor, signaling that it's OK for them to participate. Everyone will be happier. More fun in the workplace can involve establishing a feeling of camaraderie and help alleviate unnecessary competition. As the boss, you can take advantage of the opportunity to recognize the individual employee and show appreciation of his work without being overly demonstrative. For instance, here's a memo from a boss to a salesperson: "Congratulations on earning still another savings bond. At this rate, I figure you'll be able to retire by the year 3271!"

BEING THE BOSS IS NO JOKE

No one is advocating that as a manager you should become an entertainer to be laughed at rather than laughed with, or that you should become so permissive that you lose the respect of your employees. What we *are* suggesting is that you consider humor as one additional way to communicate effectively with your workers.

As a manager, you want to have a positive influence on the behavior of your employees. You have to know how to handle them, because their attitudes will affect productivity as well as their relationship with management. It makes sense that happy workers are good business.

It is also true that all managers aren't human relations experts. But, if you choose to, you can learn to manage more effectively. If you decide to, you can learn how become a better boss through humor.

DEFUSING ANGER AND LESSENING TENSION

As a manager, you don't want to diminish a person or situation with humor. So the humor you use to defuse anger should not ignore or devalue the problem; rather, it should allow employees to let off steam when under pressure.

J. Burton Gruber, C.P.A. of Expedite, Inc., had a contest for the entire accounting firm during the height of tax season. A bottle of champagne went to the person with the most suggestions about what to do with a tax form. Some suggestions:

1. Fold them and see which one is properly weighted to fly.
2. Prop up a wobbly chair.
3. Envy it.

The contest gave employees something fun to think about as they worked non-stop under deadline and helped them control their work instead of their work controlling them.

J. Burton Gruber, C.P.A. of Expedite, Inc., had a contest for the entire accounting firm during the height of tax season. A bottle of champagne went to the person with the most suggestions about what to do with a tax form. Some suggestions:

1. Fold them and see which one is properly weighted to fly.
2. Prop up a wobbly chair.
3. Envy it.

The contest gave employees something fun to think about as they worked non-stop under deadline and helped them control their work instead of their work controlling them.

MORALE: IF YOU NEVER HAVE ANY FUN, YOU'RE NOT DOING IT RIGHT

Closely related to defusing tension is building good morale, which we measure not by a total lack of complaints, but by how employees express and temper them. Just as employees can vent frustrations through humorous griping, managers can boost morale by giving employees tacit permission to voice those complaints. As a manager, you will find that employees appreciate being heard, even if you can do little to alter the situation.

One executive responded to his secretary's complaint this way:

"Yesterday was very hectic. My harried secretary complained, 'I haven't stuck my nose out of the office all day.' I replied, 'That would look silly! If somebody walked by and saw your nose sticking out of the building, what kind of impression would that make? If you're going out,

One executive responded to his secretary's complaint this way:
"Yesterday was very hectic. My harried secretary complained, 'I haven't stuck my nose out of the office all day.' I replied, 'That would look silly! If somebody walked by and saw your nose sticking out of the building, what kind of impression would that make? If you're going out, take your whole body with you.' We both laughed at the mental image that conjured up and got back to work."

take your whole body with you.' We both laughed at the mental image that conjured up and got back to work."

The humor defused the tension, but it still acknowledged the complaint. It put the problem into perspective and helped maintain their relationship, keeping lines of communication open for the future.

Maintaining morale is more delicate when you're handing down an unpopular decision. Facing the problem head-on, people in authority can find humor a useful ally in wielding power gently.

A company president wanted to soften the news that he had already made a decision on a half million dollar capital investment. Meeting with middle management, he said "Those in favor of spending $500,000, raise your hands." All raised their hands. "Opposed, raise your hands." He alone raised his hand. "Boy," he smiled, "that was close. You folks almost outvoted me."

SENDING A MESSAGE

Humor can help you get and maintain people's attention, make a point, and illustrate a problem. At one sales meeting the president of the company asked those present to stand up and look under their chairs. Taped underneath each chair was a nickel. What did it mean? No one could solve the mystery until one salesman finally caught on. "It proves," he concluded, "You can't sit on your duff and make a nickel." The boss had gotten their attention, pointed out the problem, made his point, and his employees never forgot the palatable way he did it.

Reinforcing good behavior is as important as correcting counter-productive habits. When a man arrived on time to work after being habitually late for a week, his supervisor said, "I'm glad you're not the first to be last anymore!" And another company has instituted the "One Small Step Award," a bronzed baby shoe, which goes to the bill collector who adeptly handles the toughest call of the week.

A company president wanted to soften the news that he had already made a decision on a half million dollar capital investment. Meeting with middle management, he said "Those in favor of spending $500,000, raise your hands." All raised their hands. "Opposed, raise your hands." He alone raised his hand. "Boy," he smiled, "that was close. You folks almost outvoted me."

CRITICIZING: YOU CAN LAUGH OR YOU CAN CRY, BUT IF YOU LAUGH, YOU WON'T HAVE TO BLOW YOUR NOSE

Constructive criticism is only constructive when the other guy gets it. No one likes to be criticized. Unfortunately, as the boss, criticizing is part of your job. The trick is to offer it without putting your employee on the defensive. One executive's secretary agrees. "It amazes me that I can't get mad at my boss. Yesterday, I was typing a letter to my parents. He walked by, noticed, and teased, 'That's right, just keep typing that sales letter, keep at it.' He made his point, but when he jokes, I don't have to be defensive." Managers must also be even-handed with their criticism. Here again, humor makes it palatable. A habitually late worker at D.C. Comics found production manager Bob Rozakis running a lottery based on his tardiness. The late employee had to pay a dollar to the worker who estimated his arrival time most accurately. Humor helped cure the tardiness in a nonaccusatory way and softened the criticism, but also let the department know that the boss was dealing with the problem.

COHESIVENESS: WHEN THINGS GET STICKY

According to research conducted by Jack Duncan, professor of management at the University of Alabama's Graduate School of Management, humor often influences group cohesiveness.[5] In a work group, for instance, cohesiveness may be strongest when an external threat is great. (Think about machinists taking a pay cut against the wishes of their union, or auto workers pulling together during a threatened company collapse.)

An effective manager can increase cohesiveness by humorously focusing on the competitive relationship with other groups within the organization, with another company, or even with foreign competition. An American plant foreman told this joke about foreign trade to his crew: "One thing about asking the Europeans to buy as many products from us as we buy from them: it lets you know who your friends were."

UNPLEASANT SURPRISES: BUT SERIOUSLY, FOLKS . . .

By foreseeing various stressful situations that may occur, you can prepare and practice appropriate light-hearted responses. This preparation will increase the likelihood of your success in calming the anger when the actual situation arises.

For instance, when you have disagreeable news to announce to your employees or co-workers, humor can soften the blow and make it more bearable. If you have to ask several people to work late, you might use a good news—bad news format. "Group, I've got some good news and some bad news. The good news is that we have to work late tonight to meet our deadline. The bad news is, I'm making the coffee."

GIVING PERMISSION FOR HUMOR

Most employees will cut down on their joking and bantering in the presence of a boss, especially one who does not participate in the humor. So if you often work alongside your employees, you can enhance a cooperative atmosphere by participating to some extent in the humor. Your participation lets your employees know you are human. If you are secure enough to laugh with them, you will encourage their good will.

And as one manager said, "I like having a happy department. If we can't enjoy a laugh together now and then, the place will become a morgue. I think that humor provides a common ground as much as music or sports or any other 'interest.' The people in my department know that, no matter how tight the deadline, if I can make a joke, we're not going to have problems getting the work done. They know I expect them to work hard, but I'm on their side and appreciate what they're doing."

Public relations executive Dale L. Brown took it one step further, using his puppet "Chip Martin" to shed a more personal and positive light on his executives for employees. At meetings, when Chip the puppet looked at the managers and asked Brown who they were, Brown answered, "They're the company's executives." And Chip would reply, "Shows you that all the clowns aren't in the circus!" The employees loved it.

Public relations executive Dale L. Brown took it one step further, using his puppet "Chip Martin" to shed a more personal and positive light on his executives for employees. At meetings, when Chip the puppet looked at the managers and asked Brown who they were, Brown answered, "They're the company's executives." And Chip would reply, "Shows you that all the clowns aren't in the circus!" The employees loved it.

HUMANIZING A PRESENTATION: IN LIFE, FUN COUNTS

Many business people associate intentional humor with giving a presentation or a speech, where humor can be quite effective. Humor can help the audience identify with the speaker and thus become more receptive to the points he or she wants to make. And, if you win your listeners over initially by gently poking fun at yourself, you will be setting a tone for cooperation in the future (see hints on bringing humor into your speeches in Chapter 5).

Erwin Zaban, chairman of National Service Industries, a company with annual sales that top the billion dollar mark, learned this lesson well. Shortly after buying Block Industries, a shirt company, he addressed a large group of anxious Block employees who were somewhat in awe of his position.

Meeting them for the first time, Zaban explained his decision to buy their company. "We checked out your shirts—as a matter of fact, I'm wearing one right now. We found the *collars* beautifully tailored, the *neck* fits well and the *color* lasts. The only detail we overlooked was: What about the *rest* of the shirt?" Zaban then removed his jacket, revealing his shirt, which he had shredded to pieces. The employees exploded with laughter, and Zaban had won them over.

Erwin Zaban, chairman of National Service Industries, a company with annual sales that top the billion dollar mark, learned this lesson well. Shortly after buying Block Industries, a shirt company, he addressed a large group of anxious Block employees who were somewhat in awe of his position.

Meeting them for the first time, Zaban explained his decision to buy their company. "We checked out your shirts—as a matter of fact, I'm wearing one right now. We found the collars beautifully tailored, the neck fits well and the color lasts. The only detail we overlooked was: What about the rest of the shirt?" Zaban then removed his jacket, revealing his shirt, which he had shredded to pieces.

TRAINING AND PRESENTING NEW INFORMATION: "THE NEW ROBOT HAS ARRIVED AND HE'S ALL YOURS"

Most managers, at one time or another, find themselves in a teaching situation—either training a new employee, or more frequently introducing new procedures or equipment to their department. An effective leader can use humor to cushion the impact and help employees learn and retain information. By relieving the apprehension that blocks understanding, your humor will also free up the creative problem-solving abilities of your employees. Here are six possibilities for using humor in both formal and informal training:

1. *To break the ice, relax people and reduce anxiety.* Begin a training session with a five-minute brainstorming of funny names for the new piece of equipment.

2. *To help people retain information.* A young woman manager in our workshop had to conduct a one-week training session to teach her employees five different machines so they could in turn sell them to their customers. She said that the sales staff had trouble remembering the names of the different components in each machine. We took the first letter of the component names and created a funny mnemonic (memory device) for each machine's parts. The first letters for one machine's

parts were F, L, P, A, N, M, F, P, I, T, S. We came up with Fat Lipped Pigs Are No Match For Paris In The Spring.

She used this strategy, and reported to the seminar that the humorous associations had helped with memory retention, had made the normally dull presentation more fun for her as well as for those being trained, and the task had been shortened by a half hour. As Chapter 11 indicates, studies show the effectiveness of using humor to help people retain information.

Advertising executives are well aware that humor as a creative tool can sell ideas and help people remember their products. Of all the commercials on television, which ones catch your attention, and which ones do you remember with pleasure? Which ones stay with you even after they are no longer aired? Most often they will be ads embedded in your memory with a clever bit of humor. Many people still remember and use in conversation that classic Alka-Seltzer ad, "I can't believe I ate the whole thing!"

3. *To keep employees' attention.* Sitting in a darkened room watching a slide presentation is a nap waiting to happen. You'll lessen the odds of dozing or daydreaming by occasionally slipping in a funny or incongruous slide. "Here's the graph of projected industry growth for the next five years . . . here's a pie chart of foreign competition . . . here's my dog at the beach last summer . . ." A relevant cartoon would work just as well.
4. *To recharge employees' batteries in the midst of a long day.* Take a humor break and have each person tell a funny (and appropriate!) joke: "There's nothing worse than getting stuck in traffic with your carpool, no air conditioning, and a dang-blasted motivational tape." If the training lasts several days or weeks, you might assign several people each day to be responsible for providing the group with a funny anecdote.
5. *To facilitate hands-on learning.* Role-playing and exaggeration of incorrect methods naturally bring forth a lot of laughter while bringing the point home. Some medical school instructors are finding value in placing interns in the patient's position, asking future obstetricians/gynecologists to carry large weighted bags around their middles for several days, or to lie on an examining table with their feet immodestly draped over

stirrups. Abundant laughter accompanies these assignments, but as the doctors experience some of the discomfort of their patients, they also learn to empathize with them. Or, in teaching proper customer relations for cashiers in a discount store, exaggerating the totally wrong way to be friendly to customers ("How old is your baby? Are you planning to have more? Why so many? Are you crazy?") will drive the point home far more effectively than "Don't get too personal" reminders.

6. *To add an ongoing sense of fun to the learning process.* An instructor can make having fun contagious and can spread knowledge while fostering an atmosphere of cooperation. To humanize what's being taught, one boss, instead of talking about case studies of anonymous companies, makes up funny names, such as the Idaho Spud and Mud Company, The Civil Savings and Loans, and the Munch 'N Crunch Demolishing Company. The joking also relaxes everyone and makes the learning situation less threatening.

A Cautionary Note Watch out for miscommunication in humor. As with any other strategy, humor can occasionally misfire. As a boss you have to be particularly wary, especially with new employees who might not realize that you are kidding.

One boss made a habit of joking with his employees when they slowed down, arrived late, or took more time than usual for lunch. The old hands knew he had confidence in their ability because a trust relationship had been established. So they knew he was kidding when he'd say something outrageous like, "Let me guess why you're late. Someone hijacked your bus and drove it to Newark, and when they discovered who *you* were, threw you into the Hudson River!"

The day he tried that joke on a newcomer to his department, she took him seriously. "She felt I was picking on her, singling her out for being late. She hadn't seen my routine before, although I thought she had. She came into my office and told me to stop picking on her, but when I explained the situation, she smiled." After that when she came in late, she told her boss that her bus had been hijacked.

A manager who initiates humor should feel flattered when employees are comfortable enough to use humor back—as long as neither the boss nor the employee ridicules the other. Humor can be a smoothly paved two-way street.

Any boss should expect his employees to work hard and get the job done. But after a hectic race to meet a deadline, there can be room for a laughable, "Well, that was easy, wasn't it!"

HOW TO ADD HUMOR TO YOUR ORGANIZATION: OK, SO NOW WHAT?

"It took hard work to get where I am today. That, and a rich father."

Perhaps it isn't important to you whether or not your employees like you. It's true, they don't have to like you to get the job done. But chances are, an employee will be more loyal to a boss she likes and trusts. Although the nature of the work may necessitate a hectic work atmosphere, that climate doesn't have to be unpleasant. With a congenial atmosphere, an employee is more likely to look forward to coming to work every day and more likely to want to stay with your company (assuming the work is satisfying, the pay is fair, and the hours are reasonable). Humor is one way to come across as a person of goodwill. If you feel that you and your organization could use some constructive humor and don't know where to start, several humor sources are at your disposal.

1. Buy books with humorous stories, quotes or jokes, and find some that you can personalize.

2. Offer free doughnuts for a week to the employee who comes in with the most appropriate humor for whatever is happening at work that week. For instance, the president of one company received a "take-a-number" dispenser as a gift to use as his appointment calendar.

3. Put something humorous in your office that also makes a point. One vice-president has a life-size picture of her infant grandson with his toe in his mouth, and she captioned it, "Don't let our customers catch you this way." Another manager made a "Crisis Meter" for his door. The chart has a movable arrow with such readings as "All Clear," "Batten Down the Hatches," "Watch Your Step," and "Meltdown." He changes the arrow as a situation develops. On one occasion two staffers embroiled in an argument were reduced to laughter when he stood up and changed the meter reading.

4. Put up a humor bulletin board for employees to read in the company cafeteria line. Laughing always makes the wait easier.
5. When appropriate, brighten some of your memos and correspondence with a touch of humor. Thomas Edison interspersed funny sayings in the margins of his ponderous experiment notebooks to lighten the load for his overworked assistants.
6. Join an organization like Toastmasters if you want to learn to sprinkle humor into presentations or speeches.
7. If you hire a professional writer for your speeches, hire one who knows how to write humor tailored to your *personality* and *style*.
8. Take a humor awareness course at your local college or university in their continuing education department (see Chapter 14). You will meet other business people and will be able to share ideas and compare the atmosphere in your workplace with that in other businesses.
9. Bring in a humor consultant who can do some on-the-job problem solving with you, your managers and your employees, and who will make specific suggestions keyed to your business (listings in Chapter 14).
10. Take a humor break yourself, at least once a day.

Finally, consider this from Renn Zaphiropoulos, co-founder and president of Versatec, Inc. "A person who doesn't laugh may be a ruler, but he will get only what he asks for and nothing more. In high-tech companies you can't survive by having people do merely what you ask them to. You hope for pleasant surprises."

"It took hard work to get where I am today. That, and a rich father."

Humor With Co-Workers: Nobody Complains About the Weather When They're Laughing

On the first day of its annual August White Sale, a department store opens its doors at ten AM, and customers in a buying frenzy rush to the linens department. One harried sales clerk says to the other, "I never knew people could be so desperate for sheets." His co-worker replies, "The only sheets I'd like to get right now are four sheets to the wind."

One young physician in a Chicago hospital emergency room, after a particularly bloody, accident-filled night, remarks to the other resident working with him, "Cleaning up after the St. Valentine's Day Massacre must have been a breeze compared to this."

A shipping clerk banters with her co-worker, "The specifications on this invoice state that this order can only be filled by a redhead. And because you are the only redhead in the department, I guess it's all yours." Her colleague replies, "Tomorrow I'm a blonde."

These are all examples of humor in the workplace used constructively by co-workers. In the department store incident the humor implied, "It's a bad situation, but we are in this together."

On the first day of its annual August White Sale, a department store opens its doors at ten AM, and customers in a buying frenzy rush to the linens department. One harried sales clerk says to the other, "I never knew people could be so desperate for sheets." His co-worker replies, "The only sheets I'd like to get right now are four sheets to the wind."

The gallows humor was appropriate for the hospital situation and relieved the enormous pressure momentarily. To avoid conflict, the shipping clerk delegated the assignment with humor, and in turn her colleague used humor to register the complaint noncombatively. When you joke with co-workers, you are joking with peers, so you have a little more latitude both in the kind of humor you use and how you use it. First, rank and status among peers aren't as much an issue as between boss and employee. Therefore, you may use more personal humor without worrying about jeopardizing your job or making a bad impression on the boss. Second, you are likely to be closer to your co-workers to begin with, so the foundation for humor is already there. Last, even if you sometimes fail in using humor with co-workers, you don't have as much at stake. Because the risk factor is negligible, you may feel freer to experiment with humor among your co-workers.

For colleagues who are also good friends outside the office, humor often erupts spontaneously.

Two friends, Faye and Dian, accepted a time-shared job assisting the director of a senior citizens' apartment house. On Faye's first day, a new resident spent thirty minutes objecting loudly to the mandatory dining room plan. Faye left a detailed note for her friend Dian.

A shipping clerk banters with her co-worker, "The specifications on this invoice state that this order can only be filled by a redhead. And because you are the only redhead in the department, I guess it's all yours." Her colleague replies, "Tomorrow I'm a blonde."

The next day the same tenant stormed into the office, saw Dian's face behind the desk, and demanded, "Where's the lady in charge?" Immediately recognizing the situation, Dian replied sweetly, "She'll be back tomorrow," and left a note, "Dear 'Boss Lady,' your friend of the dining room complaint is looking for you."

Good friends like these two can get away with stunts like that and can use personal humor more easily without offending each other than can co-workers who do not know each other well and may not even like each other much. Therefore, for the sake of discussion, we will define our co-workers to be people working in the same office with relatively equal job standing, whose friendship does not extend beyond the work day. Let's examine, then, what humor between co-workers can accomplish.

ESTABLISHING RAPPORT: MEETING OF THE MINDS WITHOUT BUMPING HEADS

Have you ever sat at a business seminar among strangers and then laughed together at the speaker's amusing story? If you made eye contact with another person across the room, you probably smiled and nodded, indicating, "That was really funny, wasn't it?" In that brief connection, the act of sharing a laugh gave you and that stranger something in common, and chances are you no longer felt alone.

Humor in a work environment can serve a similar function, establishing rapport between two people, where no other common ground has yet been discovered.

> One young physician in a Chicago hospital emergency room, after a particularly bloody, accident-filled night, remarks to the other resident working with him, "Cleaning up after the St. Valentine's Day Massacre must have been a breeze compared to this."

BRIDGING THE GAP

Consider, for instance, a young, single secretary—we'll call her Amanda—fresh out of college, working in an office with a fifty-three-year-old married mother of four—we'll call her Margaret. Eventually, if they work well together, they may like each other enough to be interested in each other's lifestyles. But in the beginning, Amanda finds Margaret's settled home life dull, and Margaret is wary of Amanda's college education and fears possible airs of superiority. How can they bridge that gap?

That's where humor comes in, establishing a sense of rapport, however tenuous at first. Humor creates a shared experience. It lets you set up a shared moment *actively,* rather than waiting *passively* to find something in common. So what could Amanda and Margaret do?

Well, Amanda could lightly joke about her own inexperience on the job. "Learning to use this word processor is nothing compared to finding a new printer ribbon in the supply room." In addition to providing a mutual laugh, Amanda is signaling that she is aware of her own inexperience and open to help. By kidding herself about it, she is giving Margaret tacit approval to do the same. Margaret might reply, "Finding that ribbon in the supply room is a little like looking for my sixteen-year-old son in his room. I know he's under all that mess somewhere."

Margaret could also tell Amanda some harmless, amusing anecdotes about past experiences with their boss or other employees in the office. In doing so she not only establishes a link with Amanda, but also imparts useful information to her about the way the office functions.

GUIDELINES FOR HUMOR IN THE INITIAL STAGES OF WORKING TOGETHER:

1. Joke about yourself, not the other person. Many people will resent a stranger poking fun at them or their friends, and it is risky to do so before you are aware of their sensitivities and idiosyncrasies.

2. Don't put yourself down professionally. Although it is acceptable for Amanda to joke about her inexperience, it would be unwise for her to joke about her *ability* to handle the job. Her co-workers may believe her!

3. Share humor that is related to your job or the business in general. This keeps humor off the personal level completely and eliminates any worry about offending anyone.

4. Keep the amount of humor in line. If you are just starting to experiment with humor, you may be tempted to over do it. Humor can establish rapport, but remember this equation: appropriate humor + inappropriate timing = inappropriate humor.

By following these guidelines and finding a humor connection with your colleagues, you are on your way to building a good working foundation.

Two friends, Faye and Dian, accepted a time-shared job assisting the director of a senior citizens' apartment house. On Faye's first day, a new resident spent thirty minutes objecting loudly to the mandatory dining room plan. Faye left a detailed note for her friend Dian.

The next day the same tenant stormed into the office, saw Dian's face behind the desk, and demanded, "Where's the lady in charge?" Immediately recognizing the situation, Dian replied sweetly, "She'll be back tomorrow," and left a note, "Dear 'Boss Lady,' your friend of the dining room complaint is looking for you."

INCREASING COOPERATION: KEEP SMILING—YOU'LL DRIVE THE COMPETITION NUTS!

As we mentioned earlier, the boss sets the tone for the work atmosphere. As part of this atmosphere he or she may choose to arouse competition among employees. Competition in the workplace is a fact of life. But some competition is unnecessary, self-generated, and self-defeating.

In the long run, when it undermines cooperation by making short-term individual gain more important to a worker than long-term gain for the company, excessive competition can actually decrease the smooth running and overall effectiveness of a business (to say nothing of heightening stress levels for all involved). Management can use humor to stimulate a spirit of camaraderie among colleagues and encourage a teamwork atmosphere.

Where unnecessary competition goes, antagonism usually follows. Using humor to defuse that anger, you can often de-escalate the competitiveness, if only for the moment.

To impress the boss, one shoe salesman takes on more customers than he can handle at once, and his customers grow impatient waiting for him to help them. The other salesperson says, "Remember, we're all in this together. You don't have to sell out the store by yourself. There are plenty of feet to go around."

To impress the boss, one shoe salesman takes on more customers than he can handle at once, and his customers grow impatient waiting for him to help them. The other salesperson says, "Remember, we're all in this together. You don't have to sell out the store by yourself. There are plenty of feet to go around."

HOW TO POKE FUN WITHOUT OFFENDING

Some research studying the joking relationship of people at work indicates that joking among peers is common. As you get to know your co-workers better, the joking relationship becomes more personal.

Researchers define a joking relationship as one in which a participant has permission to gently kid a co-worker, and the co-worker tacitly agrees not to be offended. Until your relationships get to this stage of familiarity, you can still rib someone gently, without offending, by following these guidelines:

1. *Joking about something trivial and unimportant*—someone's habit of misplacing her glasses—that does not reflect negatively on either your colleague's job performance or on her personality.

2. *Joking about something that is obviously not true.* One teacher remarks to another, returning from a county-wide field trip, "You left with fifty-six students. I see you returned with fifty-six. You got the number right, but are you sure you came back with the same kids?" The incongruity, the gap between what you pretend is real and what everyone knows is really true, is the source of the humor.

3. *Joking about whatever a co-worker kids himself about.* This requires a bit more familiarity and good judgment than the previous suggestions, but you will still be on relatively safe ground. For someone who never bothers to read memos, send him a huge, pink, oversized memo with a "Try to lose this one" note attached (available at gift stores or the *Whole Mirth Catalog*).

At one insurance agency, rather than just complaining about the constant stream of paperwork, a hazard that comes with the territory, agents began gathering funny explanations for accident claims to circulate within the office. "Coming home, I drove into the wrong house and collided with a tree I don't have."

Joking within the group allows you to vent in an acceptable way frustrations about dealing with clients without your being labeled as the Office Whiner. And laughing about complaints that may have no quick solution serves as a coping mechanism to help control angry feelings. In one employee lounge, for instance, a worker tired of other people's continued grousing brought in a miniature basketball hoop for the garbage can. He taped a line on the floor a few feet away, with this sign: "Complaint Department: Write, wad, and shoot your complaints from here."

EXPRESSING A RISKY OPINION

JOB-RELATED AGGRAVATIONS

Humor is a constructive pressure valve and a lot more tolerable than banging your head against your all-too-thin office wall. Gripes, humorously expressed, transform your frustrations into a shared, collective one that opens the door for others to offer their opinions. In other words, the humor invites communication.

At one insurance agency, rather than just complaining about the constant stream of paperwork, a hazard that comes with the territory, agents began gathering funny explanations for accident claims to circulate within the office. "Coming home, I drove into the wrong house and collided with a tree I don't have."

Joking within the group allows you to vent in an acceptable way frustrations about dealing with clients without your being labeled as the Office Whiner. And laughing about complaints that may have no quick solution serves as a coping mechanism to help control angry feelings. In one employee lounge, for instance, a worker tired of other people's continued grousing brought in a miniature basketball hoop for the garbage can. He taped a line on the floor a few feet away, with this sign: "Complaint Department: Write, wad, and shoot your complaints from here."

PEOPLE-RELATED AGGRAVATIONS

When people work closely together, handling minor irritations and divisive tensions requires tact. With humor you can make your point indirectly, without provoking retaliation. Used in this manner, humor becomes a verbal shield.

A newspaper reporter, tired of constantly lending pens to a colleague who never returned them, finally attached a large helium balloon to her favorite pen that said, "Borrowed from Abby." That one came back with a sheepish apology. She could just as easily have sent an official looking bill with an "easy finance plan" to pay her back.

RELIEVING BOREDOM: IS IT SOUP YET?

To the untrained ear, employees joking on the job may sound unproductive, as if they are goofing off and not taking their work seriously. On closer examination, however, this behavior (in moderation) is probably helping them do their jobs.

In any job involving repetitious tasks, boredom is a real hazard that can lead to sloppy work, lack of motivation, and decreased productivity. Occasional humor helps break up the tedium, relieves some of the tension that repetitive work often provokes, and allows the workers to resume their task refreshed and alert.

The computer room in the E & W Bank is a small interior room with no windows. It contains six desks for the computer operators. Their data entry job requires concentration and attention to detail, but no creativity, little physical movement, and no change in the work from one day to the next.

Martin, their supervisor, observes that every day after working a couple of hours (and often again in mid-afternoon), someone spontaneously initiates a humorous exchange or physical bit of silliness—perhaps making designs out of computer paper edges or stringing paper clips together and inventing new uses for them. The incident usually lasts five to ten minutes and involves the entire group with a lot of hearty laughing. Then they resume work.

At first the supervisor is tempted to put a stop to the shenanigans. But after a while he realizes that his workers always seem to be in a better mood and able to work well after a few moments of horsing around. The humor breaks release pent-up energy, break up the monotony, and make the work environment more enjoyable.

So whether you are the employer or the employee, listen with an educated ear to the humor around you at work, and listen for the hidden message tucked inside. Even if you don't find new opportunities to initiate humor yourself, you will become more aware of how your office really functions.

The computer room in the E & W Bank is a small interior room with no windows. It contains six desks for the computer operators. Their data entry job requires concentration and attention to detail, but no creativity, little physical movement, and no change in the work from one day to the next.

Martin, their supervisor, observes that every day after working a couple of hours (and often again in mid-afternoon), someone spontaneously initiates a humorous exchange or physical bit of silliness—perhaps making designs out of computer paper edges or stringing paper clips together and inventing new uses for them. The incident usually lasts five to ten minutes and involves the entire group with a lot of hearty laughing. Then they resume work.

At first the supervisor is tempted to put a stop to the shenanigans. But after a while he realizes that his workers always seem to be in a better mood and able to work well after a few moments of horsing around. The humor breaks release pent-up energy, break up the monotony, and make the work environment more enjoyable.

Here are a few exercises for co-workers to try, either singly or together:

1. *Isolate common aggravations shared by the group,* such as irritating phone calls, unreasonable complaints from customers, or flimsy excuses from suppliers. Classify and rank them with varying point values for each. Keep a weekly score and give the winner of the week an Aggravation Trophy for her desk. (For five dollars, be a sport and pick up a small one from a trophy store). This has the added advantage, when others ask what it is, of airing the more irritating aspects inherent in the job in a natural way.

2. *Look for opportunities to use a running joke.* For example, in the office where the woman who arrives late now says, "Someone hijacked the bus," that could become the catchall excuse for anything that goes wrong. Thus, the next time food in the cafeteria is tasteless, a co-worker might say, "Someone must have hijacked the cook." Running jokes are the origin of many so-called "in-jokes," unintelligible to an outsider. The humor here is a code between people, much like verbal shorthand.

3. *Try the humor strategy.* Make a list of unpleasant situations that repeatedly arise in your office, and then come up with several relevant humorous responses. Use one next time. Waiting in line at the copying machine—"Somebody must have run out of five-dollar bills again."

4. *Start a joint collection of office anecdotes.*

5. *Put up a humor bulletin board* and encourage people to post funny cartoons, newspaper ads, articles, anecdotes, or original material, all relevant to your office. Use your imagination and come up with your own categories.

6. *Provide a few tape recorders and tapes of old radio shows* like "The Jack Benny Show" and "The Fred Allen Show" in the coffee room for employees to sign out. Or, begin a humor shelf there and encourage everyone to add books to it. A ten-minute coffee break might also become a nine-minute humor break.

So what's the bottom line? Even if two different companies offer the same job description, their "corporate cultures" and work atmospheres will vary. Responsibilities and pressures differ as much as the people who are asked to accept them.

But unless you have applied for the position of "resident hermit," you undoubtedly will at some time during your working day have to interact with other people. If most of that conversation is positive, you will probably perceive your work environment as pleasant.

Humor is no panacea that will make the burdens of organized life disappear. It can, however, make them much more bearable. As Mark Twain observed, "It is your human environment that makes climate."

YOUR UNOFFICIAL CO-WORKERS: MAKING AND MAINTAINING YOUR NETWORK OF BUSINESS CONTACTS

When the president of a large company retired, his biggest friendly competitor told this story: "David and I started out in the same business the same year, and David thought it was time for us to get acquainted, so he invited me to dinner at the most expensive restaurant in town. I put the date on my calendar and looked forward to our first 'one-on-one' with nervous anticipation. I got the day right, but mistakenly recorded it on the following week, thus standing up my formidable competition. Not realizing my mistake, I didn't even call to apologize.

"That evening he called my wife, introduced himself and asked if all was well with my family, expressing concern about my absence. Naturally I was upset when she called me to the phone. Before I could say a word, he said, 'Sam, I am so relieved to find out you really aren't perfect.'

"I am convinced that his generosity that day long ago contributed not only to the growth of both our businesses but more importantly to me as a human being."

When the president of a large company retired, his biggest friendly competitor told this story: "David and I started out in the same business the same year, and David thought it was time for us to get acquainted, so he invited me to dinner at the most expensive restaurant in town. I put the date on my calendar and looked forward to our first 'one-on-one' with nervous anticipation. I got the day right, but mistakenly recorded it on the following week, thus standing up my formidable competition. Not realizing my mistake, I didn't even call to apologize.

"That evening he called my wife, introduced himself and asked if all was well with my family, expressing concern about my absence. Naturally I was upset when she called me to the phone. Before I could say a word, he said, 'Sam, I am so relieved to find out you really aren't perfect.'

"I am convinced that his generosity that day long ago contributed not only to the growth of both our businesses but more importantly to me as a human being."

RAPPORT GALORE

If you were asked what you find especially valuable in your life, perhaps near the top of your list you'd name friendship. If we asked, "What specifically about that friendship do you cherish?" along with trust, admiration, and respect, you will likely add laughter. Few moments in life exhilarate like those filled with laughter between close friends.

Likewise, in order to build a network of business friendships, you must be willing to open yourself up to new possibilities and relationships, taking risks. If you want to develop a relationship, even one confined to your world of work, you must risk trusting another person.

There's always the chance that you will be disappointed, but the alternative is being isolated in your work and cut off from valuable sources in the quasi-social arena of business friends. The savvy work warrior actively seeks these new friendships rather than passively waiting for them to appear from thin air. This isn't always easy, but it doesn't have to be terribly difficult, and your sense of humor can be your best ally as you:

1. Distinguish between business and personal friendships.
2. Connect with others.
3. Disagree without being disagreeable.

DISTINGUISH BETWEEN BUSINESS AND PERSONAL FRIENDSHIPS

Some people run into problems with business relationships because they don't recognize and distinguish between the different levels of business friendships: close friends, casual friends, and friendly acquaintances. Although all three can add flavor to what could be a vanilla workday, they each require a different level of communication. When using humor to communicate, you should keep your remarks on the appropriate level.

You are likely to give to close friends a tacit approval to joke about personal subjects that you would not give to casual friends or acquaintances. For instance, you might feel free to joke with a close friend about her job or boss, whereas you might limit your humor with a casual Rotary Club acquaintance to less personal subjects such as the merits of opposing football teams. You might limit yourself to a humorous remark about the elevator service in your office building with someone you occasionally ride up with in the morning rush.

People get into trouble when they mismatch the joke and the person. The man in the elevator might not find jokes from a casual acquaintance about his baldness or potbelly funny, in the same way he might feel uncomfortable if you confide in him that the bank just turned down your request for a loan to buy a franchise. If he were a close friend, he'd be more willing to accept your teasing or listen to your problem.

CONNECTING WITH OTHERS: THE SUPERGLUE OF LAUGHTER

How often have you sat in a crowded airport watching the briefcase brigade on a Monday morning and wondered, "Where are they going? What are they thinking?" Although we all have separate lives, work constantly throws us together with total strangers. The decision to connect with another person in this situation is up to you. Sometimes you might choose to read a book on that cross-country flight. But occasionally you may prefer to converse with the stranger sitting next to you, and many a spontaneous work connection has been made waiting for the seat belt light to be turned off. Then humor is your best entrée.

On a flight to Pittsburgh a woman sat next to a man engrossed in paperwork. She mentally practiced her upcoming presentation until the flight attendant brought their meals and the man put his briefcase away. Having ordered wine, she was amused when the attendant handed her a small flip-top can of Chablis. Opening the wine, she remarked to her seat mate, "Do you suppose I'm supposed to sniff this aluminum tab?" Laughing together about the canned wine opened the way to a dinner conversation. He was a Pittsburgh native and offered helpful suggestions about the best restaurants in which to entertain clients during her stay.

On a flight to Pittsburgh a woman sat next to a man engrossed in paperwork. She mentally practiced her upcoming presentation until the flight attendant brought their meals and the man put his briefcase away. Having ordered wine, she was amused when the attendant handed her a small flip-top can of Chablis. Opening the wine, she remarked to her seat mate, "Do you suppose I'm supposed to sniff this aluminum tab?" Laughing together about the canned wine opened the way to a dinner conversation. He was a Pittsburgh native and offered helpful suggestions about the best restaurants in which to entertain clients during her stay.

Lose Your Cool Without Blowing Your Stack

Unless you have an affinity for the comatose, you aren't going to find business friends who agree with you all the time, and you shouldn't expect them to. Getting along with people means being realistic about the boundaries of business relationships, accepting them the way they are, and not expecting them always to have the solutions to your questions. Networking with your connections is a two-way street, and you've got to be willing to offer ideas and information as readily as you receive them.

When frustrations arise between business associates whose relationship may be grounded more in convenience than in mutual admiration, humor can blunt the sting of disagreement. After an especially heated faculty meeting, one professor noted to his friend who had opposed him on the issue, "Only in academia are the disagreements so big and the issues so small."

And when Eugene Cafiero, former president of Chrysler, flew to England to meet with riled up unionists at one of his plants, he faced off with a worker who yelled, "I'm Eddie McClusky, and I'm a Communist." The executive, nonplused, extended his hand and replied, "How do you do? I'm Eugene Cafiero, and I'm a Presbyterian."

Humor With New Business Friends

It is not unusual to be apprehensive when you face the prospect of meeting new people, even if you are a high ranking executive. Perhaps you dread going to a meeting of your professional organization because you might be called on to speak, or you fear being left out or ignored. These are leftover insecurities born in childhood and nurtured in adolescence. It's time to remind yourself of your accomplishments and reaffirm your ability to meet this challenge.

Bolster Your Knowledge Supply to Meet the Demand for Humor

Take off your blinders. Read and know what's going on in the world beyond your own narrow field, so that after you smile, you will have something to say. And if you hear a funny anecdote, remember it. You never know when it might come in handy.

Discussing innovative thinking at a national meeting, an advertising executive remembered an experience his wife had had recently: "My wife really brought the message home during the 1992 presidential race. She was working as a volunteer when a group of non-English-speaking Japanese tourists came to the Democratic headquarters seeking souvenirs. Thanks to my wife's quick thinking, the travelers continued their tour of our city proudly wearing extra-large buttons proclaiming themselves, 'Republicans for Clinton-Gore.'"

Discussing innovative thinking at a national meeting, an advertising executive remembered an experience his wife had had recently: "My wife really brought the message home during the 1992 presidential race. She was working as a volunteer when a group of non-English-speaking Japanese tourists came to the Democratic headquarters seeking souvenirs. Thanks to my wife's quick thinking, the travelers continued their tour of our city proudly wearing extra-large buttons proclaiming themselves, 'Republicans for Clinton-Gore.'"

USE HUMOR AS SOCIAL GREASE

Most strangers at business gatherings want to meet each other, but at the same time may be hesitant to initiate a conversation. So learn to ask open-ended questions that are likely to elicit humorous responses rather than "yes" or "no" answers.

For instance, if you meet an accountant, you might say, "You must get all kinds of questions about tax deductions. What are some of the strangest?" The question, "What was the first job you ever had?" often elicits amusing stories or may offer you some insight into that person's background and motivation. One dietitian started out shucking corn in Iowa, and decided she'd rather work higher up on the food chain. And a building contractor's first job cutting women's coats in a factory convinced him he never wanted to work inside four walls again.

Almost anyone has funny work experiences to relate, if only you'd ask. In sharing the humor, you start building rapport.

Smile . . . The Instant Facelift

If you are trapped in a boring conversation, don't feel stuck. Excuse yourself. A touch of humor will do nicely: "Excuse me, but I promised the treasurer I'd help twist some arms to collect dues. It was the only way I could get an invitation to hear the speaker." Or, "Excuse me, but there's someone over there I have to start an argument with." That one will clear your path immediately!

> "Excuse me, but I promised the treasurer I'd help twist some arms to collect dues. It was the only way I could get an invitation to hear the speaker."
>
> "Excuse me, but there's someone over there I have to start an argument with."

Stay Flexible

Discuss subjects you're enthusiastic about and ask other people about their interests. If your first goal is genuinely to learn about them and have fun, your enthusiasm will be contagious and people are more likely to be attracted to you.

Remember That First Impressions Aren't Always Right

Don't be too judgmental. A blank stare might mean that person is near-sighted and can't see you clearly. If someone doesn't recall meeting you before, try not to be offended, and handle it with a laugh.

When a short brunette saw a man at a meeting whom she had met several months before at a real estate closing, he obviously didn't remember her at all. But rather than react with an accusatory, "You *should* know me," she responded, "We met several months ago at the Cantwell closing. I was the tall blonde with the big check." This time she made a lasting impression with humor, and she did it without putting him on the spot.

VINTAGE BUSINESS FRIENDSHIPS: USING HUMOR TO STAY IN TOUCH

In our mobile society with changing life-styles, old business friends are sometimes left to simmer on the back burner while we become fired up with new opportunities. If you don't want these connections to evaporate, you must season and stir them, if only occasionally, as you get on with your work. The most pleasant way to stay in touch with longtime business associates is to use humor.

The most obvious humorous tack, and one that takes the least time, effort, and creativity, is sending a funny greeting card or cartoon that reflects some shared moment with your friend. One account executive sent his former mentor, Bob, a button he found that said, "Bob for President. Why not?"

There are other ways, however, humor can convey the message that although you are both busy people, you still value the friendship. Here are some ways a few people let their networking friends know, "I'm thinking of you and haven't forgotten how helpful you've been." Perhaps their creativity will inspire you to find humorous ways to stay in touch with some of your own vintage business friends.

Friendship #1 One woman sent her longtime newspaper contact an empty McDonald's hamburger carton with the note, "Lunch just isn't the same without you."

Friendship #2 After getting a Ph.D. in chemistry and laughing at the "stuffy establishment" for five years with his favorite iconoclastic professor, David took a job with a prestigious firm. He sent the former mentor a picture of himself which had appeared in the company newsletter. For the first time in many years, he was clean-shaven and short-haired, wearing a suit, a button-down shirt, and a silk tie. Turning the photo into a cartoon by pasting a little white balloon above his head, he captioned the picture with these words coming out of his mouth: "Thank God, Professor Wesson's not here!"

Friendship #3 A young woman also used a photograph to get her message across to a business friend who had just given birth to her first baby. She sent a picture snapped at an all-night brainstorming session at their publishing company ten years earlier. On the back she wrote, "This may have been your first sleepless night, but it sure won't be your last."

Friendship #4 Two stockbrokers at competing firms enjoyed a running joke about a garish necktie one had given to the other. The recipient tried to rid himself of the tie by hiding it in the other's file cabinet, and thus began a tradition of "secretly returning the tie." Finally, when the original giver moved hundreds of miles away, he arrived at his new office for the first time and was surprised to see the old faithful tie hanging on a doorknob.

However, that wasn't quite the end of the running gag, because several years later when the other broker's wife gave birth, a champagne bottle mysteriously appeared in the hospital room with no message except a bright garish bow made out of the tie. Over the years, the tie made many more surprise appearances. In this case, affectionate humor was the tie that binds.

Two stockbrokers at competing firms enjoyed a running joke about a garish necktie one had given to the other. The recipient tried to rid himself of the tie by hiding it in the other's file cabinet, and thus began a tradition of "secretly returning the tie." Finally, when the original giver moved hundreds of miles away, he arrived at his new office for the first time and was surprised to see the old faithful tie hanging on a doorknob.

However, that wasn't quite the end of the running gag, because several years later when the other broker's wife gave birth, a champagne bottle mysteriously appeared in the hospital room with no message except a bright garish bow made out of the tie. Over the years, the tie made many more surprise appearances. In this case, affectionate humor was the tie that binds.

Whether or not business contacts net friendships that last into retirement and beyond, networking with a touch of humor is invaluable to a career on the move.

P A R T

Communication

CHAPTER 5

Humor in Communication: When the Laughter Rings as Clearly as the Message, You're Really Talking

HUMOR IN SPEECHES

After a glowing introduction, the distinguished speaker stepped up to the podium, and a horrified audience watched helplessly as his written notes dropped from his hands, scattering across the floor. With the aid of the master of ceremonies, he took only a few moments to gather the papers. Silently the lecturer rearranged his notes, looked out at the audience, and said, "For my next trick . . ."

With humor he established an emotional link between himself and his audience, relieving the tension that his accident created. Laughter saved the day—not just for him, but also for everyone else.

It is not surprising that when Americans are asked, "What is your greatest fear?" more respond, "speaking in front of a group," than any other single apprehension. When you face an audience as a public speaker, not

After a glowing introduction, the distinguished speaker stepped up to the podium, and a horrified audience watched helplessly as his written notes dropped from his hands, scattering across the floor. With the aid of the master of ceremonies, he took only a few moments to gather the papers. Silently the lecturer rearranged his notes, looked out at the audience, and said, "For my next trick . . ."

only are you the center of attention, but you are there completely on your own. No matter how well you may have prepared your talk, you are always aware of the possibility of something going wrong, as well as those nagging questions: Will the meeting begin on time? Will I be delayed by heavy traffic on the way? Will I find a parking place when I get there? Will anyone attend? What about the microphone system? Will they remember to provide a podium for my notes? Will the slide projector work? Who will introduce me? And the ever persistent—Will my talk be well received? With preparation you can minimize the external hazards. If you learn to use it judiciously, humor can be your best ally.

You can eliminate most of the problems you might confront during a talk by developing a professional approach to your speechmaking. Even though your purpose may not be to entertain, view yourself as a performer and apply the principles of show business to your onetime appearance—whether it's in the board room, at a professional meeting, or at a ceremonial dinner.

Regardless of the content of your talk, you can avoid many problems by checking out the facilities and the technical equipment ahead of time. Allow plenty of time to locate parking as well as the meeting room itself. Get information about the makeup of your audience as soon as you accept the invitation to speak. How many people are expected? Will there be both men and women? Will you be the only speaker? Where in the program will you appear?

However, no matter how foresighted and organized you might be, like any other performer you know that the unexpected may lurk around the corner. A microphone can go dead, a waiter might drop a tray at a crucial point in your talk, or you may lose your place.

You can't anticipate every mishap, but you can fortify yourself with prepared humorous remarks for some of the more common hazards public speakers confront. Using humor to deal with these occurrences (and knowing you are prepared) will not only lessen your stress, but will also enable you and the audience to slough them off and refocus attention on the subject.

Some people, through practice and experience, have a more developed humorous perspective than others and find it easier to react spontaneously with a funny remark to the unexpected.

Just as everyone was seated and the speaker at a hotel banquet was about to begin her talk, two maintenance men carrying a ladder sauntered through the room. She could have ignored them and begun her talk. Instead, she silently watched them enter, stroll through, and exit. A nervously giggling audience watched her mute reaction until she finally began her speech with, "Well, now that we are alone . . ."

Just as everyone was seated and the speaker at a hotel banquet was about to begin her talk, two maintenance men carrying a ladder sauntered through the room. She could have ignored them and begun her talk. Instead, she silently watched them enter, stroll through, and exit. A nervously giggling audience watched her mute reaction until she finally began her speech with, "Well, now that we are alone . . ."

For most people, however, spontaneous humor does not come that easily. But you can learn to make prepared humorous responses look both easy and spontaneous. Books of one-liners specifically geared for public speakers are available in your library and bookstores. These collections contain categories dealing with some of the problems we have discussed. You can also subscribe to newsletters of current jokes and one-liners written specifically for public speakers by professional speech writers. For starters, try *Current Comedy, The Jokesmith,* and the *Executive Speechwriter Newsletter* (see Chapter 14).

Even if you approach your audience prepared with a few backup jokes for the unexpected, you may not cover every problem that might crop up. But you will be prepared for quite a few. Here are some to use as a springboard for creating your own.

1. When you lose your place: "I'm sorry. While I was running off at the mouth, my train of thought seems to have derailed."
2. When lights go out: "Everybody's a critic."
3. When lights come back on: "Was it good for you?" (Use with discretion!)
4. When something is being repaired: "When you are finished here, my car could use an oil change."
5. When you have to raise the mike: "I prayed my talk would be well received, but I wasn't planning on kneeling throughout the whole thing."

6. When you have to lower the mike: "I guess when_______suggested I give an elevating speech, he meant I should give it on stilts."
7. When someone drops a folding chair: "Why can't you carry a briefcase like everyone else?"
8. When you trip on the way to the podium: "This is like starting your own business—a fast slide down and a slow climb up."

"It has been a great honor for me to introduce tonight's speaker. But before I turn the podium over to him, I have to add that I am pleased that so many of our ladies are present this evening. What would we men be without you? After all, you ladies have been created for the erection of mankind!"

The Host's Introduction—Will It Be a Hard Act to Follow?

"It has been a great honor for me to introduce tonight's speaker. But before I turn the podium over to him, I have to add that I am pleased that so many of our ladies are present this evening. What would we men be without you? After all, you ladies have been created for the erection of mankind!"

It took the audience at this large national convention almost ten minutes to stop laughing after this faux pas. When the audience finally calmed down, the speaker thanked the meeting chairman for his "edifying remarks." By acknowledging the humor in the situation, the speaker brought the episode to a conclusion. He took charge of the laughter and redirected the audience's attention to him, winning them over before he had even begun.

A rabbi was invited to speak at a large church dinner. The woman chosen to introduce him had obviously done her homework and presented a beautifully written introduction. When she began to improvise, however, she ran into trouble. She beamed as she concluded, "I now present to you a Jewish rabbi and true Christian gentleman." The rabbi thanked her for her kind words and then added, "You called me a Jewish rabbi. Have you ever heard of any other kind? And as far as being a Christian gentleman, my dear friend, I hope you are at least half right."

Gaffes on the part of people introducing you are not uncommon. When they do occur, acknowledging them good-naturedly, with humor, spares the audience embarrassment and lets them know that no offense was taken.

Another problem is the overeffusive introduction. Again, humor is the best way to cope. By poking fun at yourself, you can release some of the hot air from the emcee's overinflated words. It is a good way to relate to the audience, letting them know you appreciate the compliments but that you are, after all, one of them.

On one occasion, we were invited to entertain at an employee appreciation banquet. The emcee must have confused us with Joan of Arc and Madame Curie, because his overstated introduction of our professional accomplishments created a barrier, putting too much distance between us and the audience. We had to topple that barrier before we could reach them. Humor accomplished this without offending the well-meaning host who introduced us. We did it by responding, "That was a beautiful introduction (pause). It's too bad those two women didn't show up."

Many professional speakers, accustomed to receiving poor introductions, write their own. You can do the same, mailing it ahead and carrying a copy with you as a backup if five minutes before your speech you are confronted with a hasty, "What do you want me to say about you?" Nine times out of ten the emcee will be relieved to receive it, because he hasn't really prepared his introduction anyway. Unfortunately, many people are careless with introductions, not realizing that they are your warm-up act and can help set the mood for your speech.

A rabbi was invited to speak at a large church dinner. The woman chosen to introduce him had obviously done her homework and presented a beautifully written introduction. When she began to improvise, however, she ran into trouble. She beamed as she concluded, "I now present to you a Jewish rabbi and true Christian gentleman." The rabbi thanked her for her kind words and then added, "You called me a Jewish rabbi. Have you ever heard of any other kind? And as far as being a Christian gentleman, my dear friend, I hope you are at least half right."

THE INGREDIENTS OF A SUCCESSFUL SPEECH

Keep It Short

Professional speech writer Robert Orben emphasizes, "A good twenty-minute speech will always be perceived as being better than a good long one. After twenty minutes, only twenty percent are listening, thirty percent have dozed off, and the other fifty percent are having sexual fantasies."

Make a Few Good Points

Limit what you plan to discuss. There is only so much material you can cover in a given amount of time. Once you have picked your subject, stick to it. Use language understandable to your audience and illustrate points with humorous examples and anecdotes when appropriate.

Give People Something to Think About

How many times after listening to a speaker is your initial reaction, "Whew, am I glad that's over!" or, "I thought he'd never finish!"? Later, when someone asks you what was said, it takes a few minutes to recall even one memorable point.

As members of an audience it has happened to us all. But you can avoid this reaction by making each person feel you are talking directly to him or her—sharing your thoughts and occasionally a good laugh.

There is no substitute for knowing your material. But your purpose should not be to overwhelm your audience with facts, but rather to challenge them and give them something to think about. Respecting people's capacity to think and feel, you can use relevant humor to appeal to their intellect as well as to touch them emotionally.

Leave Them With a Satisfied Feeling or Move Them to Action

Again, although your purpose may not be to entertain, you would do well to follow the show business axiom, "Always leave them wanting more." This doesn't mean incomplete or dissatisfied; it means, "I enjoyed her talk. I could have listened all night." Or, "What did you think about the point she made about . . . ?" "I think I'm going to read more about..." "I'm going to vote for her." Or, "Wasn't that funny when she told the story about . . . "

HOW CAN HUMOR HELP?

Even though you are not an entertainer, a smattering of humor can:

1. help your audience identify with you,
2. get them to like you,
3. get their attention,
4. help you make a point, and
5. help them remember what you said.

There are several kinds of speeches you might be called upon to deliver. So before discussing where to use humor in your talk, how to do it, and what to avoid, let's examine some different kinds of speeches.

THE IMPROMPTU SPEECH

Has this ever happened to you? "Before we close the meeting, I know you would all like to hear a few words from our good friend . . ." And the only words you can think of are, "Oh, nuts! What am I supposed to say?" For some people the impromptu speech is an accident waiting to happen. They either spend the evening hoping they won't be called on to say anything, or they are caught completely off guard when they are.

Others, however, when confronted with the unexpected, manage to say a few meaningful words seemingly without effort, with grace and a touch of humor. How do they do it?

The answer, of course, is that their remarks are often not completely impromptu. They are partially planned. And if they can do it, you can do it.

Although you may not expect to be called to speak, you can prepare for the eventuality. On one occasion at a large banquet when a prominent member of the community was unexpectedly asked to say a few words, he began, "As King Solomon said to the Queen of Sheba when he entered her tent, 'I did not come here to speak.'"

> "As King Solomon said to the Queen of Sheba when he entered her tent, 'I did not come here to speak.'"

Obviously he had stored away this humorous anecdote to be recalled if necessary, and it worked. While the audience was laughing, he was able to gather his thoughts for a few short, more serious remarks in keeping with the auspicious occasion.

You can do the same thing. Begin collecting and storing away in your memory a few appropriate anecdotes or jokes. If your story is related to the occasion, and your remarks that follow are short and to the point, you are bound to be a success as an impromptu speaker.

THE PERSUASIVE SPEECH: WINNING PEOPLE OVER TO YOUR POINT OF VIEW

This is the speech where you tell people what the situation is and what they should do about it. You pose a problem or an idea, and you try to win them over to your point of view. The purpose of your speech is to move people to act upon your words, to contribute something of themselves—time, money, or votes.

Often, however, you are not the only person vying for their support. Consequently your pitch needs to be more effective than your competitor's. Humor can sometimes give you that competitive edge, because if you embrace that audience with a blanket of laughter, they will be more warmly receptive to what you have to say.

Politicians have found that once they have won an audience over, they can take humor one step further, using its negative side to their advantage by ridiculing their opposition.

In the Reagan-Carter presidential debates, Ronald Reagan used this technique effectively. To counter charges thrown at him by Jimmy Carter, Reagan responded with his four seemingly innocent words, "There he goes again."

Senator Barry Goldwater tried it when he ran against Lyndon Johnson with, "Would you buy a used car from Lyndon?" But you have to be sure of your ground before using ridicule to cloak a verbal attack, because it can backfire, leaving your opponent with the last laugh.

"There he goes again."
Ronald Reagan

"Would you buy a used car from Lyndon?"
Barry Goldwater

If you want to win people over to your point of view, you first need to get them to like you. A hostile audience won't be receptive to your ideas. Obviously you should avoid offending them with sexist, racial, or ethnic slurs. If your humor is going to be risqué, use discretion.

Don't talk down to your audience with your humor, but be aware of the educational level of the people you are addressing. Adlai Stevenson's wit was sharp, but too esoteric for many people. His intellectual use of humor backfired when his opponents stuck him with the label "egg-head."

THE ILLUMINATING SPEECH—LIGHTING THE WAY

You, the lecturer, are the authority on the subject you are covering. As a teacher of facts, you are in a position to enlighten people with new information and leave them with something to remember. It won't work if they're fast asleep.

Most people attend your presentation or sign up for your course because they want to learn about the subject. Regardless of how difficult the material, a little bit of humor interspersed throughout your talk, combined with your own enthusiasm about your topic, can help you present factual material.

For example, you can interject one or two relevant cartoons among your slides or handouts. Add a couple of suitable jokes or anecdotes, where appropriate, to lighten your presentation. If that's not possible, at least begin your talk with a touch of humor for the audience, the topic, or yourself.

THE CEREMONIAL SPEECH—BRING OUT THE BIG GUNS

The ceremonial speech has a definite purpose, and it is usually an honor when you are chosen to give one. Often this speech commemorates a momentous occasion, a milestone in someone's life such as an award, honor, dedication, graduation, or celebration of a charity event.

This type of speech often has room for humor, but that doesn't mean the whole speech ought to be funny. As a matter of fact, this is often a forum for enlightening, as well as winning people over to your point of view. Beginning your ceremonial speech with a touch of relevant humor will put people in a good mood. Whether you realize it or not, audiences have come to expect it.

Dr. Jesse L. Steinfeld, former president of the Medical College of Georgia and former Surgeon General of the United States, gave a commencement address to the graduates of Georgia State University. His speech on the moral, ethical, legal, and medical issues of the future was exceptionally well received. His opening remarks are an excellent example of the impact of using humor tailored to both the audience and the ceremonial occasion.

> *It is an honor, privilege, and a pleasure for me to be with you at commencement. Of the limited number of messages that speakers bring to graduating students, few are remembered and for good reason. You have other things on your minds. Accordingly, I shall try to maintain this high standard and not distract you from your chosen careers.*
>
> *Let me begin with a story about a women's college. Some years ago, Vassar had an application form requiring parents to complete a questionnaire providing financial and other data. In response to one of the questions, "Is your daughter a leader or a follower?" Mr. Jones thought for a while and then wrote "follower." There were few other questions that required much thought, and the completed form was mailed.*
>
> *The usual sequence, because there were many more applicants than acceptances, was that Mr. Jones would not hear until the following March or April regarding his daughter's September application.*
>
> *To his surprise he received a letter by return mail from the president of Vassar. The letter said, "Dear Mr. Jones: It is a pleasure to inform you that your daughter has been accepted*

into next year's class at Vassar. From her application we can tell that she has all the qualifications that we seek in our students and graduates. She is academically highly qualified and has been successful in all her pursuits, scholastic and otherwise. P.S. Miss Jones will be in a class of 112 students. There will be 111 leaders and one follower."

Now, I'd like to summarize any number of commencement speeches so that you may be relieved of having to listen intently to my later discussion of health issues.

Be a good person and be kind to your fellow man. This will astound your friends and confuse your enemies and will lead to success in all walks of life except business, politics, the academic, social, military, and governmental worlds. These exceptions unfortunately cover all walks of life.

Don't forget your Alma Mater.

Continue your education lifelong.

Work hard and success will come to you—eventually, and if you live a long time.

Be true to your profession.

Be a good citizen.

Don't plagiarize . . . unless you think you can get away with it.

Get involved in society's problems.

Donate generously to your Alma Mater.

Don't watch television too much, unless you work in the industry.

Be a leader, not a follower. What this country needs is 230 million leaders.

Donate generously to your Alma Mater.

Keep healthy.

Avoid sinful companions.

Maintain the high morality exemplified by your fellow sinful students. I mean, maintain the high morality exemplified by your fellow students.

Be wary of government intervention, unless you happen to work for the government.

Be skeptical.

> *Don't go into debt . . . unless it is for donations to your Alma Mater.*
>
> *For every complex social issue there is a simple solution . . . and it's wrong.*
>
> *Give a full day's work for a full day's pay . . . especially while your boss is watching.*
>
> *Cultivate activities outside of your chosen profession.*
>
> *Remember the family is the foundation of our society, as accurately portrayed in prime-time and daytime TV.*
>
> *There is no problem that cannot be solved in the allotted thirty or sixty minutes, minus time for commercials, of course.*
>
> *Study the issues and candidates, thereby fulfilling your civic duty. Vote in every election.*
>
> *Encourage government support for higher education, particularly for your Alma Mater.*
>
> *Now that you are amply supplied with commencement messages, what I propose to do is discuss some selected health statistics so that you will have an idea, particularly those of you who are not in the health professions, of the kind of society you will face in the next fifty years, not only medically, but economically, morally, and ethically . . .*[6]

Occasionally the purpose of your ceremonial speech will be sheer entertainment. You may be asked to interject some levity on the occasion of honoring an employee or at a retirement dinner. This is the time to find out the office "in-jokes," poke fun at problems and frustrations common to that audience, and include in your humor some of the people present. Personalize it by good-naturedly poking fun at those things that they joke about themselves. But do your homework, taking care not to offend. If you don't know the people being honored, elicit the help of a tactful person who does.

WHEN YOU ARE IN CHARGE

INTRODUCING THE SPEAKER

It is better not to accept the task of introducing a speaker unless you are willing to do a little research. If you don't know the speaker personally, contact him or her ahead of time to discuss their topic and what they would like emphasized in your introduction. If a speaker sends you a résumé, highlight a few interesting things, but don't enumerate all accomplishments and every school attended. That's boring. Try to tell the audience something personal that will make them want to listen to what the speaker has to say.

Humor in an introduction depends on the subject of the speech, how formal or informal the gathering, how well the audience knows the speaker, and how well you know both the audience and the speaker. But please keep in mind that you are not the main attraction. Your task is to make the audience receptive to someone else.

If you do decide to use humor, you should relate it in a positive way to the person you introduce.

A magazine editor who was well known for his abrupt manner was invited to speak at a writers' meeting. The woman who introduced him began, "The first time I met Mr. S. was at a party. The hostess introduced us and when I said, 'How do you do,' he said, 'Get to the point.'"

After the laugh, she was able to emphasize that it was this business-like attitude, as well as his talent, that had led to his success as an editor.

A magazine editor who was well-known for his abrupt manner was invited to speak at a writers' meeting. The woman who introduced him began, "The first time I met Mr. S. was at a party. The hostess introduced us and when I said, 'How do you do,' he said, 'Get to the point.'"

After the laugh, she was able to emphasize that it was this business-like attitude, as well as his talent, that had led to his success as an editor.

TOASTMISTRESS OR MASTER OF CEREMONIES

"Have you heard the one about . . ." How many times have you attended a wedding dinner, only to have the happy mood ruined by a loud-mouthed band leader who has carelessly been given the job of master of ceremonies and who manages to offend everyone with his inappropriate, unfunny patter? Have you been subjected to the well-intentioned roast which turns the honored guest into shish kebab before your very eyes?

As a toastmistress or master of ceremonies, you have to be a helmsman of humor, setting a steady course geared for the occasion. You must steer clear of inappropriate humor that can sink the best planned party.

You can be more effective if you know the people involved personally. But if not, you can still shine by learning as much about them beforehand as possible. Then you can choose enjoyable material that is suitable for the occasion.

Find out who will participate in the program and what they plan to say, so you can prepare related humorous material. Having an agenda will also help you keep the momentum going and will encourage unprepared guests to organize their thoughts. If you can, it is a good idea to offer these people a specific time limit, because lack of preparation leads to rambling.

MODERATOR—LET ME MAKE ONE THING PERFECTLY CLEAR

As a moderator your job is to keep the meeting on track, to ensure each participant a fair share of time, to cool tempers (if necessary), and to field questions from the audience. A touch of humor can make your job much easier. Opening a meeting with a funny story related to what will follow often relaxes the participants and heightens the audience's expectations.

Several experts were invited to speak on a panel about "Starting Over After Retirement." The moderator opened the meeting with this story.

When John Kennedy was running for the presidency, he was found early one morning shaking hands at a factory gate in West Virginia. One grizzled worker asked him, "Is it true, young fellow, that you have a rich daddy and didn't have to work for a living if you didn't choose to?" And Kennedy replied, "It's true. I have a rich daddy, and didn't have to work for a living." The workman shook his head and said, "Believe me, young fellow, you didn't miss a damn thing."

When John Kennedy was running for the presidency, he was found early one morning shaking hands at a factory gate in West Virginia. One grizzled worker asked him, "Is it true, young fellow, that you have a rich daddy and didn't have to work for a living if you didn't choose to?" And Kennedy replied, "It's true. I have a rich daddy, and didn't have to work for a living." The workman shook his head and said, "Believe me, young fellow, you didn't miss a damn thing."

Besides getting a big laugh, her story provided a vehicle for thinking about needing to work, not needing to work, and people's relationship to their jobs.

As a moderator you should let each panelist know ahead of time the format of the meeting and the allotted length of speaking time. Emphasize that you will hold him to his time by slipping him a series of cards with warnings—"You have two minutes," "One minute left," and "Your time is up." If the speaker does not sum up after receiving the last card, your final message could be a funny cartoon of a face with taped lips saying, "That's it!" Then, out of respect for the other speakers, you need to cut him off gently but firmly.

Moderators who must field questions from the audience find that having a few prepared humorous comments can help. (Consult humor books geared specifically for speakers.)

When someone in the audience makes a long, drawn out statement instead of asking a question, you could say, "Well, sir, now that you've given us your in-depth answer, could you please dive in and find your question? I'm sure it must be in there somewhere."

A competent moderator who knows how and when to use humor can mean the difference between a well-run, informative meeting and a disorganized flop.

NAILING IT DOWN WITH HUMOR

WHERE TO USE HUMOR

The occasion and the audience determine where you use humor in your speech. Your first sentence doesn't have to be funny, but it should be an attention-grabber.

Generally, however, it's a good idea to include some relevant humor near the beginning of your talk. Don't announce you are going to be funny by saying, "By the way, something funny happened to me on the way to the meeting," but rather slip the humor in, adding the advantage of surprise to your funny story.

A political scientist once spoke on the subject, "Running for Political Office in the 1990s," and he began: "The main thing when running for political office is not to be hypocritical. The public likes a sincere person. If you are able to fake sincerity, you've got it made." His bittersweet joke opened the way for further comments about the role of television, computers, and advertising agencies in modern political campaigns.

As you prepare your speech, interject humor sparsely, where it can help you make a point, illustrate an idea, or help the audience visualize what you are saying. Keep in mind that in most cases humor is only a facilitator to the success of your message, not an end in itself.

> Novelist Frances Patton Statham was invited to speak at a dental convention in a busy downtown hotel. She allowed plenty of time to get there, but after driving around for half an hour, she couldn't find a parking space anywhere. Becoming desperate and realizing she had only a few minutes to get to the meeting on time, she spotted a gasoline station across the street from the hotel.
>
> She drove in and said to the attendant, "I'd like you to change the oil and grease the car. I'll be back in two hours." Not only did she get to the meeting just in time, but by telling them about her twenty-five-dollar parking place, she established immediate rapport with a laughing audience who readily identified with her problem.

HOW TO USE HUMOR

If you don't know what you are talking about, a few jokes aren't going to make much difference to an unimpressed audience. If you don't know how to organize or deliver a speech, you can get help from many good books in your library, as well as from courses at high schools, colleges, and recreation centers, such as the YMCA. To improve your public speaking skills, you can also join the Toastmasters organization.

But for the purpose of this section, let us assume that you are knowledgeable about the material you are going to cover, you know how to organize a speech, and, although you are nervous, your stage fright is manageable.

After you have written the body of your speech, and you have selected appropriate jokes or stories from your humor journal (collection), and you know where you want to use them, follow these basic suggestions on using your humor effectively with your audience:

1. Know your material well. Don't memorize it, but be intimately familiar with it so you can tell your joke or story in a conversational, believable tone.

2. Alter your story or joke so you can bring individuals who are present into the story. When talking at a banquet to a group of food service workers, we found out the dietitian's name. After joking about the large quantities of food these workers have to deal with every day, we pondered the question, "I wonder how Mrs.______ prepares an intimate dinner for two? She probably says, 'There are only twelve dozen left, they shouldn't go to waste. Eat!'"

3. Make sure you deliver your joke in a conversational style.

4. Besides sharing your ideas and expertise with an audience, share a bit of yourself. Poking a little fun at yourself humanizes you and helps the audience warm to your talk.

   Novelist Frances Patton Statham was invited to speak at a dental convention in a busy downtown hotel. She allowed plenty of time to get there, but after driving around for half an hour, she couldn't find a parking space anywhere. Becoming desperate and realizing she had only a few minutes to get to the meeting on time, she spotted a gasoline station across the street from the hotel.

   She drove in and said to the attendant, "I'd like you to change the oil and grease the car. I'll be back in two hours." Not only did she get to the meeting just in time, but by telling them about her twenty-five-dollar parking place, she established immediate rapport with a laughing audience who readily identified with her problem.

5. Find out the "in-jokes." Discover what people in that particular group kid about and work it into your talk. When entertaining at a hospital employees' awards banquet, we found out that recently all the room numbers in the hospital had been changed, resulting in a great deal of confusion. So we added that bit of information to another joke:

   ESTHER: "The last time I was in the hospital I had a private room. My room was so private the nurse never found it."

   LYNNE: "Well, maybe they changed your room number . . ."

   ESTHER: "Don't be ridiculous. What hospital would change patients' room numbers ?"

6. Make your stage fright work for you by converting that energy into vitality and enthusiasm in your voice.

ESTHER: "The last time I was in the hospital I had a private room. My room was so private the nurse never found it."
LYNNE: "Well, maybe they changed your room number . . ."
ESTHER: "Don't be ridiculous. What hospital would change patients' room numbers ?"

7. Practice your talk in front of a mirror. Practice telling your funny stories with a straight face. If you laugh before or during your joke, you will lose the element of surprise and ruin the story. Also look out for physical gestures that may distract attention from your words. If they're busy watching your flailing arms, or nervous adjustments of your necktie, they won't be concentrating on your words.

8. Use pauses. Don't rattle off your funny story. Give the audience a chance to absorb it. As comedian Stanley Myron Handelman said, "When an audience doesn't laugh, give them more time, torture them. They deserve it."

9. Speak slowly, distinctly, and loudly enough to be heard by people in the back row. Nothing kills a joke faster than, "What did she say?"

10. Keep your humor short, conversational, and sparsely scattered throughout your speech, and keep it meaningful to the audience, the occasion, and yourself. Instead of going for the biggest laugh possible, go for one that leaves the listener nodding in recognition at the message wrapped in laughter.

WHAT TO AVOID

1. *Avoid offensive jokes.* A hostile audience won't be receptive to your ideas. They are also capable of throwing rotten eggs and fruit. Remember, you are on your own.
2. *Don't tell long, involved stories* that lose half your audience before you get to the punch line. It's difficult to be heard over the sound of snoring.
3. *Don't underestimate your audience's capacity for humor.* Even if you don't get a laugh, it's better to approach them with a joke that makes them say, "I should have understood that," than to insult them with jokes they heard from their four- and five-year-old children. At least then if they miss the point, they can blame themselves instead of you.
4. *Don't explain a joke.* Humor is too fragile to be publicly dissected. If people don't laugh out loud, they may acknowledge the humor with a smile of recognition. If there's *no* reaction at all, either ignore it or, if you're feeling adventurous, dismiss your joke with a prepared funny reaction, such as crumpling a piece of paper, tossing it over your shoulder, and saying, "So much for that one."
5. *Always remember that humor merely enhances the material in your talk.*
6. *Keep in mind that some occasions do not lend themselves to laughter.* Then humor is both inappropriate and insensitive, and you should avoid it. Use good judgment.

THE NUTS AND BOLTS OF JOKE-TELLING

For several chapters we've been telling you that humor is much more than reciting funny stories. And it is. But for many people, telling jokes is either a considerable part of their style or a talent they would like to develop. Therefore, for those of you who want to improve your technique, we want to mention several elements of effective joke-telling. If you're serious about getting better laugh mileage out of your storytelling, try this:

1. Tape record five jokes in your usual style, trying hard not to "play" to the machine.

2. Tell the same jokes again, alone, in front of a mirror.
3. Think about the facets of joke-telling listed below in conjunction with your own style. Decide which need work.
4. Practice and refine your technique, each session concentrating on only one element. At the end of each practice, retape the same five jokes, and listen only for the one problem you're currently working on.
5. When you are satisfied that you're improving, make a final tape. Relax, have fun, forget about technique, and see how it sounds.

   If you have fortitude but no recorder, ask a brave and sympathetic friend for a (relatively) objective evaluation of progress. As you build on the following techniques, allow enough time for each lesson to mold to your natural speech patterns and cement your skills.

ELEMENTS OF EFFECTIVE JOKE-TELLING

Enunciation

Like a magnet, your mumbled speech will draw listeners' attention to the sound of your voice and away from the story itself. Results? No laugh.

EXERCISE: Open your mouth wide and recite the jokes several times at an abnormally slow pace, concentrating only on speaking the words clearly and precisely.

Volume and Projection

Speaking too softly can kill a joke just as quickly as mumbling. Become aware of your low voice level, and be on guard against poor speech habits or nervousness that can worsen the problem.

EXERCISE: Practice breathing deeply from your diaphragm for more power in your voice. Always take a deep breath immediately before beginning. And because proper breathing relaxes your muscles, including your vocal cords, it can lower your voice pitch, making it easier to hear. Lower pitch plus increased volume will add power and confidence to your delivery.

Gestures

Well-timed hand or body movements can add emphasis to your story and punch line. Moreover, they can energize your voice, infusing it with expression. Do, however, curb your impulse to overuse gestures, lest your listeners become transfixed by your histrionics. Observe professional comics.

Timing: Rhythm, Pace, and Momentum

All jokes have their own rhythm, maintained by your pace and supported by the momentum of accelerating anticipation. Here, lack of practice is the most common cause of problems. Even Steve Martin can't save a joke once he's stumbled over his words. Dragging out the story unnecessarily or speaking too slowly will cause you to lose the audience's attention and destroy the setup for your punch line. And above all, tell the *entire* story beforehand so you don't have to add anything after your punch line—explaining a joke afterward is sudden death.

Pauses

Don't ignore the effectiveness of pauses. They create anticipation, add emphasis to the punch line, and keep you from speeding through the setup. Try this joke with and without pauses to test its effectiveness: "One good thing I can say about his speech: he must have been alive when he wrote it."

TA-DUMMmmm . . .

After sufficiently practicing the nuts and bolts of joke-telling, it's time to quit thinking about technique. Relax, have a good time, and when the opportunity arises, try out your new style. And if ultimately you want to try your own hand at writing jokes, Gene Perret has written an instructive guide, *Comedy Writing Step by Step: How to Write and Sell Your Sense of Humor.*

Professional comedians, of course, have good material that is usually written by professional writers. It relates to their personality and meets the expectations of their audience. However, with outstanding professional material, almost anyone can be funny.

Do you doubt it? Take this copy of a portion of the classic Bud Abbott-Lou Costello routine, "Who's on First?" Read it aloud with a friend and see if you get a laugh. However, be forewarned—once you make other people laugh, it can become habit-forming.

WHO'S ON FIRST?

ABBOTT: You know, strange as it may seem, they give ballplayers nowadays very peculiar names. Now, on the St. Louis team, Who's on first, What's on second, I Don't Know is on third.

COSTELLO: That's what I want to find out. I want you to tell me the names of the fellows on the St. Louis team.

ABBOTT: I'm telling you. Who's on first. What's on second, I Don't Know is on third.

COSTELLO: You know the fellows' names?

ABBOTT: Yes.

COSTELLO: Well, then, who's playin' first?

ABBOTT: Yes.

COSTELLO: I mean the fellow's name on first base.

ABBOTT: Who.

COSTELLO: The fellow playin' first base.

ABBOTT: Who.

COSTELLO: The guy on first base.

ABBOTT: Who is on first.

COSTELLO: Well, what are you askin' me for?

ABBOTT: I'm not asking you. I'm telling you. Who is on first.

COSTELLO: I'm asking you, who's on first?

ABBOTT: That's the man's name!

COSTELLO: That's whose name?

ABBOTT: Yes.

COSTELLO: Well, go ahead tell me!

ABBOTT: Who.

COSTELLO: Have you got a first baseman on first?

ABBOTT: Certainly.

COSTELLO: Then who's playing first?

ABBOTT: Absolutely.

COSTELLO: Well, all I'm trying to find out is what's the guy's name on first base.

ABBOTT: Oh, no, no. What is on second base.

COSTELLO: I'm not askin' ya who's on second.

ABBOTT: Who's on first.

COSTELLO: That's what I'm trying to find out.

ABBOTT: Now, take it easy.

COSTELLO: What's the guy's name on first base?

ABBOTT: What's the guy's name on second base.

COSTELLO: I'm not askin' ya who's on second.

ABBOTT: Who's on first.

COSTELLO: I don't know.

ABBOTT: He's on third.

COSTELLO: If I mentioned the third baseman's name, who did I say is playing third?

ABBOTT: No, Who's playing first.

COSTELLO: Stay offa first, will ya?

ABBOTT: Well, what do you want me to do?

COSTELLO: Now, what's the guy's name on first base?

ABBOTT: What's on second.

COSTELLO: I'm not asking ya who's on second.

ABBOTT: Who's on first.

COSTELLO: I don't know.

ABBOTT: He's on third.

COSTELLO: There I go back to third again.

ABBOTT: Please. Now what is it you want to know?

COSTELLO: What is the fellow's name on third base?

ABBOTT: What is the fellow's name on second base.

COSTELLO: I'm not askin' ya who's on second.

ABBOTT: Who's on first.

COSTELLO: I don't know. (Makes noises) You got an outfield?

ABBOTT: Oh, sure.

COSTELLO: The left fielder's name?

ABBOTT: Why.

COSTELLO: I just thought I'd ask.

ABBOTT: Well, I just thought I'd tell you.

COSTELLO: Then tell me who's playing left field.

ABBOTT: Who's playing first.

COSTELLO: Stay out of the infield. I want to know what's the fellow's name in left field.

ABBOTT: What is on second.

COSTELLO: I'm not asking you who's on second.

ABBOTT: Now take it easy, take it easy.

COSTELLO: And the left fielder's name?

ABBOTT: Why.

COSTELLO: Because.

ABBOTT: Oh, he's center field.

COSTELLO: Wait a minute. You got a pitcher?

ABBOTT: Wouldn't this be a fine team without a pitcher?

COSTELLO: Tell me the pitcher's name.

ABBOTT: Tomorrow.

COSTELLO: You don't want to tell me today?

ABBOTT: I'm telling you, man.

COSTELLO: Then go ahead.

ABBOTT: Tomorrow.

COSTELLO: What time tomorrow are you gonna tell me who's pitching?

ABBOTT: Now listen. Who is not pitching. Who is on—

COSTELLO: I'll break your arm if you say who's on first.

ABBOTT: Then why come up here and ask?

COSTELLO: I want to know what's the pitcher's name.

ABBOTT: What's on second.

COSTELLO: Ya gotta catcher?

ABBOTT: Yes.

COSTELLO: The catcher's name?

ABBOTT: Today.

COSTELLO: Today. And Tomorrow's pitching.

ABBOTT: Yes.

COSTELLO: I'm a good catcher too, you know.

ABBOTT: I know that.

COSTELLO: I would like to catch. Tomorrow's pitching and I'm catching.

ABBOTT: Yes.

COSTELLO: Tomorrow throws the ball and the guy bunts the ball.

ABBOTT: Yes.

COSTELLO: Now when he bunts the ball—me being a good catcher—I want to throw the guy out at first base, so I pickup the ball and throw it to who?

ABBOTT: Now, that's the first thing you've said right.

COSTELLO: I DON'T EVEN KNOW WHAT I'M TALKING ABOUT.

ABBOTT: Well, that's all you have to do.

COSTELLO: Is to throw it to first base.

ABBOTT: Yes . . . [7]

AND SO, IN CONCLUSION . . .

When you give a speech it is important to respect your audience. Granted, it takes additional time and effort to find appropriate humor for your talk, but sharing a bit of humor lets them know that you like them and appreciate their capacity for laughter. Humor helps the audience identify with you, accept you, and become more willing to listen to what you have to say.

By being prepared, you can help minimize your own stress, enhance the material, and cope with difficult circumstances. Imagine being in front of a large crowd. You step up to the microphone as the chairwoman concludes her introduction: "I am happy to see such a great attendance for today's talk. If you continue this kind of cooperation, we shall be able to get better speakers next year."

OK, speaker, you are on your own.

CHAPTER 6

Difficult Situations: No One Spits on a Smiling Face

SAYING NO WITH HUMOR

After telling them "no" in a memo, a business owner walked into a meeting of unhappy employees. Handing each of them a pair of scissors and a copy of his photo, he said, "Go ahead. Now you can finish cutting me to pieces." His gesture broke the ice and opened the way for a rational talk about the problems at hand.

In this example, the boss used humor to let his employees know he was sensitive to their feelings and vulnerable to their reactions. By putting business on a person-to-person level, he enabled his employees to identify with him and to listen to the reasoning behind his "no."

"No," regardless of how you phrase it, is a disappointment, and it is often misinterpreted as a personal rejection. By adding a touch of humor, you can help others save face, letting them know your rejection of their request is not a rejection of them personally.

You can use humor to say "no" when dealing with unreasonable or untimely demands as well as with demands you don't wish to accept.

> After telling them "no" in a memo, a business owner walked into a meeting of unhappy employees. Handing each of them a pair of scissors and a copy of his photo, he said, "Go ahead. Now you can finish cutting me to pieces." His gesture broke the ice and opened the way for a rational talk about the problems at hand.

When Joanne Black, senior vice-president of marketing at MasterCard International, was being interviewed for a management job, she realized it was a "stress interview" where it was appropriate for the interviewer to be tough. He laid it on thick with, "You'll have to live, breathe and sleep the job, and work night and day." Finally she smiled and asked, "Do I get to go to the bathroom?" Breaking the tension, he laughed and replied, "Only if you take something to read."

At a party, a pediatrician was accosted by a mother who asked him about her baby's rash. He smiled, turned over his lapel, showed her his "Off Duty" button, and recommended she bring the baby to his office in the morning.

DEMANDS FOR YOUR COOPERATION

You can say no directly to a request, then offer a humorous explanation.

A graduate student asked permission to record the professor's lectures. "I don't allow tape recorders in my classroom," the professor answered. "This is, after all, a benevolent dictatorship." The class laughed but got the point. The professor was really saying, "The answer is no, because that's the way I want it." He left no room for argument, only direct truth lightened by humor. The student in turn accepted his refusal without feeling intimidated, put down, or embarrassed.

When Joanne Black, senior vice-president of marketing at MasterCard International, was being interviewed for a management job, she realized it was a "stress interview" where it was appropriate for the interviewer to be tough. He laid it on thick with, "You'll have to live, breathe and sleep the job, and work night and day." Finally she smiled and asked, "Do I get to go to the bathroom?" Breaking the tension, he laughed and replied, "Only if you take something to read."

DEMANDS FOR YOUR MONEY AND TALENT

Who wouldn't like to erase poverty, disease, and ignorance, if it were in their power to do so? Realistically, though, time and financial limitations force you to be selective of good causes to support. Thus, sometimes you are faced with the most difficult "no" of all—refusing to help when you would really like to be able to say "yes."

Although you don't want to sound flip when refusing to support a worthy endeavor, adding a soft touch of humor to your refusal sometimes makes it easier for you, as well as for the other person. Keep in mind that asking you to contribute can be as difficult for many people as refusing is for you.

Being confronted by these requests may make you feel cornered and embarrassed. Consequently, too often your first response may be abrupt or angry: "I haven't got another minute to spare." "I gave at the office." "I raised my pledge last year."

A laugh can relieve an awkward situation and smooth the way for a graceful exit:

"I wish I could give more, but Uncle Sam got here first, and I'm doing my share to pay off the national debt."

"I really would like to help you, but the problem is that, as a child, I saved my pennies. Unfortunately, I should have saved five-dollar bills."

"I wish I could accept your offer to speak to your club, but I've done my share of community service this year. As a matter of fact, I've done more community service than the City Council."

"I wish I could give more, but Uncle Sam got here first, and I'm doing my share to pay off the national debt."

"I really would like to help you, but the problem is that, as a child, I saved my pennies. Unfortunately, I should have saved five-dollar bills."

"I wish I could accept your offer to speak to your club, but I've done my share of community service this year. As a matter of fact, I've done more community service than the City Council."

HUMOR AND ASSERTIVENESS

To whom do you have the most trouble saying no? In what situations, or on what subjects, is saying no the hardest? How do you react when returning merchandise to a store or when speaking up in a group? How do you handle guilt-invoking requests from friends and family? How do you deal with a salesperson, the repairman, a charity worker, or an authority figure?

For many people, saying no doesn't come easily because it involves swimming upstream. It's harder than going with the current. You want to be strong and assertive enough to disagree but you don't want to seem unnecessarily contrary and unpleasant.

Assertiveness coupled with humor can either help you tone down a tendency to be overly aggressive, or help you conquer timidity and stand up for your rights.

In discussing how to say no with humor, let's assume that you know—and usually practice—basic assertiveness skills. That is, in response to someone's request, you:

1. *Acknowledge the other person's position.*
   ("I know you want to finish the project today.")

2. *Express your own position.*
   ("I have a full afternoon of appointments.")

3. *State what you want.*
("I'd like you to bring in the reports at nine o'clock tomorrow morning and we can be finished by lunch time.")

For those of you who are aware of the directness involved in the assertive model, humor may seem to be an unwelcome note of indirectness. In many serious situations, indiscriminately used humor may indeed be inappropriate and may undermine the importance of what you're saying. Still, in everyday circumstances humor can often maximize your assertive skills.

USE HUMOR TO:

MAINTAIN YOUR FOCUS ON SOLVING THE PROBLEM

In any discussion where two opposing viewpoints need to be resolved, someone can veer off on a tangent, wasting time and energy on side issues. Humor can bring the focus back to the real problem.

In traffic court, a Realtor pointed out to the judge that the college student who ran into her car as she exited the parking lot at her business had exceeded the speed limit, coming over the hill too fast. The other driver talked at length about the signs around the business property, trying to distract the judge from his speeding.

When the judge asked the Realtor if the signs had interfered with her vision, she replied, "If I removed all of the signs and attached a propeller and periscope to my Toyota, I still couldn't have slowed him down as he came over that hill. I was a sitting duck."

With humor she refocused the discussion on the other driver's reckless speeding that had caused the accident.

In traffic court, a Realtor pointed out to the judge that the college student who ran into her car as she exited the parking lot at her business had exceeded the speed limit, coming over the hill too fast. The other driver talked at length about the signs around the business property, trying to distract the judge from his speeding.

When the judge asked the Realtor if the signs had interfered with her vision, she replied, "If I removed all of the signs and attached a propeller and periscope to my Toyota, I still couldn't have slowed him down as he came over that hill. I was a sitting duck."

With humor she refocused the discussion on the other driver's reckless speeding that had caused the accident.

BUY TIME

Laughter—yours and theirs—gives you time to gather your thoughts and think of an appropriate response. It also helps you to control your own tension and anxiety in difficult situations so you can continue calmly and effectively. In turn, your self-control may also keep the other person's emotions in check.

Investigating a family disturbance call, San Francisco police officer Adelle Roberts saw a television set crash through the front window. She rang the doorbell while hearing the sounds of a heated argument. A gruff voice demanded, "Who is it?" Instead of answering, "Police," she said, "TV repairman." The shouts dissolved into laughter, and set the scene for a peaceful solution.

Investigating a family disturbance call, San Francisco police officer Adelle Roberts saw a television set crash through the front window. She rang the doorbell while hearing the sounds of a heated argument. A gruff voice demanded, "Who is it?" Instead of answering, "Police," she said, "TV repairman."

CHANGE YOUR NEGATIVE VIEWPOINT TO A LIGHT-HEARTED, I-KNOW-THERE'S-SOMETHING-FUNNY-ABOUT-THIS VANTAGE POINT

An architect shared a taxi with two other people from the hotel to the airport. When they arrived at the terminal, he discovered that the cab driver had failed to put his suitcase in the trunk. Instead of getting angry, he said, "On the way back to the hotel, I want you to point out the sights—I really want my money's worth. And if I miss the next plane to New York, I hope your wife is a good cook."

Replacing the usual anxiety-provoked gut response with a humorous one will interrupt non-productive and potentially harmful behavior patterns and help you cope, while at the same time allowing you to remain assertive.

An architect shared a taxi with two other people from the hotel to the airport. When they arrived at the terminal, he discovered that the cab driver had failed to put his suitcase in the trunk. Instead of getting angry, he said, "On the way back to the hotel, I want you to point out the sights—I really want my money's worth. And if I miss the next plane to New York, I hope your wife is a good cook."

TEMPER YOUR OWN AGGRESSION

Learning the appropriate way to stand up for your rights is just as important for the aggressive person as for the passive one. Using humor indirectly as part of an assertive statement relaxes you physically, decreases your anger, and takes the edge out of your voice. Humor can make subtle changes in your body language, making your demeanor less threatening to the person you are dealing with, but still leaving the message clear.

A man had allowed two people with single item purchases to go in front of him in the grocery store checkout line. As he finished putting his purchases on the conveyor belt, a woman with a few items came up behind him and said, "I'm in a hurry. You won't mind if I go in front of you, will you?"

His first impulse was to say, "Hell, yes, I'd mind!" But tempering his anger with humor, he instead responded calmly, "Lady, I'm an obstetrician, and I was just in the process of delivering twins when I realized I was out of a few things. I'd let you go ahead of me, but the second one is ready to pop any minute now, and I really need to get back."

Another appropriate response to her question could be, "I can't let you cut in today, but I'll let you go ahead of me the next time we're in line together."

On the Other Hand, Who Says You Have to Accept No?

When McIntyre, the Texas rancher, ordered turtle soup at Maxim's in Houston, owner Camille Bermann said there were no turtles available. Later that afternoon, McIntyre phoned Bermann. "Camille, there's a turtle waiting for you across the street in the garage." Sure enough, McIntyre had gone out and unearthed—as only millionaires can—a five hundred pound turtle, glued a broom handle to its hefty shell, and chained it to a post in the parking garage.

Bermann was speechless but not surprised. After all, McIntyre was also the man who, not finding watermelon on the menu, had an entire truckful of the juicy fruits unloaded on the busy downtown street smack-dab in front of the restaurant. He didn't accept the "no" and got his watermelon.

And even though you might not have the clout of a turtle soup-loving millionaire, when you hear, "It's not possible," you still have the power to answer, "I'm sure you're sure you're right, but whom do I talk to now?" The story of McIntyre and Bermann shows that good-natured persistence pays off, and that a good business owner doesn't take him- or herself too seriously.

> A man had allowed two people with single item purchases to go in front of him in the grocery store checkout line. As he finished putting his purchases on the conveyor belt, a woman with a few items came up behind him and said, "I'm in a hurry. You won't mind if I go in front of you, will you?"
>
> His first impulse was to say, "Hell, yes, I'd mind!" But tempering his anger with humor, he instead responded calmly, "Lady, I'm an obstetrician, and I was just in the process of delivering twins when I realized I was out of a few things. I'd let you go ahead of me, but the second one is ready to pop any minute now, and I really need to get back."
>
> Another appropriate response to her question could be, "I can't let you cut in today, but I'll let you go ahead of me the next time we're in line together."

The Written No

All of these suggestions on using humor to say no are just as effective when using the written no. A written refusal can have several advantages over face-to-face confrontations, because the written refusal:

- adds distance
- can be re-read to clarify meaning
- offers no body language (which sometimes conflicts with the spoken message)
- states your complete argument without interruptions, and
- removes gnashing of teeth that would exist in a vocal answer.

Although humor can be part of your written "no," it can be just as effective in your method of delivery as in the message itself.

A boss found many typographical errors in a letter his tired secretary had hurriedly typed before leaving work. The next morning she found the letter with penciled corrections. Stuck to it was a Band-aid with this notation: "I tried this, but it didn't work. Please do it over. Thanks."

A note to your spouse could be left under the car's windshield wiper. One to your child could be impaled on his toothbrush. (Of course, in this case, you are taking a chance he might never see it!)

This sign in front of one store gets due attention:

"This Loading Zone is Not a Creative Parking Space."

Humor is not the only way to say no, nor is it necessarily the best. But as a supplement to your own assertive skills, humor can make refusals less painful for others as well as for yourself.

When McIntyre, the Texas rancher, ordered turtle soup at Maxim's in Houston, owner Camille Bermann said there were no turtles available. Later that afternoon, McIntyre phoned Bermann. "Camille, there's a turtle waiting for you across the street in the garage." Sure enough, McIntyre had gone out and unearthed—as only millionaires can—a five hundred pound turtle, glued a broom handle to its hefty shell, and chained it to a post in the parking garage.

Bermann was speechless but not surprised. After all, McIntyre was also the man who, not finding watermelon on the menu, had an entire truckful of the juicy fruits unloaded on the busy downtown street smack-dab in front of the restaurant. He didn't accept the "no" and got his watermelon.

OILING THE WAY FOR INFORMATION

"Please pay attention while your flight attendant gives instructions concerning the safety features of this airplane." All passengers' eyes are focused on the attendant standing at the front of the cabin, holding a demonstration seat belt. For a change, *everyone* is paying attention because she is wearing a gorilla mask. And everyone is laughing as she gives the required instructions.

"Please pay attention while your flight attendant gives instructions concerning the safety features of this airplane." All passengers' eyes are focused on the attendant standing at the front of the cabin, holding a demonstration seat belt. For a change, everyone is paying attention because she is wearing a gorilla mask. And everyone is laughing as she gives the required instructions.

On her own, this attendant, one of our students, had devised this method to capture and hold passengers' attention. But she wanted other humorous but less drastic ways to improve the task of giving instructions. It is not only annoying but also potentially dangerous when passengers ignore routine preflight instructions.

People often resist heeding new information or listening to material they assume they already know. Your job, then, when giving this information, is to get and hold their attention, and to make them receptive enough to listen from beginning to end. By making it as pleasant and palatable as possible, you help your audience retain the information after you finish. Oiling the way with humor is an excellent method to get your information across to the listener. It can work in all kinds of interactions, whether between parent and child, trainer and trainee, teacher and student, or organization president and club member.

Our class came up with two practical humorous techniques that the attendant successfully incorporated in later demonstrations. These techniques can be adapted to other instances when it is necessary to break down resistance while presenting information.

1. *Involve the participants.* Involve a willing passenger (participant) seated near the front by asking him to hold your materials and to hand them to you as needed. Announce to the passengers that "Joe" is your assistant during the demonstration, and that he would appreciate their undivided attention. Then demonstrate (or give the information), keeping your helper involved—"Joe, could you please hand me the seat belt?" "If the oxygen mask drops in front of Joe, this is what he should do." Personalizing the demonstration makes it interesting and even fun.

2. *Inserting a few jokes can also be effective.* "Joe travels a lot. He flies so much that he's a natural. The last time he flew to New York, he arrived ten minutes before we landed."

3. *Tantalize your listeners.* Announce to the passengers (participants) that you will insert a bit of trivia related to the demonstration, and that when you are finished, the first passenger to raise his or her hand with the correct answer will get a free drink. The trivia question could be the flight attendants' names, something about the type of plane, or the cruising altitude, just to mention a few possibilities. Including a couple of humorous historical facts about air travel could also make the presentation more interesting and help hold their attention.

These are only a couple of examples of using humor creatively to ease the tedium of presenting factual material. Invent others that apply to your own situation. You will also find examples throughout this book which are adaptable to many different circumstances.

When presenting information, you might encounter people who fear that they will not understand the materials. Their anxiety level will increase if they feel that the information is vital to their success, whether on the job or at school.

When you deal with anxious people in a learning or training situation, you can use humor at the outset to relax them, making what follows less threatening. Here's how it can work:

Example 1: In its push to modernize, a supermarket converts from traditional cash registers to the computerized variety. For some long-time employees with no exposure to computers, the change is quite traumatic. For the first time in a long time, many of them feel mechanically inept, inadequate on the job, and extremely threatened.

The boss reassures them, explaining that once they learn how to use the new machines, they will come to prefer them, because computers will make their jobs easier. He adds, "Just try to look at this new cash register as a real shot in the arm. Of course, I realize that right now, some of you feel as if that shot is coming from a cannon, but give it a chance."

His humorous remark lets them vent some of the tension as they laugh, and they realize he will be sympathetic during the transition.

Example 2: A biology teacher instructs her first-day students on what they will need to bring for their first unit on frog dissection. "You will need to bring your lab notes, your dissecting kit, surgical gloves, and a brain . . . preferably your own."

Example 3: After initially relaxing anxious people, you should encourage them to ask questions. When answering the questions, you shouldn't ridicule their concerns, but you can, on occasion, minimize them with gentle humor.

Another teacher gives his students fifteen minutes in class to write "What it means to be an American." When a student asks, "How long should this paper be?" the teacher good-naturedly responds, "At least eleven inches." His joke relaxes the entire class as he seriously adds, "All I want are a few thoughts as a basis for tomorrow's discussion."

Example 4: A committee chairwoman instructs her members on making paper flowers for table decorations. One member wails, "My flower looks as if it just died." Whereupon the chairwoman replies, "Hang on, I'll be there in just a minute with my watering can," letting her know, through humor, "Don't get discouraged, I'll help out, it can be fixed." Humor in this instance also serves to make you—the instructor, teacher, or trainer—one of the group.

Example 5: The trainer asks a trainee, "Show us the five worst ways to approach this problem." After the participants laugh at the overstated mistakes, they are then receptive to learning the five best methods.

In these examples, the authority figure, needing to pass on information, used humor to stay in control and facilitate the assimilation of the new information. If it can help people listen, learn, and remember new material, then laughter is indeed a key to success.

REFUSING TO LET GO

Have you ever told a funny story to someone who didn't laugh? Making people laugh is serious business for those who earn a living at it. One famous comedian takes his craft so seriously that he feels he has failed if he notices a single person in the audience not responding to his humor.

On one occasion, the entire audience except for a man in the fifth row was howling with laughter. Noticing the man's blank expression, the comic "played" his jokes and stories directly to that man for the rest of his performance.

Powerless to evoke even one laugh, he felt he had failed, even though he had drawn laughs from everyone else. Only later did he learn that the man was a visitor to the United States and spoke no English.

Sometimes people don't laugh because they don't see the point of the story. Perhaps you haven't told it well, or maybe that particular story simply doesn't strike them as being funny. But what about the person who *never* laughs when others are smiling and laughing? What's his problem?

Presuming that he understands the language, you may guess that he is preoccupied, unhappy, or depressed. You might sense, however, that he is simply unwilling to lose control of his feelings, even for a brief moment.

Some people are unwilling to give up that much power to someone else. They will not risk being vulnerable or losing control to another person, even long enough to laugh. And more's the pity, because in their unwillingness to open up to humor, they close themselves to all the mental and physical benefits laughter can offer.

Being skillful enough to break down this kind of resistance is a difficult challenge but well worth the effort. The real power in using humor is not in controlling other people, but in gaining their trust and approval which in turn makes them more receptive to your ideas. Laughing together creates cracks in the walls people mentally build around themselves. Once laughter gets through, the opening is sometimes wide enough to slip in new ideas or unpopular subjects. This requires not only skill but a certain degree of courage.

On one occasion, the entire audience except for a man in the fifth row was howling with laughter. Noticing the man's blank expression, the comic "played" his jokes and stories directly to that man for the rest of his performance.

Powerless to evoke even one laugh, he felt he had failed, even though he had drawn laughs from everyone else. Only later did he learn that the man was a visitor to the United States and spoke no English.

During the Civil Rights crisis of the 1960s laughter empowered a young black comedian, Dick Gregory, to bring black comedy to white audiences. He told the jokes that had been popular with black audiences for many years. But now some whites were confronted with their own racial bigotry for the first time. Although he created laughter, the message was clear when he asked questions about blacks being required to sit in the back of the bus, such as, "Can you imagine how it will be when they hire the first Negro bus driver in the South and the steering wheel is twenty-five feet long?"

Humor also allows George Burns to talk about growing old and dying—subjects many people don't want to discuss, let alone laugh about. His warm and gentle wit disarms his audience as he says, "Eighty is a beautiful age. It takes very little to turn me on, and sometimes when I think I'm turned on, I find out I'm not even plugged in. What's the use of kidding? I've reached the point now where I can get by on about one-half inch of happiness. A whole inch would over stimulate me! But who cares, I'm enjoying it." [8]

After describing the daily exercises he does for his ailing back, he adds, "I've always had a bad back, but don't worry about it. If I outlive my back, fine. If my back outlives me, I'll stop doing my exercises." [9]

Burns advises his audience to make the most of every day and to appreciate and accept life. The message is serious, delivered on wings of laughter.

A humorist's attempts to break down resistance can backfire when the technique overpowers both the comedian and his ideas. For example, when the brand of humor used is offensive or socially unacceptable, then the ideas behind the humor, no matter how noble, may not get through as intended. Then the spigot is turned off, and laughter no longer flows.

The late Lenny Bruce's attempts to illustrate through humor that war, poverty, and bigotry are the ultimate obscenities were clouded by his use of offensive language. Many people in the 1950s found his language—relatively mild by today's standards—so unacceptable that they never heard, much less accepted, his message. When the laughter died, unfortunately so did his ability to open people's minds to new ideas.

OFFICE POLITICS AND THE POWER OF HUMOR

When Woodrow Wilson was governor of New Jersey, he got a call that one of New Jersey's U.S. senators had suddenly died. As soon as he hung up the phone, he got another call from an ambitious politician who said, "I'd like to take the senator's place."

Wilson replied, "If it's OK with the undertaker, it's OK with me."

The only difference between the political machinations that go on in government and those that go on in every ordinary office are the stakes at hand and the names of the players.

When Woodrow Wilson was governor of New Jersey, he got a call that one of New Jersey's U.S. senators had suddenly died. As soon as he hung up the phone, he got another call from an ambitious politician who said, "I'd like to take the senator's place."

Wilson replied, "If it's OK with the undertaker, it's OK with me."

And humor is often the best way to smoke out overambitious, competitive people who are jockeying for advantageous positions in ways that hurt the company. Using laughter publicly to defang those people who play office politics can expose their flanks and let them know that everyone is aware of their shenanigans.

A smart boss who at the outset defines the parameters of acceptable competitive behavior can create a healthy work place.

When assigning a large group project, a company president informed the project director, in front of the group that would be working on the project, that he wanted to be kept abreast of progress throughout the various stages.

He added, "By the way, the only time I was impressed by the words, 'and staff,' was when the group leader used it to hit a rock and get wine. Unless you're able to do that, I'd appreciate a complete list of names of those involved in this project and their contributions to it." Everyone chuckled, including the project coordinator, and the game was played on an even field.

Many writers, cartoonists, and stand-up comics have built and sustained careers with satire. Art Buchwald, Ellen Goodman, Mort Sahl, Gary Trudeau, Linda Ellerbee, Mark Russell, and Russell Baker are just a few personalities who dissect every aspect of life with wit, extracting laughter and exposing a modicum of truth when power brokers in politics or business overplay their hands.

When assigning a large group project, a company president informed the project director, in front of the group that would be working on the project, that he wanted to be kept abreast of progress throughout the various stages.

He added, "By the way, the only time I was impressed by the words, 'and staff,' was when the group leader used it to hit a rock and get wine. Unless you're able to do that, I'd appreciate a complete list of names of those involved in this project and their contributions to it." Everyone chuckled, including the project coordinator, and the game was played on an even field.

Humor is also a powerful shield to deflect verbal assaults. Ronald Reagan, "the great communicator," sustained a tone of light banter when dealing with the press and often used a preplanned joke to endear himself to an audience or to avoid a direct answer. Humor was part of his presidential style.

Whether in the Oval Office or in the corporate boardroom, those in power often take advantage of humor to present ideas, influence opinions, avoid scrutiny from the press, and disarm opposition.

A university president knew he'd need all the protection he could muster at a difficult faculty meeting, so he entered wearing a suit of armor.

He knew, like others in authority, that humor can help define the role of leadership. Harry Truman demonstrated this eloquently with the now famous sign on his desk:

"THE BUCK STOPS HERE."

Leading Groups: You've Got the Baton—Now Get Them to Play

OK, YOU'RE IN CHARGE. NOW WHAT?

Whether you call it a committee, conclave, assembly, convention, club, rally, or get-together, it's still a meeting. Whether you like it or not, meetings—big or small, formal or informal—are a fact of business and community life. Meetings allow you to get things accomplished while sharing a group experience with other people, and someone has to be in charge of them.

Accepting the position of leader or chairperson is a big responsibility, because the success or failure of the group's working relationship depends on your ability to work with them while maintaining control.

One group leader put it this way. "When I accepted the job of heading this committee, it reminded me of what the hen said to the pig. 'We make a perfect combination. Think of what ham and eggs have done for the breakfast table over the years.' And the pig replied, 'That's easy for you to say. You only have to give a small donation, but for me it means a total commitment.'"

If you are heading a committee, you want to accomplish a few basic things:

1. Get the committee members acquainted.
2. Present the problem and get them to share their ideas.
3. Keep them interested and active.
4. Get people to work together.
5. Reach a workable solution or logical conclusion to the task at hand.

Simply stated, your job as leader is to get ten committee members to do the job of ten committee members.

HOW HUMOR CAN HELP

"When I attended the company's general meeting one week ago, Harold came to my table and told me I had a telephone call. When I asked him where the telephone was, he told me, 'You go down the corridor, turn right at the elevator, go past the men's room, take a left, and it's in the third office on your right.'
"Well, when I finally found the phone, it was Harold. He said, 'Congratulations! You have just won a five-week chairmanship of the planning committee.' Well, let me tell you, I ran back down that corridor, past the elevator, didn't even pause at the men's room, because I was in such a hurry to congratulate Harold on his long-distance ploy—and to grab volunteers for this committee before all of you locked the door."

Example 1: "When I attended the company's general meeting one week ago, Harold came to my table and told me I had a telephone call. When I asked him where the telephone was, he told me, 'You go down the corridor, turn right at the elevator, go past the men's room, take a left, and it's in the third office on your right.'

"Well, when I finally found the phone, it was Harold. He said, 'Congratulations! You have just won a five-week chairmanship of the planning committee.' Well, let me tell you, I ran back down that corridor, past the elevator, didn't even pause at the men's room, because I was in such a hurry to congratulate Harold on his long-distance ploy—and to grab volunteers for this committee before all of you locked the door."

This chairman, with his amusing anecdote, let the group know that "I'll do it, but you'll have to help." His good-natured teasing also helped establish a cooperative atmosphere for his first meeting.

Example 2: To be an effective leader you must avoid doing all the talking. But on occasion you do need to interrupt to keep people on the subject. Humor can help you round up a stray conversation and guide it back to the corral:

"Well, Claire, you certainly don't make any bones about people who pick flowers in the park. But speaking of bones, we're supposed to be voting on whether the awards dinner is going to be chicken or fish."

People will laugh when they realize how you've steered the conversation back to the point, but they will not be laughing at Claire, because the humor was not a put-down. Although she may be disgruntled, she will probably be willing to defer to your leadership.

EXAMPLE 3: Being in control of a meeting means beginning on time and ending on time. One punctual chairman of a charity began his meeting at the appointed hour with this story: "It's eight o'clock and we are going to get started as promised, because as my minister always says, 'It's never too late to repent, but you might as well start on time.'"

Being in control of a meeting means beginning on time and ending on time. One punctual chairman of a charity began his meeting at the appointed hour with this story: "It's eight o'clock and we are going to get started as promised, because as my minister always says, 'It's never too late to repent, but you might as well start on time.'"

EXAMPLE 4: A humorous approach can often help you express your enthusiasm and encouragement: "I'm as excited about that suggestion as my cat was the day my son brought home our pet parakeet. The cat purred, 'Now this has possibilities!'"

AVOIDING CLOGS AND DEALING WITH CLODS

DISSOLVING "CLOGS"

Before you can incorporate humor into conducting meetings, you must first learn how to stay in control of the group you are managing, whether it is a mandatory committee at work or a volunteer group at your civic association:

1. *Clearly explain each member's assigned task* and designate leaders to whom each should report. The leaders in turn report to you.

2. *Don't try to supervise more people than you can manage effectively.*

3. *Be sure that people's jobs don't overlap.* Their efforts should mesh, but no one wants to find out he or she has done busy work that has already been accomplished by someone else.

4. *If you have people in charge of small subgroups, be sure their authority doesn't overlap.* Otherwise you end up with clashing egos, confusion, and arguments about who is in charge of what. This puts you into an arbitrator position, wasting energy and valuable time.

5. *Remain flexible and objective.* Approach your responsibility with a positive attitude and good humor. If you are in control, you can set the tone for an enjoyable group experience.

How Can You Run the Race When the Horse Has Died, and Other Problems

No matter how careful you are when managing a group of people—whether it's in an office or social setting—you are bound to run into a few problems. Unless you have the funds to take your committee to Lourdes, you'd best not depend on miraculous solutions.

However, well-placed humor can help you reduce errors when relaying information and can make correcting mistakes easier.

Using Humor to Minimize Errors

1. "I've provided pencils and paper for all of you, because I think it will be helpful if you take notes during the meeting. I know I wrote a few things down here that you might want to copy: 'one quart of milk, two dozen eggs, onions, bread.' Oops! Sorry, wrong notes." So began one chairwoman. She provided a laugh while letting her committee members know her expectations of them.

"I've provided pencils and paper for all of you, because I think it will be helpful if you take notes during the meeting. I know I wrote a few things down here that you might want to copy: 'one quart of milk, two dozen eggs, onions, bread.' Oops! Sorry, wrong notes."

2. "If you can tell me what I just said, I know it would end *my* confusion. Please don't tell me you don't have questions, because I sure do." The committee knew this competent businessman was joking. But with his joke, he got them to repeat the details he had just outlined to be sure they understood, and at the same time encouraged their questions.

3. If you use visual aids, a relevant cartoon or humorously captioned picture can help underscore the point you are trying to make. One coordinator interjected a picture of Prince Charles falling off his polo pony captioned, "Coordinating schedules can be a royal pain."

4. If you want to reach people, you need to take your time. Speak slowly and distinctly, and use humor only as an enhancer to help you stay in control, taking care not to offend. Much of their cooperation will depend on the goodwill you can generate.

Sorry About That: Putting Things Right

A company representative was negotiating with another company. His superior, out of frustration at the drawn-out delays, chewed the rep out sarcastically. The rep thumbed through his wallet, pulled out two pictures and stuffed them into his briefcase. "Please wait," he admonished, "I have a wife and children, and I don't want them to hear this kind of language." The boss realized that he had gotten carried away and apologized.

1. *Cool off.* Don't try to correct the problem or reprimand anyone while you are angry. It is at these times that humor is likely to get distorted. Sarcasm takes over and wounds with its half-hidden aggression. If you have to retreat for a while, do so mentally with a humor break.

2. *Find out exactly what happened.* "City Hall just called, and we don't have the correct permit to use street vendors at our fund-raising festival."

3. *Don't call a general meeting right away,* but first talk *privately* to the person responsible. Try to cushion the bad news with a little humor, keeping in mind that most errors aren't intentional. "Hi, Tim, we have a little problem. But don't worry. I think there's enough money in the kitty to post your bail."

4. *Give the person responsible for the error a chance to review it.* Then take the opportunity to make his responsibilities clear. Correct the error, not the person: "Tim, I'm not sure what kind of permit City Hall sent us, but I don't think we're supposed to ask all the vendors to get distemper shots."

5. After you solve the problem, *figure out how to avoid making the error again.* In this case a humorous notation in the final report for next year's chairman would be appropriate: "Be sure to review the permit sent by City Hall. Mayors come and mayors go, but red tape never fades."

DEALING WITH CLODS

Staying in control of a meeting when confronted by cloddish people is difficult, but not impossible—especially if you maintain your sense of humor. Perhaps you have done everything correctly until now.

Using humor techniques you have:

1. *Helped people get acquainted.* Perhaps you asked them to design simple name tags which reflected a hobby or other interest. Then, pairing them up, you invited them to introduce each other to the group, guessing what the other's tag represents. For example, one man put his name on a loaf of bread he has drawn. The woman introducing him said, "I guess this means Hank likes to bake bread." And Hank replied, "No, I just love to eat." Laughter helped the group establish rapport and get acquainted.

2. *Reinforced people's remarks kindly with humor.* "Eating is my favorite sport, too."

3. *Used humor when passing out your agenda.* "Today we will cover points one through ten," and as point five you've listed "an in-depth examination of the cafeteria's 'wildlife on toast' from noon to one"

4. *Planned a humorous story to end the meeting on a pleasant note.*

Then, whammo! You are confronted by the common clod. Take two aspirin and get ready for:

- The person who wants to call attention to himself: "Hey, everybody, look at me."
- The negative person who shoots down every idea: "It will never work."
- The person who belittles or challenges everything anyone says.
- The filibusterer who wants to do all the talking.
- The member who wants to impress everyone with her brilliance.

- The fellow who seems to sleep with his eyes open, waking up in time to ask an irrelevant question: "Whatever happened to that guy who used to bring refreshments?"
- The chatterer who talks to neighbors throughout and doesn't listen to anyone.
- The person with impending rigor mortis. You think she's listening, but you're not sure because she never says anything.

The most effective way to turn your gavel into a magic wand is to fortify yourself ahead of time with some humorous remarks. As we've said before, you needn't depend solely on your own inventiveness for this type of humor. It is available in publications geared for public speakers. If you have kept a humor collection, you can pull out several appropriate one-liners or anecdotes that you have saved just for this purpose. Here are a few we came up with:

"Excuse me, Frank, I think we've been around this track before. Please get to the finish line."

"George, I would like to end this meeting by saying, 'George is positively enthusiastic about one of the suggestions given tonight.' And, George, I don't want that to be the suggestion to adjourn."

"Excuse me, Helen, I hate to interrupt your conversation, but we are about to vote on whether the emperor needs new clothes, and I know you wouldn't want to miss that one."

Humor, used wisely, can elicit the support of others. The force of peer pressure can help you control cloddish behavior. But proceed with caution, because if the group feels you are using humor to tyrannize rather than facilitate, they will turn on you. And then you will have to deal with the most difficult problem of all.

"Excuse me, Frank, I think we've been around this track before. Please get to the finish line."

"George, I would like to end this meeting by saying, 'George is positively enthusiastic about one of the suggestions given tonight.' And, George, I don't want that to be the suggestion to adjourn."

"Excuse me, Helen, I hate to interrupt your conversation, but we are about to vote on whether the emperor needs new clothes, and I know you wouldn't want to miss that one."

The Hostile Group

Being fed to the lions is no pretty prospect, but often, with humor, you can pull some of their teeth before they pounce.

"When I was asked to chair this meeting, I prayed for three things. I prayed for the wisdom of Solomon, I prayed for the patience of Job, and I prayed I wouldn't end up like Jonah."

One of our students, a middle management bank employee, was asked to chair a meeting of the entire executive staff to hash out some crucial differences and agree on priorities for the coming year. Most of those attending outranked him. He couldn't refuse the assignment, but he was concerned that he might not be able to control the ensuing discussion and conflicting self-interests.

"When I was asked to chair this meeting, I prayed for three things. I prayed for the wisdom of Solomon, I prayed for the patience of Job, and I prayed I wouldn't end up like Jonah."

To help him out, we created the "Solomon-Job-Jonah" joke tailored for his predicament. The story brought constructive results, both expected and unanticipated.

By starting off with this story, he not only relaxed everyone but gained their sympathy and acceptance through his humor. He was then able to state clearly the objectives of the meeting and establish himself as the facilitator.

Interestingly, others picked up on the analogy of being swallowed by a big fish, which they referred to at various times throughout the meeting when tempers flared. Later it continued as an "in-joke" among the participants.

If you want to get something accomplished with hostile audiences, you need to maintain control while winning their acceptance as group leader. It is easier to do this when you are merely a facilitator than it is when you are a representative of the group or a proponent of the view they generally oppose.

Whatever the case, you should be aware of several basic problems:

1. Every audience is different.
2. You may find that your meeting place works against you. Woe to the speaker who has to win over a large number of people crowded into a small, windowless, smoke-filled, overheated room.
3. You may be telling the audience something they don't want to hear.

4. You may encounter vociferous protesters or hecklers.
5. You may face uncooperative or antagonistic listeners whose help you need to get the job done.

The Initial Approach

It is of the utmost importance that you approach this kind of audience with forethought, because they will take their cues from you. So before confronting a potentially hostile group, you need to plan *what you will say* and exactly *how you will say it*. The *what* is easy. All you have to do is:

- define the purpose of the meeting and the goal you want to achieve, and then,
- discuss ways to accomplish this goal.

It's the *how you will say it* that poses the difficulty. First decide how you want people to respond. Do you want them to go along with what you are saying, merely understand the issue, create ideas themselves, or act on your words? Sometimes the purpose is only one of these, but at other times it is all four. You also need to decide how formal or informal the meeting should be, because the more informal, the more relaxed. Exactly how relaxed do you want them to be?

What Makes People Mad?

There are all kinds of reasons why individuals get angry. But groups of people usually get mad when they feel they have no control over decisions that affect their lives and when they sense that someone is lying to them or treating them unjustly.

Parents become angry when a school board sends a representative to their P.T.A. for input about closing the school, if the parents feel that the board has already made the decision. Audiences get angry when they pay for tickets to a performance and the performer shows up two hours late. Voters get angry when they get a tax hike after their president has promised them no change. And employees get angry when they feel someone is treating them unfairly and no one is listening to their complaints.

FEW ARE CHOSEN

There are several possible reasons why you have been selected to lead a potentially hostile group and why you have accepted the job:

1. The task may complement your natural masochistic tendencies.
2. The person who assigned you the job hates you.
3. You didn't know what you were getting into.
4. It was generally felt that you had the personality and the ability to stay in control and get the job done. You, in turn, felt you could meet the challenge.

HUMOR—YOUR BEST ALLY

Humor can't help very much if you fit one of the first three categories. However, a humorous perspective can help you stay in control if you have taken the job with your eyes wide open.

It can help if you prepare your presentation well, maintain a steady voice, and approach the audience with sympathy for their position. Taking their cues from you, the audience may respond in kind.

If you ridicule them, however, they can retaliate in the same way. Furthermore, put-downs or other displays of hostility on your part signal a loss of control. Controlling your own anger becomes paramount when you face a hostile group.

Humor can extend the range of your control, stretching it to cover each successive caldron of conflict where otherwise anger—theirs or yours—might boil over.

For example, a man at a zoning hearing angrily shouts at you, "You represent a bunch of crooks!" You reply, "I'm sorry you feel that way. However, if that were really the case, I think it would be a lot easier to be out robbing stage coaches than here trying to work things out."

A man at a zoning hearing angrily shouts at you, "You represent a bunch of crooks!" You reply, "I'm sorry you feel that way. However, if that were really the case, I think it would be a lot easier to be out robbing stage coaches than here trying to work things out."

As you control yourself with humor, tune in to the attitude of the audience as a whole. Often the whole group may not be hostile, and you may be able to isolate the heckler with humor:

"Life really isn't fair. It took me an hour to get dressed up for this meeting, and it only took you two minutes to dress me down."

"Well, if I have a choice, I guess a tongue-lashing is better than a cat-o'-nine-tails any day."

Peer pressure may take over if you give it a chance, and you may hear, "Let her finish what she is saying," or, "Stop taking it out on her."

Also, try not to put too much physical distance between yourself and others. Staying in control is easier if you stand, relaxed, immediately in front of an audience instead of up on a stage. With a small group you can position the listeners near you, sitting around a table or in a circle of chairs.

Humor can likewise help you turn conflict into cooperation, not by minimizing people's concerns but by illustrating problems realistically. "OK, if we don't raise the price of our automobile, we'll need to figure out what to call an airbag without a frame, an engine, or four wheels."

Finally, be aware that your humorous, non-threatening attitude may make all the difference to an oversensitive audience. Essentially, you want to be accepted as a person who understands them and their concerns.

In the final analysis, getting results is what counts. If you've stayed in control, perhaps you'll still have the strength to say, "Well, now that we have solved that problem in only five hours, maybe next week we can tackle something minor . . . like the federal deficit."

"Well, now that we have solved that problem in only five hours, maybe next week we can tackle something minor . . . like the federal deficit."

Women, Power, and Humor (Laughter, The Great Equalizer)

THE UNRECOGNIZED POWER IN HUMOR: IF LAUGHTER CAN BREAK DOWN WALLS, IT CAN CRACK GLASS CEILINGS TOO

A banker, the master of ceremonies at a charity auction, spied a friendly competitor, a woman from another bank. From the podium he broadcasted, "Anne, you get the big salary at that hotshot bank you work for. I'm sure you can afford to bid much higher than I can."

"Well, Greg," she zinged back, "I probably can. At our bank we get paid in proportion to our work." The audience exploded with laughter.

Have you ever thought about what happens during a good, old-fashioned belly laugh? What happens when you provoke irrepressible, hearty laughter in another person or an audience? Usually two things happen. First, you stimulate their thoughts, memory, and imagination, and then you cause them to express their feelings through spontaneous laughter that is, at times, uncontrollable.

A banker, the master of ceremonies at a charity auction, spied a friendly competitor, a woman from another bank. From the podium he broadcasted, "Anne, you get the big salary at that hotshot bank you work for. I'm sure you can afford to bid much higher than I can."

"Well, Greg," she zinged back, "I probably can. At our bank we get paid in proportion to our work."

If you continue on the same track, the laughter will be loud, some people's bodies will shake, heads will be thrown back, people might hold their stomachs or sides, tears may begin to flow as muscles squeeze tear glands, and in extremely funny moments people may even lose bladder control.

After the laughter subsides, they feel exercised, relaxed, and sometimes weak with laughter. You have made them feel good.

However, for a brief time, you also held sway over their emotions. They were powerless and vulnerable. *You were in control.* By using humor you can gain the upper hand and place yourself in an advantageous position in business dealings.

From the assembly line to the board room, men have always used the power of humor to persuade, to illustrate, and to bond with one another. However, some have also used it to bait, to undermine, and ultimately to slice-and-dice anyone too unsure, defenseless, or ill-equipped to respond in kind.

As more and more women become viable business team players, they, too, are developing humor styles of their own and discovering the empowerment that comes with the ability to create laughter in the workplace.

Rosemary T. McFadden, first woman president of the New York Mercantile Exchange, recommends that a young businesswoman get a "broad-based education and make a commitment to work very hard." However, she also advises that the businesswoman needs more—a sense of humor and the ability to deal effectively with other people.

Prominent women in the public eye are making news with their humor skills. Supreme Court Justice Sandra Day O'Connor earned a television sound bite when she read a portion of a letter to a group of women she was addressing. The letter writer recommended, "Don't let those men on the court intimidate you. They put their robes on the same way you do!"

And Ann W. Richards, Governor of Texas, hasn't let one of the toughest jobs in the nation diminish her famous wit, which propelled her into national prominence with her historic keynote address at the 1988 Democratic National Convention. She raised howls of laughter poking fun, in a low-keyed voice, at Republican opponent George Bush. After listing his faults she delivered a stinging one-liner, "Poor George, he can't help it, he was born with a silver foot in his mouth." After the election,

President-elect Bush, in recognition of her humorous home run—as a member of the other team—sent her a small silver pin in the shape of a foot as a peace offering.

Sometimes in business and politics men and women have to play hardball. Richards has learned not to take herself too seriously, and her comedic sense has helped her "open doors and bring down walls." Recognizing that laughter is an eminent equalizer, she observes, "If you give us women a chance, we can perform. After all, Ginger Rogers did everything Fred Astaire did. She just did it backward and in high heels."

"If you give us women a chance, we can perform. After all, Ginger Rogers did everything Fred Astaire did. She just did it backward and in high heels."

SUGAR AND SPICE AND EVERYTHING NICE. THAT'S WHAT LITTLE GIRLS ARE MADE OF

As the sugar melts in the boiling caldron of feminist change in the 1990s, connotations of "everything nice" have also changed. A young woman can now aspire to be an astronaut or president of the United States. No longer is physical fitness considered solely a manly pursuit.

Most people have finally acknowledged that after a jog around the park, a game of tennis, or a soccer match, nice girls do sweat—and they don't sweat just on the athletic field. It takes a great deal of courage and sweat for women to become assertive enough to catapult themselves into competitive positions in the formerly male domains of business and government.

Until recently, our culture encouraged women to be passive rather than active, receivers rather than initiators. Reinforcing expectations and stereotypes of femininity, mothers would give their daughters such misguided advice as "Don't be too smart," "Act interested in a man's work," and "Always laugh at his jokes."

Each quarter in our humor awareness class, at least one well-educated, articulate woman, who most often holds a responsible business position, will plaintively lament, "I can't tell a joke." And despairingly ask, "Why?" She is usually taken aback by our response, "Because you're not supposed to."

For generations women in our society were told that creating humor was unladylike. Women could react to men's jokes with laughter (society tacitly recognized that women did have the capacity to appreciate humor), but they should not initiate humor.

When a male client called his accounting firm, he was told that his C.P.A. was out of town, so he asked to speak to another of the firm's partners. When a woman answered the phone, he remarked with surprise, "I thought all C.P.A.'s were men." She good-naturedly replied, "I can read the numbers to you gruffly and three octaves lower, if that will put you at ease." Her sense of humor and self-assuredness gained his confidence and trust.

In the past many people believed that women had limited cognitive abilities, and that men alone possessed intellectual power, including the inventiveness to create humor. It is important for women to understand that it's not only OK, it is desirable to initiate humor, because humor can sometimes give you the edge.

When a male client called his accounting firm, he was told that his C.P.A. was out of town, so he asked to speak to another of the firm's partners. When a woman answered the phone, he remarked with surprise, "I thought all C.P.A.'s were men." She good-naturedly replied, "I can read the numbers to you gruffly and three octaves lower, if that will put you at ease." Her sense of humor and self-assuredness gained his confidence and trust.

WHEN POWER BECOMES AN ISSUE

As more women take positions of authority, power comes into play, putting women into direct competition with their male counterparts. The use of power is an aggressive act, and for many women it is a hard act to follow, because whoever has the power doesn't want to share it, let alone give it up. And you can't blame them.

Consequently, as women learn to use and share humor effectively, the laughter they create can help break down barriers, opening communication for cooperative effort. However, in their reluctance to give up control, some people are not willing to let women wield that much power through humor, because they fear that to laugh is to admit vulnerability.

To compound the problem for many men and women, until recent years their *only* shared experience was not business, sports, or politics, but love, sex, and marriage.

PROBLEMS WOMEN FACE: BREAKING PAST HUMOR PATTERNS, FINDING ROLE MODELS FOR YOUR HUMOR, AND CONFRONTING SEXIST HUMOR

BREAKING PAST HUMOR PATTERNS

"Attention, everybody. It's a woman driver. Get off the sidewalk."

"I just got a Siamese cat for my wife."
"Not a bad trade."

"She's a good nurse, but I have to watch everything she writes on the patients' charts. Like the other day, I had to tell her, 'Miss Jones, the man's appendicitis condition is acute . . . not adorable.'"

It's easy to find jokes that reinforce the stereotype of women as both inferior and incapable. That's not surprising, however, because until recently, the business of humor has been more open to men both as stand-up comedians and as comedy writers. Consequently, men (with a few exceptions) drew the guidelines on what kind of humor was culturally acceptable.

"Attention, everybody. It's a woman driver. Get off the sidewalk."

"I just got a Siamese cat for my wife."
"Not a bad trade."

"She's a good nurse, but I have to watch everything she writes on the patients' charts. Like the other day, I had to tell her, 'Miss Jones, the man's appendicitis condition is acute . . . not adorable.'"

In the past, talented women comics responded by developing an act based on putting themselves down, or playing the part of the dumb-but-lovable blonde or the naive foil for a male partner. Gracie Allen, Judy Holliday, and the young Goldie Hawn endeared themselves to their audiences through playing characters who reinforced people's preconceived expectations.

Their roles were stereotypically feminine, cute, cuddly, naively funny; they reinforced the notion that women only said funny things by accident or out of ignorance. Comediennes memorized, rehearsed, and delivered their lines brilliantly while audiences felt superior and laughed at their "little girl" qualities. They were indeed funny, but the images they projected were limiting.

However, as roles in society began to change and opportunities opened up to women, the old humor stereotypes began to dissolve. Many comedic actresses, like Goldie Hawn, still lovable, are now more sophisticated. The woman comedy partner rarely portrays the dumb blonde or the perennial foil, and the public is still laughing.

"He took his clothes off and asked me how he stacked up. I told him, 'Next to home-grown cucumbers, not very well.'"

"My husband is very versatile. The minute he gets me into bed it's slam-bam-shazam The Incredible Shrinking Man."

Women have always had the ability to make each other laugh when joking about common experiences, but only now can women tell these jokes in public and be accepted. Stand-up comic Marjorie Gross observes, "Ever notice how whenever you're in pain, guys think you've got your period? You're lying on the floor with a spear coming out of your chest, and he says, 'What's the matter, you got cramps?'"

Other contemporary female comics, reacting angrily to male humor directed at women, entertain with a now-it's-our-turn mentality. They hurl their jokes powerfully, not only to wound but also to permanently cripple male egos. Instead of breaking free of the "put-down" humor pattern of the past, these comics fall into the same rut: they hit below the belt and try to draw more blood than their male counterparts did in the past.

> "He took his clothes off and asked me how he stacked up. I told him, 'Next to home-grown cucumbers, not very well.'"
>
> "My husband is very versatile. The minute he gets me into bed it's slam-bam-shazam The Incredible Shrinking Man."

These jokes polarize men and women rather than finding a common ground for laughter, and they are trading the fun of laughing together for equality of animosity.

Each individual must judge whether or not this kind of humor is funny. If you are in a nightclub, you can demonstrate your decision by laughing or not laughing, or by staying for the rest of the performance or going home.

Before you judge these comics too harshly, keep in mind that they learned their craft by imitating male comedians who for years told jokes denigrating the intelligence and ability of women rather than by poking fun at universal human imperfections. The "civilized" world, shocked when Native Americans collected scalps, ignored the fact that according to some historians the skill was introduced to the Indians by "civilized" Europeans who encouraged the practice by paying bounties on scalps collected.

ROLE MODELS

In the 1940s and early 1950s, several talented actresses brought to life Hollywood's comedy image of the woman with a key to the executive bathroom. The late Rosalind Russell epitomized the corporate woman, dressed in her square-shouldered, pinstriped suits and armed with clever, humorous barbs, outmanning the men. She was most often engaged to a "wimp" until a "real" man appeared on the scene and became her employee. With funny repartee and reminders that underneath it all she was a woman, he turned her into a vision of loveliness in a soft evening gown designed by Edith Head. They fell in love, and at the end of the movie he became her partner or boss.

The audience was left with the implicit promise that he would soon be taking over, and she would be sent scurrying back home where she belonged and had always wanted to be anyway. The writers came up with better punch lines for him to deliver to put her in her place. And, to top it all off, he even had access to a better tailor.

The pseudo-macho role was funny because it didn't fit the feminine mold, and the laughs came when the framework began to crumble. Hollywood writers demonstrated what happens when a woman oversteps her prescribed boundaries.

Until the 1970s, few women could demonstrate intelligent humor and yet remain "ladylike." Although a thinking person's humor was somehow out of bounds for women, slapstick and clowning were not. Because it wasn't accepted that a woman could be intelligent, pretty, well-dressed, and funny at the same time, attractive comics like Lucille Ball, Phyllis Diller, and Carol Burnett dressed in outlandish costumes, messed up their hair, distorted their femininity, and clowned their way into people's hearts. They were funny—but certainly not role models for humor in the corporate world.

Who wants to vote for a coy and cute Congresswoman? If past role models don't work for women in the 1990s, then they are going to have to create new ones for their daughters and granddaughters.

Many women in business and politics are aware of the positive aspects of humor, but they sometimes run into problems knowing when and how to use it. You can't go around the office snapping your gum at the boss like Roseanne Arnold, or joking about being flat-chested as Joan Rivers does, and expect to gain your co-workers respect. Who wants to vote for a coy and cute Congresswoman? If past role models don't work for women in the 1990s, then they are going to have to create new ones for their daughters and granddaughters.

THE DIRTY DUO: SEXIST HUMOR AND OFF-COLOR JOKES

Sexist Humor

Two young people have worked hard to excel on the company sales force. They are good at their jobs, and they are the only women among many men employed in these competitive positions. As they enter the room together for the weekly sales meeting, a co-worker once again elicits a few laughs with, "Here come the Buns Sisters."

Two young people have worked hard to excel on the company sales force. They are good at their jobs, and they are the only women among many men employed in these competitive positions. As they enter the room together for the weekly sales meeting, a co-worker once again elicits a few laughs with, "Here come the Buns Sisters."

Those words wield power, and he knows it. By making his women competitors the sexual butt of the joke, he is telling them and the other men in the room, through his condescension (masked with humor), that he considers these women inferior—even if they can do the job. Excluding them from the group hinders their effectiveness. The one or two men who laugh at his remark not only seem to concur, but encourage his behavior.

Most women don't like sexual humor that degrades women, and many men don't enjoy that kind of humor either. But the inappropriate use of humor is still too common, even though the legal profession has made progress in the field of sexual harassment.

The experience of the two young saleswomen is only one of many similar stories that women have shared in our workshops. Interestingly, when the men in these seminars see the embarrassment and pain that this type of sexist humor causes, they empathize with them. Not once has a man responded to a woman in the class with the standard defense, "What's the matter, can't you take a joke?" By discussing it in a classroom situation, the men realize that this kind of humor puts women in an unfair, no-win situation.

Unfortunately, men who use humor to mask lewd remarks about women's bodies get a power charge from the discomfort they cause, and they have used it often in the past, knowing that few women wanted to compete at that level. It is the technique of the schoolyard bully. The vagueness of innuendo often makes this subtle form of annoyance, or even harassment, tough to pinpoint.

Widespread insensitivity to the problem by many men and even some women ("It never happened to me, so it doesn't exist") is shocking. Even more shocking is the number of women who have acknowledged, in the post-Anita Hill-Clarence Thomas hearings atmosphere, the pervasiveness of the problem. According to attorney Mary Ann Oakley, who practices in the area of employee discrimination, "I've seen numbers ranging as high as ninety percent for working women who have been harassed."

> "The Equal Employment Opportunity Commission definition boils down to unwelcome verbal or physical conduct of a sexual nature. That could be physical touching, heavy propositioning, or just the environment—for instance, dirty jokes or nude calendar pictures."
>
> Mary Ann Oakley

So before we address "low-key" sexual humor and light-handed strategies to discourage the unwitting (perhaps witless) perpetrator, let's get specific. Where does harmless joking end and harassment begin?

Says Ms. Oakley, "The Equal Employment Opportunity Commission definition boils down to unwelcome verbal or physical conduct of a sexual nature. That could be physical touching, heavy propositioning, or just the environment—for instance, dirty jokes or nude calendar pictures."

Truly unintentional offenses depend on the perception of the receiver. However, after the 1993 U.S. Supreme Court ruling, cases have moved away from "what a reasonable man would find offensive," or a "reasonable person," to "what a reasonable *woman* would find offensive." Adds Oakley, "Judges will no longer tolerate a 'boys will be boys' attitude."

And a one-time offense? Should women take action? "Depends on the act," considers Ms. Oakley. "A one-time dirty joke may not mean anything. On the other hand, if a guy grabs a woman's breast, once is enough. In other words, one dog bite is a bite, two dog bites are trouble.

"It is important to establish that you, the employee, neither elicited nor incited the offensive behavior," emphasizes Ms. Oakley, "and you *must* inform your supervisor." Without that official complaint, you cannot hold a company responsible.

There's nothing funny about sexual harassment. So if you find yourself in that predicament, take appropriate action.

But if it's just a tasteless joke, a onetime offense, what are the front-line alternatives that will make your point while discouraging a repeat performance?

Light-Handed Strategies

1. *At the first off-color remark, stare at the offender and do not laugh.* It is amazing how often women laugh because they have been programmed to do so, even if they don't think something is funny. Sometimes they laugh out of nervousness or embarrassment.

2. *Do not react with anger.* That opens you up to the responses, "I was only joking," "You can't take a joke," or "You are not a good sport." By not being a good sport, you automatically eliminate yourself from the team. It is more effective to muzzle a *relatively tame* sexual remark firmly, but with a smile if possible. For instance, you could answer the old line, "Hey, Babe, where have you been all my life?" with this rejoinder: "Well, let's see, for the first twenty-five years I wasn't even thought of, conceived, or born yet."

3. *Use peer pressure.* There are plenty of male co-workers who are willing to accept capable women in the work force and who dislike a destructive, counter-productive atmosphere. Many are sensitive enough to pick up on your reactions to this kind of humor and are aware of its interference with the common good. Sometimes a simple "That's not funny" from you will be enough to encourage your co-workers to speak up the next time an unpleasant remark is made.

4. *Elicit the help of co-workers.* Here is an imaginative solution women colleagues devised to solve a vexing problem at their office.

   The women noticed that while they were seated around a large conference table during office meetings, one male co-worker would look under the table to silently admire their legs. Although in all other situations he worked appropriately with them, at least once during each meeting,

> The women noticed that while they were seated around a large conference table during office meetings, one male co-worker would look under the table to silently admire their legs. Although in all other situations he worked appropriately with them, at least once during each meeting, without fail, he would drop his pen or a piece of paper, or tie his shoelaces. However, one day his clumsiness was sent into permanent remission when he peeked under the table and saw neatly lettered on seven kneecaps (one letter per knee) the illuminating words, "H-I R-A-L-P-H." Before complaining to their over-worked boss, they worked together to plan a creative, humorous solution, and at the same time allowed Ralph to save face (as long as he kept it above the table).

without fail, he would drop his pen or a piece of paper, or tie his shoelaces.

However, one day his clumsiness was sent into permanent remission when he peeked under the table and saw neatly lettered on seven kneecaps (one letter per knee) the illuminating words, "H-I R-A-L-P-H." Before complaining to their overworked boss, they worked together to plan a creative, humorous solution, and at the same time allowed Ralph to save face (as long as he kept it above the table).

5. *Involving the boss for this kind of irritation should be your last resort.* If you choose this route, instead of just complaining about insensitive treatment, offer a positive suggestion. Propose a workshop to improve office communication or the office humor level with a communications expert in group dynamics, or a humor consultant who, as an impartial observer, can make people aware of the differences between productive and destructive humor. *Again, serious harassment requires different procedures.*

Whether or not you find bawdy, off-color jokes funny is a matter of individual taste. Plenty of people like this kind of humor as long as they don't feel victimized by it.

On the other hand, some people run into problems with these jokes, not so much because the jokes aren't funny, but because they tell them at the wrong time, in the wrong place, and to the wrong person.

To pose the problem so that both men and women could relate personally to it, we presented the following situation to a business group. Participants then created some imaginative, workable solutions. What strategies would you add?

Problem: Your mother is a secretary in a large company. She makes a good salary, likes her boss, and finds the working conditions ideal. But one man in her office insists on telling dirty jokes in her presence, and she finds it both embarrassing and upsetting. On the other hand, she doesn't want to look like a bad sport. How can she best handle this problem?

Possible solutions: The group agreed that in a nightclub setting your mother would have the option of leaving if the entertainer's material was not to her liking. But walking out of an office situation is impractical, and it will not cause a change in the man's behavior—her real goal.

Perhaps he is purposely using offensive humor as a put-down or intimidation technique. Let's assume, however, that he is merely insensitive and doesn't realize his jokes are inappropriate in the business setting.

There are several ways she can make her feelings known in a humorous, nonthreatening way and muster some good-natured support from others in the office. She could:

1. Reply, "That joke is so interesting, I'm going to submit it for the company newsletter in your name."
2. Keep a large bar of soap on her desk. Each time he tells a joke, hand him the soap to wash his mouth out. Soon the soap itself will become a joke, and as soon as he begins telling a joke, colleagues may also reach for the soap.
3. Reply, "That joke wasn't funny when I heard it twenty years ago."
4. Place a bell on her desk. Each time he tells an offensive joke, she rings the chimes. Everyone will come to associate the sound with his jokes, and she will make her point without saying a word.
5. Place a large, lidded, empty jar in a conspicuous place on her desk labeled "Dirty Joke Jar," accompanied by these typed instructions: "Whisper your dirty jokes in here. Then please put a lid on them."

The humorous gimmicks may stop the joke teller. But even if they don't they can open up communication about the problem of inappropriate humor. If used constructively, humor can be a powerful bonding agent between you and others. A pleasant atmosphere benefits everyone. And sometimes a picture can demonstrate succinctly how easy developing a healthy humor atmosphere can be, whether at home or at work.

"Remember, we are all in this together."

One office bulletin board displays the picture of a crew team. One team member is rowing in the opposite direction. It is captioned, "Remember, we are all in this together." The real power in humor lies in everyone pulling together.

JESTING FOR SUCCESS

The same basic rules for using humor apply to men and women. Keep the humor relevant, fit it to your personality and style, and take care to know when and with whom to use it. So why do some women run into trouble when trying to be funny in a work setting?

Many women feel they have only three choices: being cute and coy, emulating men by joking about what the men in the office are joking about, or taking the safe route and avoiding humor altogether.

Cute is a mistake because when you're trying to compete and win, "cute" is not the appropriate image to convey. Who wants a "cute" team player? Emulating men by trying to be "one of the boys" usually doesn't work either. And by deliberately avoiding humor, you tend to shut yourself off. If you are capable and articulate, use humor to show people you can communicate effectively, meeting them halfway.

> *Be proud of the woman you are.*
>
> *Little girls are cute and coy; women hold positions of responsibility.*
>
> *You are not "one of the boys," but that's OK.*
>
> *Don't be afraid to tell a joke or make a funny remark when it is appropriate.*
>
> *If you don't get a laugh, let it go. Don't get discouraged.*
>
> *Ease the threat of being a woman boss.*

Here are a few hints that should help:

1. *Be proud of the woman you are.* Whether you're a homemaker or a corporate officer, you should value yourself and be valued because you are good at what you do. You don't have to imitate anyone else, and neither does your humor.

2. *Little girls are cute and coy; women hold positions of responsibility.* Reverting to the laughs you got from Mom and Dad and the kids at school won't help you accomplish your goals. It's time to grow up with your humor.

   Make it your business to know what's going on in the world, and include on your reading list contemporary women writers who are adept with humor: Ellen Goodman, Judith Viorst, Erma Bombeck, Fran Liebowitz, Gail Parent, and Molly Ivins, to mention a few.

3. *You are not "one of the boys," but that's OK.* Steer the laughter toward subjects you and your co-workers have in common.

4. *Don't be afraid to tell a joke or make a funny remark when it is appropriate,* and don't announce that you are going to say something funny. You'll lose the element of surprise.

5. *If you don't get a laugh, let it go.* Forget it. Try it again on someone else. If it still doesn't work, find a better story to tell next time, but don't take it personally. No one hits the humor bull's-eye every time.

6. *Don't get discouraged.* Breaking new ground isn't easy, and in many respects it is still a man's world. But it can be challenging, fun, and well worth the effort. Who knows? If you succeed, younger women may one day look to you as a role model, much as they now look to Jane Evans, who at twenty-five became president of I. Miller Shoes.

   Now, after twenty-five years in retailing, marketing, and merchandising, Evans is president and C.E.O. of the Inter-Pacific Retail Group. She says that one reason she has succeeded is through her use of a sense of humor. "It is the one great equalizer. And particularly as a woman climbs up the ladder, to learn how to make men comfortable in your presence has been the critical variable of my being accepted and has certainly played a major role in my ability to advance."

7. *Ease the threat of being a woman boss.* Let people know you are human. The president of a successful small business has two items framed in her office: a kindergarten report card which says, "Susan must work on following instructions," and her award for "Business Entrepreneur of the Year."

PART

Specific Professions

CHAPTER 9

Secretaries: On the Firing Line

The project was ready to go, the workers had agreed upon all matters, and they were eager to meet the deadline, but the project manager couldn't set things into motion without the department head's signature on some simple paperwork. After a week with no response from the overworked department head, the anxious manager approached his boss's secretary and explained his dilemma. She immediately attached a stickum note to the paperwork, took it into the boss's office, and returned to her desk.

The attached note read:

"If you want to fill out form 258-B, you'll have to fill out 258-A first, which will give you permission to fill out 258-B and all subsequent forms. But if you don't want the hassle, please just sign the enclosed paperwork and return to me by the end of the day." A loud guffaw boomed from the other side of the door, and the boss came out a few minutes later with the signed documents.

This secretary used humor to get out of the middle between two superiors and to break the force field that was blocking progress.

> The project was ready to go, the workers had agreed upon all matters, and they were eager to meet the deadline, but the project manager couldn't set things into motion without the department head's signature on some simple paperwork. After a week with no response from the overworked department head, the anxious manager approached his boss's secretary and explained his dilemma. She immediately attached a stickum note to the paperwork, took it into the boss's office, and returned to her desk.
>
> The attached note read:
>
> "If you want to fill out form 258-B, you'll have to fill out 258-A first, which will give you permission to fill out 258-B and all subsequent forms. But if you don't want the hassle, please just sign the enclosed paperwork and return to me by the end of the day." A loud guffaw boomed from the other side of the door, and the boss came out a few minutes later with the signed documents.

Later, the little yellow stickum note became an entertaining story for the department head to relate at a dinner party. Although the boss received full credit for meeting the project deadline, unfortunately he never fully comprehended his "right hand's" contribution to his success. He did know, however, that in his very responsible position, he "couldn't get along without her," because of her expertise with electronic office paraphernalia and her ability to recognize and deal with his moods. She understood how he thought and perceived that humor would work in that particular situation—with that particular boss.

Michael Williams, economist, Women's Bureau, U.S. Department of Labor, a man who enjoys the world of statistics, hummed a little tune over the phone as he related these numbers: In 1991, 3,791,000 secretaries (37,000 men) were working in the United States and 540,000 more secretaries will likely join the work force by the year 2005.

SO WHAT IS A SECRETARY?

Professional Secretaries International defines a secretary as "an executive assistant who possesses a mastery of office skills, demonstrates the ability to assume responsibility without direct supervision, exercises initiative and judgment and makes decisions within the scope of assigned authority."

In plain English that means today's secretaries are not only experts in modern machine technology, but also know how the business works, have managerial skills, and must make vital judgment calls every day that affect the organization, their bosses, and their co-workers.

And a capable secretary is expected to deliver the whole package with finesse and grace. The demands are challenging; the pressures, enormous. Karen Nussbaum, then executive director of 9to5, the National Association of Working Women, said their organization received seventy thousand calls in 1991 from secretaries trying to deal with problematic situations, difficult people, and unreasonable demands.

"From the founding of the organization, we always felt humor was important. If you just looked at the issues, you'd have to cry. You have to have a humorous outlook just to get the energy to try to change things for the better."

HOW CAN YOU KEEP YOUR BALANCE WITH HUMOR?

In our workshops, we have found many secretaries who have used humor to raise serious issues as well as to poke fun at office situations concerning bosses, clients, and co-workers. One group of secretaries for an insurance adjuster keeps a fire bucket in the middle of the office. Every day they jot down their most frustrating calls, toss them into the bucket, and at the end of the week, they take the pot outside, set fire to the contents, and have a marshmallow roast.

Secretaries get it from both sides. They have to walk a tightrope between the in-house people (bosses and co-workers) and, as one secretary put it, the "out-house" folks (the clients, customers, and salespeople). It isn't easy!

Nancy, long-time secretary to three lawyers, jokes, "I'm always on the firing line. By the time I'm sixty, I'll be a tough bird. I may even carry a sidearm." The first day on the job, she was introduced to the three attorneys. Later that day, a client called in, saying, "This is Red Dog One calling Red Dog Two, put me through immediately." So she put him through to the attorney she thought fit the bill. "I had sized up this boss the minute I walked in the door."

Nancy, long-time secretary to three lawyers, jokes, "I'm always on the firing line. By the time I'm sixty, I'll be a tough bird. I may even carry a sidearm." The first day on the job, she was introduced to the three attorneys. Later that day, a client called in, saying, "This is Red Dog One calling Red Dog Two, put me through immediately." So she put him through to the attorney she thought fit the bill. "I had sized up this boss the minute I walked in the door."

Because she had noticed this lawyer's joking attitude and demeanor, she could correctly guess which of her three bosses had a bantering relationship with his clients.

As routine clerical tasks are now accomplished electronically in most offices, many secretaries can enjoy the intellectual and creative functions formerly reserved for their managers. And more and more secretaries are finding that a touch of humor is indispensable when dealing with the boss, colleagues, and clients.

IT'S LONELY AT THE TOP: HUMOR WITH THE BOSS

Working for more than one boss at a time can be advantageous because sometimes your advancement is linked to one boss's mobility within the company. If you work for more than one boss, you may later be able to choose which one you want to follow, as each one progresses within the company.

Problems multiply, however, if you have more than one boss.

"Am working on current crisis. Please rate your crisis before interrupting. Choose between 'Emergency, semi-emergency, critical emergency, vital emergency, just wanted to see a friendly face.'"

1. *How do you set priorities?* How do you deal with interruptions from several bosses? One administrative assistant puts a crisis appointment sheet on her door and turns it over on especially harried days. It warns:

   "Am working on current crisis. Please rate your crisis before interrupting. Choose between 'Emergency, semi-emergency, critical emergency, vital emergency, just wanted to see a friendly face.'"

   The sign doesn't discourage all interruptions, but since she uses it only on especially busy days, it does give pause to those who might otherwise not give her hectic schedule a second thought.

2. *Humor can often anticipate potential rough spots, set standards, and define parameters for acceptable behavior.* After someone had shouted at her, a savvy young woman put this sign on her desk. "Hold your breath and count for ten minutes before yelling at me." A variation on this theme appeared in another office: "Take a number from the dispenser and stand in line if you want to yell at me. But please remember, loud yelling breaks my glasses."
3. *Secretaries have to deal with unreasonable demands from all sides.* One boss would always bring that last letter to be typed at five PM. The secretary had missed the bus many nights because of the boss's poor planning. Finally, at 4:45 PM the secretary put a fish net over the "in" box with a sign, "I have bagged my limit for the day. No fishing in these waters after five PM by order of the Fair Game Department."

Most smart bosses not only realize that a good secretary is hard to find, but they also know that the better the skills, the broader the options. Therefore it behooves the boss to make the atmosphere as pleasant as possible. The secretary for the president of a large chemical company told us that she continually received other job offers at higher salaries, but her boss had such a good sense of humor and was so considerate that she just couldn't leave, because she loved coming to work every day.

One boss would always bring that last letter to be typed at five PM. The secretary had missed the bus many nights because of the boss's poor planning. Finally, at 4:45 PM the secretary put a fish net over the "in" box with a sign, "I have bagged my limit for the day. No fishing in these waters after five PM by order of the Fair Game Department."

4. *Occasionally, however, you find the completely unreasonable boss.* Karen Nussbaum recalls the boss who asked his secretary to get him a corned beef sandwich. She brought it to him on white bread, and he fired her on the spot.

   Members of 9to5 picketed his business with signs, "No Rye—No Bread," and the story made the front page of the Boston Globe. Two other secretaries also came forward with stories of his equally unfair treatment of them. His former secretary didn't get her job back, but their humorous protest brought national attention to the boss's unprofessional behavior, and put other bosses on notice that they wouldn't tolerate unreasonable behavior.

5. *Sometimes humor can draw attention to an inequity.* During one pay dispute, the secretarial staff framed a dollar bill which had been torn in half. They added the caption, "We can't make it stretch anymore," and presented it to management. It started the pay discussion off with a laugh, and the staff got their raises. 9to5 holds an annual "National Boss Contest," which gives working women (and a few men) a fun opportunity to honor good bosses and skewer bad ones. Winners in 1992 included this downright unbelievably bad boss: A department head of a local government office in Eastport, New York,

A department head of a local government office in Eastport, New York, required a married, thirty-seven-year-old mother of two to bring a note in from her parents verifying that she was out sick, so she wouldn't be docked pay.

who required a married, thirty-seven-year-old mother of two to bring a note in from her parents verifying that she was out sick, so she wouldn't be docked pay. And one "good boss" winner was the management of the Fun Company in Atlanta, an employer of about fifty, which responded to a single complaint of sexual harassment by providing a mandatory two-hour sexual harassment awareness seminar for all employees.

Nussbaum says, "Our contest reflects what is happening out there. Health care, family and medical leave, pay equity, workplace privacy, and just plain respect are issues that our political and business leaders can no longer ignore."

Good bosses receive a certificate, bad bosses a "9to5 Job Survival Guide."

> One self-important client called an office and complained to the boss that the secretary didn't recognize his voice. The boss agreed with the secretary that the client was out of line, and he trusted her to take care of the problem.
>
> She asked her boss what the client looked like and for some particulars about his family. When the client came to the office, although they'd never met, she greeted him warmly by name and asked if his wife Mabel was enjoying the presidency of her garden club? And did his son Frank enjoy playing shortstop on the high school baseball team? She went on to ask about his mother, his father, and cousin Felix. The client flip-flopped from assuming, "she ought to know who I am," to thinking, "This woman knows everything about me," to finally realizing and laughing, "This is a joke, isn't it?"

CLIENTS, CUSTOMERS, AND THOSE UNWANTED COLD CALLERS

The relationship between boss and secretary is unlike other office associations. Often the secretary is the only person in whom the boss can confide. Seeing and knowing all, the secretary is trusted to reveal nothing. A boss depends upon a good secretary to know where information is filed and stored, and to see that things get done. The secretary functions as both memory and ultimate organizer for the boss. If a secretary loses the schedule calendar, three months of the boss's life are lost.

One secretary keeps a dart board with the boss's most important obligation of the day pinned to the bull's eye.

A boss's private secretary is living proof that the boss is valuable to the company. A good secretary is one of the perks that goes with the job, along with a fancy title, stock options, and a pension plan. Inextricably tied to his or her productivity, the secretary understands when the boss says: "I'm in to clients A, B, and C, but out to D, E, and F."

No one wants to lie, but often secretaries are caught between the boss's need for call screening and the client's need for her boss's services. They are the boss's buffers to the outside world as well as the key to the closed doors that serve as a shield. So how can the secretary juggle them all?

Whether you, as the secretary, are on the client's side or not, clients want to think you are, and it's up to you to make them feel that way. Nancy, the longtime legal secretary, says, "You have to make clients feel they are important and that you know who they are." This isn't always easy, and if you lose your composure, it's the company insulting the customer—not you!

One self-important client called an office and complained to the boss that the secretary didn't recognize his voice. The boss agreed with the secretary that the client was out of line, and he trusted her to take care of the problem.

She asked her boss what the client looked like and for some particulars about his family. When the client came to the office, although they'd never met, she greeted him warmly by name and asked if his wife Mabel was enjoying the presidency of her garden club? And did his son Frank enjoy playing shortstop on the high school baseball team? She went on to ask about his mother, his father, and cousin Felix. The client flip-flopped from assuming, "she ought to know who I am," to thinking, "This woman knows everything about me," to finally realizing and laughing, "This is a joke, isn't it?" His attitude softened. With her boss's permission, she had used humor to win him over.

From then on, they recognized each other's voice, and he treated her with the courtesy and respect she deserved. In this case, the boss knew the client could take some kidding, and he knew that his secretary could use humor appropriately. That, of course, requires a friendly, professional relationship.

When a secretary who worked for Endicott and Goldfaden law firm mistakenly answered the phone, "Endifaden and Goldicott," she laughed and said, "Please hold on while I run that by you again." The caller laughed, accepted her mistake, and was still smiling when the boss came to the phone.

WANT TO KNOW HOW BUSY YOU ARE? LEAVE TOWN AND TRY TO MAKE AN APPOINTMENT WITH YOURSELF

A frantic customer had called five times in one day about a delay with an expected order. Trying to avoid unpleasantness, the boss refused to take the calls. Finally the sympathetic secretary wrapped all five messages

A frantic customer had called five times in one day about a delay with an expected order. Trying to avoid unpleasantness, the boss refused to take the calls. Finally the sympathetic secretary wrapped all five messages in a red ribbon and handed it to her boss with this note: "The person is on hold, here are his five messages. It would be a real gift if you'd talk to him." The boss groaned, but she did take the call, because when it came right down to it, she knew her secretary was right.

in a red ribbon and handed it to her boss with this note: "The person is on hold, here are his five messages. It would be a real gift if you'd talk to him." The boss groaned, but she did take the call, because when it came right down to it, she knew her secretary was right.

When we had a magazine assignment to interview Maynard Jackson, then mayor of Atlanta, it took fifty phone calls plus one funny poster with one shiny star for each call, drawn by a sympathetic secretary pleading our case. We got the interview.

Cold-calling salespeople are another problem. They have a job to do and will often try unorthodox means to get past the secretary who is under strict orders to admit no one.

After several attempts, one salesman finally brought a bouquet of roses to the office. Before he could say anything, the secretary said, "How nice, but even though it may seem that way, my boss hasn't died. I know he will appreciate the flowers, but I can't promise you an appointment." The salesman smiled, realizing she had seen through his ploy, but her light-hearted words had let him down as gracefully as possible.

HUMOR WITH SECRETARIAL COLLEAGUES AND SUBORDINATES

OK, you might as well try to have a good time, because these are the people you have to work with every day. If you can inspire a "we are all in this together" atmosphere, we encourage you to do so, because a happy office is a productive office, and creative humor is a perma-bonding agent.

In one of our workshops, an office manager posed this problem. Although her secretarial staff was doing their work, they were making too many family calls during office hours, and it was her job to get the situation under control. She herself was a widow with two teenagers and knew that many, but not all, of the calls were necessary. How could she cut down the extra calls without seeming insensitive? We brainstormed creative ideas in small groups, and one circle of office managers came up with a possible solution. They suggested she get an "E.T." phone, shaped like the extra-terrestrial creature from the movie, put it in the middle of the office, and hang a sign around its neck. The sign would read: "After establishing essential daily linkage, this is the only extension you can phone home on."

She did it, and the message came through without offending anyone directly. It did cut down on the personal calls, and she was still one of the "good guys."

Group humor projects can also be bonding. Another secretary started a permanent list of office jargon and funny definitions for staffers to expand. For instance, what does "in basket" really mean? Answer: "I'll get to it when the cows come home." And when the boss says, "I see," it really means, "You're in my office, I hear you, and I've displayed concern. Now please don't tell me again." She recorded the jargon dictionary on her computer, and as an initiation ritual, the staff presents an updated copy to each new employee.

When you have to deal with an individual problem, humor can tilt the scales in your favor. A notorious carpool dawdler, who enjoyed chatting with others during prolonged good-byes while her driver waited, received the following coupon: "Dear Friend, I value your company, but I have to leave exactly on time. This carpool voucher is good for five rides at five PM sharp, one ride at five ten, and 'Sorry, you'll have to hitchhike' at five fifteen!"

It is difficult but vital to keep your perspective when:

1. you are secretary to a C.E.O. who is driving you nuts but who everybody else thinks is God,

2. someone is banging a fist on your desk because his crisis is more critical than the crisis you are already working on, or

3. the person at the next desk is cracking her knuckles and her gum in three-quarter time.

A balanced perspective is necessary for both your professional and personal health, and laughter is the glue that can often keep you from falling apart.

An executive secretary discovered this when, on Friday, June 5, 1992, the last afternoon of a wild, nationwide, half-price air fare sale, her boss ordered her to get him a ticket to the West Coast. She enlisted the help of her fellow secretaries, and when a paper airplane landed on one of their desks, it was that secretary's turn to hold the phone. After fifty paper airplanes and two hours on hold, they got the boss his ticket.

Time after time, humor has helped get the job done. And isn't that what it's all about?

Humor, Sales, and Customer Relations: Tell Me What You Laugh At and I'll Tell You Who You Are

THE POWER OF HUMOR AS A SALES TECHNIQUE

The fifty-year-old salesman, Mr. D., was out cold-calling (contacting business offices unannounced). He strode into an office for the first time to try to see the buyer. Sweet-talking the harried secretary, he convinced her to check with Mr. Buyer about his schedule.

Grinning, he added, "By the way, I heard a good limerick yesterday. Are you ready?

A buxom young typist named Baines,
At her work took particular pains.
She was good at dictation
And long explanations,
But she ran more to bosom than brains."

> The fifty-year-old salesman, Mr. D., was out cold-calling (contacting business offices unannounced). He strode into an office for the first time to try to see the buyer. Sweet-talking the harried secretary, he convinced her to check with Mr. Buyer about his schedule.
>
> Grinning, he added, "By the way, I heard a good limerick yesterday. Are you ready?
>
> A buxom young typist named Baines,
> At her work took particular pains.
> She was good at dictation
> And long explanations,
> But she ran more to bosom than brains."
>
> The secretary suddenly replaced the phone she was dialing. "I just remembered that Mr. Buyer is in conference now and doesn't wish to be disturbed. Leave your card and he'll call you if he's interested."

The secretary suddenly replaced the phone she was dialing. "I just remembered that Mr. Buyer is in conference now and doesn't wish to be disturbed. Leave your card and he'll call you if he's interested."

Chances are, Mr. Buyer will never see the salesman's card.

What went wrong? Aren't salespeople supposed to be funny? Isn't humor supposed to warm up a potential customer? That's what Mr. D. thinks, as he calls customers just to tell them a long shaggy-dog story or the latest ethnic joke (his way of keeping in touch). If you asked Mr. D. why he has never become more successful as a salesman, he will blame a poor product, a weak territory, the economy—anything but himself.

Mr. D. fails to observe the negative effect his attempts at humor can have when he dispenses it indiscriminately. In addition to not being selective, he tells stories that are often too long, as well as irrelevant, unprofessional, and inappropriate.

Although he may know his product, the net result is that he loses the respect of many potential clients because his humor is offensive to them. He fails to connect with them, personally or professionally, and is unable to develop rapport. This all adds up to failed communication.

Before exploring the power of humor as a sales technique, let's examine a few basics of selling.

A salesperson is somewhat akin to a circus juggler who simultaneously spins eight plates high in the air on poles. The juggler must make constant adjustments and pay adequate attention to each one. No two performances are exactly the same, even though he uses the same poles, the same size plates, and the same principles of balance. Ignore one for too long, and they all come tumbling down.

Selling and customer relations likewise involve the coordinated balancing of several elements, each vital to becoming a truly successful salesperson. These are:

1. a salable product,
2. thorough knowledge of the product,
3. hard work,
4. willingness to spend the time necessary for preparation,
5. good communication skills, and
6. a pleasing personality.

Having the first five is not enough. Given a choice, people prefer doing business with people they like, and doing business requires trust.

> Can I trust you? Will you provide good service? Can we work together? Do you understand my specific business problems? Can we communicate?

What sets you apart from other salespeople touting similar products? Frequently it is your personality and manner that clinch the deal, because you have answered the prospective client's unstated but very real questions: Can I trust you? Will you provide good service? Can we work together? Do you understand my specific business problems? Can we communicate?

A survey conducted at U.C.L.A. Medical School asked fifteen hundred high-income people who were not ill about the patient-doctor relationship. The study revealed that eighty-five percent had either changed doctors in the previous five years or were considering a change.

Of the five reasons for changing physicians cited by the respondents, the least important was the doctor's competence. The four more commonly mentioned reasons related to the physician's style were:

1. not taking enough time,
2. not allowing patients to express themselves,
3. being preoccupied with phone calls, and
4. having poor personal habits.

Medical competence was taken for granted, and it was generally "bedside manner" that made the difference.

Doctors, of course, are not salespeople in the strictest sense of the word. But they do offer a service that people can either accept or seek elsewhere. If, even when matters of personal health are involved, individuals are willing to change doctors merely on the basis of the doctor's style and personality, consider how much more vital a factor your manner is in the everyday dealings of the business world.

HUMOR STRATEGIES

If you don't like people, it's hard to sell successfully, whether in commission sales or in retail business, and it's equally hard to wield the power of humor effectively. Therefore, in discussing humor strategies, let's assume that you like people, you possess the first four elements of a good salesperson, and your salesmanship directly affects your livelihood. How, then, can humor enhance your technique in selling or customer relations? Humor can help:

- humanize you,
- make a point,
- relax customers, making them more receptive,
- get and keep their attention,
- break through an established pattern of rejection,
- control the emotional climate,
- establish rapport,
- extricate you from an uncomfortable situation,
- maintain control by keeping the conversation on track,
- allow you to make transitions smoothly,
- or maintain your own perspective, keeping the other person's irritating behavior from controlling you.

THE HUMOR BASICS

You communicate through your words, your voice, and your actions. Ideally these elements mesh harmoniously to communicate a single idea. Each can be a vehicle for humor.

Here are some questions to ask yourself in evaluating your sales skills and effectiveness in communication. Once you've honestly taken stock of your strengths and weaknesses, you can knowledgeably ascertain how you might improve your salesmanship and customer relations effectiveness with the Humor Basics that follow.

1. How often are you really speaking "on the same wave length" with your prospect?
2. Do you like most of your customers? Do they like you?
3. Do you put your sales ability down with your humor?
4. Do feelings of anxiety or desperation cause you to come on too strong?
5. Does the pitch of your voice often rise during a presentation?
6. Do you cope easily with customer objections?
7. Do people laugh genuinely at (most of) your humorous off-the-cuff remarks? Or do you sometimes sense that they are uncomfortable?
8. Is your humor generally sexist, ethnic, and otherwise emotionally charged?
9. Do you view selling as manipulative, or do you genuinely have the best interest of prospective clients at heart?
10. Do you waste customers' and your own time telling long irrelevant stories and anecdotes?
11. Which successful colleagues do you admire? How do they use humor to enhance their sales technique?
12. Do you usually notice the humorous side of whatever happens to be going on?

If you have found room for improvement, use these fifteen Humor Basics to help you achieve your goals.

Basic #1: Creativity is the cornerstone of successful selling. Experiment with humor but don't overwork it. Use it as an aid, not a crutch.

Basic #2: Know thyself, know thy customer. Successful salespeople handle each customer differently. As one woman sums it up, "First I have to be attuned to what role the customer expects me to play. Does he want me to relate to him in a quiet, unassuming manner or use a take-charge, aggressive approach? When I decide what style the customer prefers, and how much attention that person will give me, then I can determine what role humor will play."

BASIC #3: Keep humor relevant. Off-the-subject humor will keep the discussion off the subject. Irrelevant humor is both counter-productive and wasteful of time for your prospect.

BASIC #4: Speak their humor language, tailoring your level of humor to individual differences in taste and preferences.

BASIC #5: Take advantage of the opportunity for humor of the moment that arises from your customers' comments, from interruptions, or from unexpected occurrences. When we interviewed the governor of Georgia, a phone call interrupted. The governor apologized for the delay when he returned, saying he was only supposed to be interrupted for urgent calls. "But then, you know how teenaged sons are." We responded, "We were just relieved that when the phone rang, it wasn't one of ours."

BASIC #6: Look for humor in other places. If a colleague mentions a way she used humor effectively, think about how you might apply it in the future. Jot down funny sayings which also make a point. Example: "To err is human, but it takes a computer to really louse things up."

BASIC #7: Know when to pull back, sensing when your customer does not want you to top her humor. The last thing you want is to grapple with an impromptu game of one-upsmanship with a customer, fighting for who gets the last laugh. Either way, you lose.

BASIC #8: Don't joke about people's names. For most people, nothing is as personal as their names, and many don't take kindly to jokes about theirs. Just remember, they've had their names for a lifetime. You won't come up with anything they haven't heard before.

Basic #9: If you find funny remarks that work, keep using them when appropriate. Although you can plan much of your humor in advance, when you say something unexpectedly funny and effective, write it down and reuse it in similar situations.

Basic #10: Selling is a person-to-person activity, and the more you share of yourself and let the customer get to know you, the better the business rapport will be. Customers do not want to hear about your personal problems. But if they feel they are getting something from you personally, you will have a better business relationship with them.

Basic #11: Make a point to be cordial to the person at the front desk—the receptionist or secretary. Buyers may come and go, get fired, promoted, or transferred. Consequently, the person behind the front desk may be your only source of continuity. It's important to treat that person as well as you do the individual buyer.

Basic #12: Keep humor brief. No one has time to waste. Get to the point humorously and then move on.

Basic #13: Train yourself for success with humor. Preparation is important to perfect your skills. Take courses and attend lectures and seminars related to humor and public speaking.

Basic #14: Decide which humor techniques fit your style best and focus on those.

Basic #15: With humor, always behave professionally. Few clients or customers want to conduct business with Bozo the Clown.

THE ANATOMY OF A SALE

Now let's analyze the parts of a sale and see where humor fits in.

THE APPROACH

The approach is the most important part of a sale. If you don't get the customer's interest, you have already lost the transaction. Let humor open the door.

Improve your approach by using humor to:

- *Break patterns of rejection.* Linda, in computer sales, called a company vice-president for an appointment. Not seeing any need, he repeatedly said no, claiming he had no time. Finally, Linda said, "Certainly you have to eat. Let me take you to lunch."

  The vice-president answered, "I don't take time to go out to lunch."

  "Well, I tell you what," Linda suggested, "I'll bring over a loaf of bread, some cheese, a bowl of apples, and some ants, and we'll have a picnic at your desk."

  At this, the vice-president started laughing. "OK, I'll skip the picnic. So when do you want your appointment?"

  She persistently but gently chiseled away at his resistance, and her humor interrupted his "no" frame of mind.

- *Break the ice in awkward situations.* A chemical salesman, in town for the day, dropped in unannounced on a customer he knew fairly well. He walked into the buyer's office, but before he had a chance to say anything the customer barked, "We don't need anything today. Good-bye."

  The salesman turned around, went out of the door, and closed it. Then he came back in the door and said, "Now let's do this all over again." The humor broke the ice. The customer started laughing, and he realized he had been a bit too abrupt and hadn't given the salesman a chance to talk.

- *Catch the buyer's attention.* A woman regularly called on a business. After she made her presentation, the buyer would politely say, "I'll call you if we need anything." She realized that he didn't remember her from one month to the next and never placed an order. Finally she bought six

A chemical salesman, in town for the day, dropped in unannounced on a customer he knew fairly well. He walked into the buyer's office, but before he had a chance to say anything the customer barked, "We don't need anything today. Good-bye."

The salesman turned around, went out of the door, and closed it. Then he came back in the door and said, "Now let's do this all over again." The humor broke the ice. The customer started laughing, and he realized he had been a bit too abrupt and hadn't given the salesman a chance to talk.

helium-filled balloons and wrote her name and her company's name on them.

This time when she walked into his office, she smiled, said, "Good morning," released the balloons, and left. The buyer, curiosity piqued, tracked her down for an explanation.

"I realize you're a busy man and have trouble telling one salesperson from another, so I thought I'd give you something to remember me by." The buyer laughed heartily, and this time paid attention to her presentation. Then he wrote an order.

Although her professionalism and homework had ultimately closed the deal, it was her humor that had caught his attention.

Ms. L., prospecting on the phone, needs to leave a message for the buyer and asks the receptionist, "Have you got a big piece of paper?" She then leaves her own long name, the long name of her company, and adds, "I told you it was a long message, but good things don't always come in small packages."

Put people at ease. Carefully making a joke at your own expense can also evoke friendly feelings. Occasionally Mr. O. will say to an obviously busy customer, "I know in your list of priorities I rank just ahead of funeral lot salesmen and Florida swamp property agents, but I think if you can give me a couple of minutes I can show you how our new line of products can boost your sales considerably." He lets the buyer know he "knows his place" in her priorities, and they can joke about it together.

Humanize telephone conversations. Don't forget the value of humor as part of your telephone technique. You can't use body language and gestures when you're talking on the phone, but smiling to yourself will improve the timbre of your voice.

A humorous comment also humanizes the exchange. Ms. L., prospecting on the phone, needs to leave a message for the buyer and asks the receptionist, "Have you got a *big* piece of paper?" She then leaves her own long name, the long name of her company, and adds, "I told you it was a long message, but good things don't always come in small packages."

This simple comment, spoken with a smile in her voice, creates a warm, shared moment, and her message always gets delivered. In a world where too many people treat secretaries and desk personnel as nonentities, humor acknowledges the other person as an individual trying her best to do a good job. Everyone likes to be appreciated.

THE PRESENTATION

OK, you've gotten past the secretary and in to see the buyer. Now what? The task of a presentation is to get your prospects to listen and accept what you say, to convince them that your product best fits their needs, and to show them that you can solve their problems.

A successful presentation is tailored to the individual and her business, and you must tailor your humor just as individually. It's a game of matching appropriate humor with both the person and the situation.

During a presentation you might use humor to:

Hold people's interest while making your point. Mr. S. was presenting a new line to a group of manufacturer's representatives, the middlemen in the wholesale-retail transaction. When one of them grumbled that a one percent commission on the item wasn't enough to bother with, Mr. S., having anticipated this criticism, took out a handful of one hundred pennies.

He dropped them and let them clatter and roll all over the conference table. "Are any of you going to tell me that on a one hundred dollar sale, you wouldn't bother picking this up?" Smiles and nodding heads proved him right.

Create warmth and receptiveness by letting people see you as a real person. When a customer, knowing Mr. S.'s wife had a business of her own, asked, "How's your wife?" Mr. S. replied, "Marsha's remodeling the kitchen. She's making it smaller and adding vending machines." His comment didn't belittle her, and it encouraged a feeling of camaraderie. He humanized himself to the customer, who responded, "I know what you mean, my wife's in business, too."

- *Neutralize criticism and turn it to your advantage.* Ms. A. quoted a *Fortune* article that named Hewlett-Packard, her company, as one of the top one hundred corporations. Looking skeptical, the prospective client countered, "I read that article too, and I thought it was mainly referring to financial stability." Ms. A. replied, smiling, "Then perhaps you'd also like to add us to your stock portfolio." She adroitly took a negative remark and converted it to a positive one.

- *Keep the discussion under your control.* When the conversation gets off the subject, humor can guide it back without seeming abrupt. A customer couldn't decide between a pocketbook that zipped and a similar style that snapped shut. While examining them, she engaged the saleswoman in conversation about her grandson's pet gerbils and how they were always escaping from their cage. "I don't know what I'll do if one gets out when I'm visiting," she sighed. "Well," the saleswoman smiled, "You could always snap it up in this bag." The customer laughed, the saleswoman got her mind back on business, and the sale was made.

A customer couldn't decide between a pocketbook that zipped and a similar style that snapped shut. While examining them, she engaged the saleswoman in conversation about her grandson's pet gerbils and how they were always escaping from their cage. "I don't know what I'll do if one gets out when I'm visiting," she sighed. "Well," the saleswoman smiled, "You could always snap it up in this bag."

- *Drive home your point without running it over.* An investment broker showed his prospective client that with the current rate of inflation the client had only enough assets available to support himself and his wife comfortably for six years after he turned sixty-five. "You don't plan to stay retired for very long, do you?" Humor, in its indirectness, allows the customer to save face.

- *Keep the customer's attention and maintain feelings of goodwill.* In selling, where so much hinges on subjective perceptions, goodwill is no longer a luxury but a necessity. A woman who sells advertising specialties carries an item called a Stress Card. Reacting to hand temperature, it turns various colors when touched, indicating a present degree of stress. (Tension usually produces cold hands.)

Although the Stress Card is seldom purchased because of its high price, it almost always evokes a humorous reaction. Most frequently, the humor comes from the customer. The card gives him the opportunity to talk about himself, frustrations at work, or other pressures. Inspiring humor in others can be just as effective as initiating it yourself.

Make transitions. Humor allows you to cross from one point to another smoothly. It also gives you time, during the pause and ensuing laughter, to regroup your thoughts for the next subject to be discussed. Among the samples a saleswoman presented to a drugstore manager was a new brand of mouthwash. To her amazement, he uncapped it, took a swig, and spit it into the wastebasket. She looked at him, looked at the basket, and not missing a beat, whipped out her order book and said, "So how many bottles do you want to shoot for?"

Among the samples a saleswoman presented to a drugstore manager was a new brand of mouthwash. To her amazement, he uncapped it, took a swig, and spit it into the wastebasket. She looked at him, looked at the basket, and not missing a beat, whipped out her order book and said, "So how many bottles do you want to shoot for?"

Be creative. An accounting firm, needing to remind workers to use red ink, asked their supplier for an idea. He suggested red pens with the slogan, "This Time It's OK To Be In The Red." It sold.

There's more to humor than meets the eye. By examining your own sales techniques and looking for weak areas, you will discover where the power of humor can work best for you.

THE CLOSING

While closing an imminent sale, you need to maintain your professionalism. Often this is the least appropriate time for using humor. If you get sidetracked with humor, you might miss the cue to close. Telling jokes indiscriminately will get you off the subject and waste the buyer's time. (This is true any time during the selling process.) The last thing you want is to be considered a clown who's not serious about business. Your aim is to influence your customer to act now.

Sometimes humor can salvage an awkward moment during a closing. One salesman knew he was not the only supplier being considered. After presenting his products, he missed the cue to close when the manager said to her assistant, "Well, I think it's Model 203."

Unclear what she meant, he inquired, "Have we reached the point where I should take out my order pad?" Here, it was not the words that conveyed the humor so much as his quizzical expression and the bantering tone of his voice.

Humor can also smooth over a snag in the decision-making process, especially when several people are involved. Often no one wants to take the responsibility of saying, "OK, let's do it."

One salesman picked up humor from a poster and uses it often. When he makes a presentation to a group, he says. "Careful now, you all know what a camel is, don't you? A camel is a horse designed by a committee." After they laugh, he zeroes in on the problem. "OK, what can we eliminate so we can narrow this down and make a decision?" His humor allows the customers to laugh at themselves and then take action.

THE FOLLOW-UP

The sale may be closed, but your work isn't finished until you deliver the promised goods or services to a satisfied customer. Keeping in touch with customers after the transaction is vital for maintaining continuity and promoting repeat business.

Using a light touch in dealing with unexpected delays or problems that arise after the closing can make the bad news more tolerable to your customers and minimize personal criticism.

At appropriate times, one sales representative breaks bad news to customers with this comment: "Good morning, Mr. Smith, this is Mr. Land. If you haven't had your aggravation for the day, I'd like a few minutes of your time." The remark prepares the customer for the unpleasant news to come even as he laughs (and they do laugh), while also acknowledging that it is an aggravation for the salesperson as well. The anger or frustration is then more likely to be directed toward the real source of the difficulty—the heel-dragging manufacturer—than at the bearer of the news.

"Good morning, Mr. Smith, this is Mr. Land. If you haven't had your aggravation for the day, I'd like a few minutes of your time."

"I have good news and bad news. The good news is, your goods have been shipped. The bad news is, they were sent to the wrong address."

Another salesman phoned his customers about a temporary, easy-to-remedy delay in shipment and successfully cushioned the announcement this way: "I have good news and bad news. The good news is, your goods have been shipped. The bad news is, they were sent to the wrong address."

> ONE CAUTION: Tone of voice makes all the difference in how customers interpret your remarks, and a flip attitude will backfire. Your voice must convey a caring and sympathetic understanding of what this delay means to your customer's business.

YOU COUNT TOO

Now that the parts of a sale have been dissected, there's still one more area of customer relations, salesmanship, and humor left to explore. Let's turn from thinking about the customer, to thinking about you. How can humor help you, the salesperson?

Dealing with customers and selling successfully require a high level of enthusiasm and confidence. If you carry over negative feelings of rejection, frustration, or anger from one customer to the next, you will be significantly less effective.

Therefore, let humor help you unwind. Take a few minutes between appointments to look for humor in your situation, put your aggravations in proper perspective, and create an optimum frame of mind for successful selling.

Relieving your own tension by taking a humor break will relax you both physically and mentally. You will then be able to maintain a pleasant voice level (a subtle but important influence) and allow that high level of enthusiasm to shine through. As Marsha Londe, National Salesperson of the Year in the field of advertising specialties, puts it, "A humor break can make my shoulders come down from around my neck."

Dealing with customers and selling successfully require a high level of enthusiasm and confidence. If you carry over negative feelings of rejection, frustration, or anger from one customer to the next, you will be significantly less effective.

Approach humor as you would any other challenge. You probably didn't become successful at other skills overnight—it took thought, preparation, and practice. It's rather like making bread. When you first learn, you're hesitant kneading the dough. How much is enough? How much is too much? No one can tell you exactly, because "just enough" depends on other variable factors like the humidity and temperature.

But if you do it often, eventually you just know when it's enough. It's the same with applying humor to your selling techniques. You knead your customers. Not manipulating, but working with them—adding information, expertise, and humor. With practice, you'll know when enough is just right.

Let humor help you unwind. Take a few minutes between appointments to look for humor in your situation, put your aggravations in proper perspective, and create an optimum frame of mind for successful selling.

CHAPTER 11

Teaching: You're Molding More Than Clay Here

At a high school awards assembly, the "Star Student" (academically outstanding senior) thanked the science teacher she had chosen as "Star Teacher" with these few words: "You always encouraged me and found extra time to help me, and you taught me that it's OK to laugh at my mistakes."

The head of the English department at another high school awards assembly commended the eleven members of her Senior Honors English class as winners. During the year an organization had announced an essay contest, and one student observed that nothing in the contest rules prevented an entire class from writing and submitting a single essay. The teacher good-humoredly approved the idea, and each student researched and wrote one segment. The task was challenging, stimulating, educationally sound, and great fun! Standing in the auditorium, the eleven smiling students beamed as their teacher announced the $125 award that they had won and would later spend on a class party.

The head of the English department at another high school awards assembly commended the eleven members of her Senior Honors English class as winners. During the year an organization had announced an essay contest, and one student observed that nothing in the contest rules prevented an entire class from writing and submitting a single essay. The teacher good-humoredly approved the idea, and each student researched and wrote one segment. The task was challenging, stimulating, educationally sound, and great fun! Standing in the auditorium, the eleven smiling students beamed as their teacher announced the $125 award that they had won and would later spend on a class party.

A fifth-grade student excitedly showed her mother her math homework. At the top of the paper was the question, "What is raised in Brazil during the rainy season?" Then followed several math problems. Each number in the answer had a letter equivalent, and as the child solved the problems correctly, she found the answer to the riddle—umbrellas. The homework was fun. Any mathematical error became obvious immediately and the student could then re-work the problem carefully to find the correct letter for the riddle.

The three teachers in these examples used humor differently. The "Star Teacher" taught his students through humor that they can laugh at mistakes, and that mistakes aren't the end of the world. Because she knew her class would be breaking no contest rules, the second teacher could take advantage of their humorous gambit by going along with the joke. She maximized their performance by motivating them with humor. And it never occurred to the fifth-grade math teacher that arithmetic shouldn't be fun, as the riddle technique encouraged meticulous work as well as enjoyment.

What would a home be without the sound of laughter? So why have a classroom without an occasional humor break? If you accept the idea that humor is a positive approach to life—valuable and not merely frivolous—then, as a teacher, you can use it (with reasonable limitations) as a positive approach to your class. Relevant humor can be valuable with older students for enhancing instructions, managing the classroom, and imparting knowledge. And, brief occasional encounters with humor unrelated to the subject can help you hold the attention of younger children whose attention spans are short.

This is not to suggest that the teacher become a classroom entertainer—no more than the business executive should take on that role with employees—but rather that the teacher recognize humor's potential as a teaching aid.

Because of the very nature of the teaching profession, "bad teacher" is a contradiction in terms; if you're not good at it, you can't teach. Also, if you don't like young people, you are in the wrong profession, and humor won't make a difference.

Before humor can be effective in the classroom, there must be a degree of mutual respect between teacher and students. The key to using humor effectively lies in exploring its full potential and adapting it to your particular situation and teaching style.

At a high school awards assembly, the "Star Student" (academically outstanding senior) thanked the science teacher she had chosen as "Star Teacher" with these few words: "You always encouraged me and found extra time to help me, and you taught me that it's OK to laugh at my mistakes."

STAGES OF HUMOR DEVELOPMENT

Robert E. Valett, California State University expert in early and middle childhood education, classified five progressive stages of humor development in children.

1. The early childhood *giggling prankster* stage.
2. The middle childhood *foolish comic* stage.
3. The late childhood *puzzling riddler* stage.
4. The early adolescence *punning wit* stage.
5. The adolescent-to-adult *satirical critic* stage.[10]

EARLY CHILDHOOD

During the preschool years (approximately one to five years old) children love to be silly and follow their impulses, often indulging in mischief. They are concerned about motor control; they are learning to button shirts and to tie shoes as well as to govern bodily functions. At this stage noises from the body—a belch, a slurping straw—seem funny, as do physical clowning and tickling. As their language skills increase, nonsense words or nursery rhymes become enjoyable—hey diddle-diddle, hickory-dickory-dock, rub-a-dub-dub.

MIDDLE CHILDHOOD (SIX TO NINE YEARS)

At this stage children begin to feel some power and want to test the limits of their control. They may express this in silly practical jokes—hiding a friend's shoe, for instance. They also enjoy the nonsensical and "playing around":

> "You have your boots on the wrong feet."
> "Well, they're the only feet I have," or,
>
> "I'm glad I'm not a bird."
> "Why?"
> "I can't fly."

LATE CHILDHOOD (NINE TO TWELVE YEARS)

Valett observes that this is the fun and games stage, where abstract thinking comes into play. Now clichéd jokes and riddles are popular:

> "Why is an elephant so wrinkled?"
> "Because you can't iron him," or,
>
> "What is a sleeping bull called?"
> "A bull dozer."

If you find that your child's fun and games are becoming cruel "put-down humor," you can point out the hurtfulness of ethnic, religious, or racial slurs and offer harmless substitutes like knock-knock jokes rather than knock-'em jokes. Catching it early will prevent a destructive humor habit.

EARLY ADOLESCENCE (TWELVE TO FIFTEEN YEARS)

The early adolescent enjoys playing with logic and the varied meanings of words and ideas, frequently expressed in puns:

> "Librarians are people who shelve ideas."
>
> "Headaches are all in your mind," and
>
> "These trousers are getting frayed."
> "Frayed of what?"

ADOLESCENCE TO ADULTHOOD

In later adolescence or adulthood, Valett finds that "humor involves hypothetically deductive reasoning and judgment and is typified by tongue-in-cheek biting humor." [11]

A man called animal control to complain about a dead dog in the street. "Where do you live?" asked the dispatcher.

"On Chattahoochee Avenue."

"Can you please spell that for me?"

He began. "C-A . . . C-H-E . . . C-H-A . . . hang on." After a few minutes he returned to the phone out of breath and gasped. "I dragged it down the road. Now it's on Lee Street . . . that's L-E-E."

A man called animal control to complain about a dead dog in the street. "Where do you live?" asked the dispatcher.

"On Chattahoochee Avenue."

"Can you please spell that for me?"

He began. "C-A . . . C-H-E . . . C-H-A . . . hang on." After a few minutes he returned to the phone out of breath and gasped. "I dragged it down the road. Now it's on Lee Street . . . that's L-E-E."

"When I was a little girl I was really stuck on myself. But now that I'm more mature, I've come unglued."

Touting the qualifications of his favorite congressional candidate, a student said, "He has no equal." His friend agreed. "You're right. Superiors, yes; equals, no."

In this stage a young person is adept at using language and is aware enough of human folly to enjoy and initiate playful humor that is more sophisticated, original, and funny to the adult world. Asked by his teacher of advanced music to write his class goals for the quarter, sixteen-year-old Josh wrote, "By the end of this class, I would like to know more about the structure of harmony and chords. I would also like to learn composition. And by the end of the quarter, I would like to be taller."

WHAT HUMOR CAN DO

While some teachers begin the year with a don't-smile-until-Christmas attitude, others have found that humor creates an open and sharing atmosphere. That's why a sprinkling of humor can make one classroom a place of welcome relief—an oasis—in what can be a grueling and tedious school day.

A classroom consists of children with diverse backgrounds, problems, personalities, and levels of ability. A teacher with a smile on his face, who lets students know he likes them—even though he may correct their work or criticize their behavior—can make a child's school experience a positive one. And in today's sometimes volatile school environment, turning down the emotional temperature with humor can keep the melting pot from turning into a pressure cooker.

In turn, classroom humor will make the teaching experience more rewarding, since humor has a positive effect on the instructor as well as the instructed. Here then is what a Humor Oasis can accomplish:

H umanizing effect on self-image
U nderstanding
M otivating
O pening communication
R especting individual differences, and divergent thinking

O pportunity to be creative
A ttitude
S timulating learning
I nspiring and illustrating
S afety valve for tension and aggressive behavior

"When I was a little girl I was really stuck on myself. But now that I'm more mature, I've come unglued."

THE HUMANIZING EFFECT ON SELF-IMAGE

Laughter signals acceptance. It can relax students and develop a spirit of togetherness. Showing children how and when to laugh will serve them well beyond the classroom. A child's ego can be very fragile, and helping children learn to laugh at errors rather than to be overwhelmed by them strengthens their self image.

First of all, the teacher must realize that she isn't invincible, and that she sometimes makes mistakes. She should be able to laugh at her own errors. When asked a question she couldn't answer, a biology teacher replied, "I'm sorry. My mind works like a computer memory bank, but I guess I forgot to make a deposit this morning." After the laughter subsided, she told the student where to find the answer.

A student was upset because he did poorly on a quiz. The teacher told him gently, "That was the most beautiful answer I've ever read—unfortunately it had nothing to do with the question." The student reread his essay and laughingly agreed. The teacher then went one step further. "Your answer did show me that you studied the material. I'm sure if you read the questions more carefully next time, you will do better." She let him know his mistake didn't reflect on his ability or character.

Humor also tempers discipline. It conveys, "I don't like what you are doing, but I still like you." When a teenager called his high school attendance office at eight AM pretending to be "Mr. Reed" calling to excuse his son from school, the counselor recognized fourteen-year-old Jimmy's voice. She said good-naturedly, "Mr. Reed, I'm sorry Jimmy is so ill on this beautiful day. If he doesn't recover in forty-five minutes, I'll call you at your office to see how he's doing." And she hung up.

Touting the qualifications of his favorite congressional candidate, a student said, "He has no equal." His friend agreed. "You're right. Superiors, yes; equals, no."

Jimmy made a miraculous recovery and was in school in twenty minutes. The counselor cheerfully said she was glad he recovered and asked him to stay after school to make up his class work.

For the two years she worked in that school, the counselor disciplined many students, but not once did a student lose his temper or become abusive. And she had few repeat offenders. Her humorous approach maintained discipline while showing compassion.

UNDERSTANDING

When subject matter is difficult for students, some may feel stupid. If so, they often stop asking questions in class, fearing classmates will ridicule them or the teacher will think less of them. One teacher always tells her students she has only two rules: She does not allow the word "stupid" in her class ("There are no stupid questions"), and she does not allow laughing at serious questions or wrong answers.

One first-grade teacher's aide planned a daily ten-minute laughter break for her class with games, puzzles, funny stories, riddles, cartoons, and puppet projects. It was creative, constructive, and fun.

After learning that as a child this history teacher had escaped from the Nazis during World War II, one of her fifteen-year-old students excitedly blurted out, "Were you ever tortured?" As soon as the words left her mouth, she realized the inappropriateness of her question. Her embarrassment was heightened when a few students groaned at her seeming insensitivity. To ease her discomfort, the teacher responded, "Only in this class." Her remark indicated, "It's OK, she didn't mean any harm," and their laughter brought the chagrined student back into the group.

MOTIVATING

Humor can motivate students by establishing rapport, fostering cooperation, and encouraging group feelings of cohesiveness. As an intermediate reward, humor can also motivate students to keep working toward the real goal of learning.

On a history unit studying medieval times, the teacher proposed that the class create a newspaper relating real events of the day in modern terms, with sensational headlines, in sections of sports, lifestyle, business, front page, and editorial and political commentary. The class drew numbers for group assignments.

The sports page covered falconing, jousting, and other knightly activities. The lifestyle pages included an advice column, household hints (the best way to clean armor), fine-tuning your lute, a recipe for mead, and the latest medical discoveries ("Leeching: A New Frontier in Medicine").

The project was entertaining and creative. But most important, it demanded research and factual reporting, while also using humor to expand writing skills.

A high-school history teacher asked his class to find samples of presidential humor. It involved research and sparked discussions on the uses of humor in politics.

OPENING COMMUNICATION

If learning involves questioning and expanding viewpoints, then humor can provide yet another perspective in the classroom.

For instance, discussing the world during the time of Columbus, the teacher could ask the class, "What scientific objections of that era could Queen Isabella's advisors have given her to block the funding for Columbus's expedition?" And further, "What scientific objections would they have given our modern astronauts against space travel?" The students would have to be familiar with scientific thought in both centuries to enter the discussion, and the humor would be relevant to the lesson.

RESPECTING INDIVIDUAL DIFFERENCES AND DIVERGENT THINKING

If humor relates to subject matter or helps with discipline, then it is a valuable tool. However, when a teacher uses humor without a hint of playfulness—in anger, or perhaps because of fatigue—by publicly ridiculing a student or being sarcastic, then it is no longer humor, but mere aggression disguised as humor. It's not funny, and it hurts. A teacher should never take "cheap shots" at students.

A good rule is, if you have doubts about a retort, don't use it. Also, both teachers and students should avoid ethnic, racial, religious, or sexist jokes unless discussing the ways negative stereotypes are reinforced. Once you lose your students' respect, you will find that it is almost impossible to regain.

PROVIDING OPPORTUNITIES TO BE CREATIVE AND IMAGINATIVE

Humor can be used in posters, audio-visuals, bulletin boards, talks, dramas, creative writing, hand-outs, and occasionally as a tension-reliever on tests.

One first-grade teacher's aide planned a daily ten-minute laughter break for her class with games, puzzles, funny stories, riddles, cartoons, and puppet projects. It was creative, constructive, and fun.

A high-school history teacher asked his class to find samples of presidential humor. It involved research and sparked discussions on the uses of humor in politics.

An English teacher used Mark Twain's humorous quotations to teach the parts of speech.

> The varsity soccer team at a small high school had won only two games in a season of playing against bigger schools with more players. At the annual soccer banquet, the coach introduced his team to their parents as "the best team in the county. They had the best attitude, gave one hundred percent at practice both off and on the field, and they always had smiles on their faces no matter how tough things got. These boys were always ready to do their best and try again."

ATTITUDE

The varsity soccer team at a small high school had won only two games in a season of playing against bigger schools with more players. At the annual soccer banquet, the coach introduced his team to their parents as "the best team in the county. They had the best attitude, gave one hundred percent at practice both off and on the field, and they always had smiles on their faces no matter how tough things got. These boys were always ready to do their best and try again."

Few high school players become professional athletes, but each will have to learn to cope with frustration, disappointments, and failure, and their teacher or coach sets the example. Losing—whether it's a ball game, college choice, or potential job—isn't funny, but humor can reduce the pain. Laughter helps maintain balance and prevents loss of self-confidence while giving the impetus to try again.

The positive attitude this coach promotes on the field also permeates his algebra classes. His class becomes a cohesive team working toward achievement.

Professionals who teach children with learning or physical disabilities know first-hand how a poor attitude can compound the child's problems. These teachers recognize the value of humor as a teaching aid. If the children learn to laugh at their mistakes, humor will help them deal with their disabilities. Mike David, a special education teacher from Connecticut, reminds us that the main reason to use humor in teaching is to build self-confidence. "Humor is especially helpful for students with learning handicaps. It boosts self-esteem, and this is actually the most important subject we teach our students."

Gifted students need humor for a different reason. Humor not only challenges their creative ability, but provides equilibrium, keeping their vision of themselves and the world around them in focus.

At a P.T.A. Open House, after welcoming the visiting parents to her classroom, the teacher of advanced high school English began her presentation, "Working with your children this year has been an experience." She paused. The parents laughed. She got their attention and then added, "For me it has been an exceptionally good experience. And I hope, at the end of the year, your children will feel the same way. The ability to read literature is not enough. My goal is for your children to experience literature with heightened critical awareness."

STIMULATING LEARNING

Because humor stimulates your brain, you gain satisfaction in using cognitive skills to comprehend or create humor. Researchers have found that humor will not lower performance levels. It can aid the recall of material while it lessens anxiety and helps with comprehension.

Increasing numbers of researchers are examining humor as a learning stimulus and stress reliever. A study conducted with math students at Delaware Technical and Community College investigated the possible relationship between viewing humorous videos and reducing pre-test and post-test anxiety. Students who viewed the humorous video prior to the expected math exam had significantly lower post-test anxiety levels. Those who viewed non-humorous videos had slightly lower post-test anxiety levels. And the post-test anxiety levels for the control group, who saw no video, were the highest of all.

Other studies have found that in rote learning, humor related to the subject aids learning not only by imaginatively repeating the concept but also by making the learning process more enjoyable.

After being called to the telephone, a tenth-grade teacher returned to her classroom that was in the midst of a spitball free-for-all. Surprised by her early return, the children uneasily waited for her reaction. "I have not heard of this much chaos since the French Revolution," she said. For the benefit of the ringleaders she added, "Remember, some people lost their heads during that period."

INSPIRING AND ILLUSTRATING

At a P.T.A. Open House, after welcoming the visiting parents to her classroom, the teacher of advanced high school English began her presentation, "Working with your children this year has been an experience." She paused. The parents laughed. She got their attention and then added, "For me it has been an exceptionally good experience. And I hope, at the end of the year, your children will feel the same way. The ability to read literature is not enough. My goal is for your children to experience literature with heightened critical awareness."

Learning involves the ability to read, think, respond, and experiment, and humor sharpens these skills. This same teacher later gave her students the assignment to write satirical parodies of famous poems. Underestimating a child's capacity for humor is as unproductive as overestimating it.

SAFETY VALVE FOR TENSION AND AGGRESSIVE BEHAVIOR

After being called to the telephone, a tenth-grade teacher returned to her classroom that was in the midst of a spitball free-for-all. Surprised by her early return, the children uneasily waited for her reaction. "I have not heard of this much chaos since the French Revolution," she said. For the benefit of the ringleaders she added, "Remember, some people lost their heads during that period."

Another teacher might have scolded the class at length and sent the ringleaders to the principal, creating a tense class atmosphere. However, weighing the seriousness of the offense against her time constraints and the amount of material to be covered, this teacher used humor both to make her point to the students and to provide a safety valve for her own frustrations. After the laughter subsided, she emphasized the unacceptability of unruly behavior, and the students got back to work.

Another teacher observed two sixth-grade boys involved in a pushing match. She stopped them and asked what happened. The first boy said, "He poked me with his pencil."

She repeated to the second boy, "You poked him with your pencil."

The second boy said, "He poked me with his pencil."

Again she repeated it, adding, "What happened then?"

"He pushed me."

Calmly she repeated the process. The boys began to giggle. As soon as their laughter broke the tension, the teacher said, "I think starting World War II over a pencil poke isn't worth it. What do you think?" They laughed and agreed. She asked them to shake hands. Humor had subdued the rowdy boys, and she had dealt appropriately with the level of the offense.

Obvious behavior problems such as fighting, vandalism, or theft are more severe than two boys pushing each other over pencil pokes. Laughter can't solve many of the serious problems teachers face every day, but it can put the smaller problems in perspective. After all, one student caught stealing a cookie does not make a school filled with thieves.

Another teacher observed two sixth-grade boys involved in a pushing match. She stopped them and asked what happened. The first boy said, "He poked me with his pencil."

She repeated to the second boy, "You poked him with your pencil."

The second boy said, "He poked me with his pencil."

Again she repeated it, adding, "What happened then?"

"He pushed me."

Calmly she repeated the process. The boys began to giggle. As soon as their laughter broke the tension, the teacher said, "I think starting World War II over a pencil poke isn't worth it. What do you think?"

Humor is no substitute for other teaching techniques. Nor should it become an end-all in the classroom. But, tailored to the students—whether as a class or individual—relevant humor can greatly enhance the teaching and learning process.

HUMOR, THE BRIDGE TO LEARNING

Dedicated teachers all over the United States use humor to meet specific challenges in the classroom. Here are some of their examples that created positive, happy learning environments for their students. In other words, they work!

DISCIPLINE: SAVE-THE-SANITY-OF-THE-TEACHER TIME

To control traffic patterns in her classroom, Gloria Winger, an elementary school teacher in Pennsylvania, hangs a one-way sign behind her desk. It works far better than constant reminders, because no child wants to "break the law."

A first-grade teacher in San Diego, California, started "Giggle Recess." Once a week, for thirty minutes, students have one minute to make the class laugh—following her guidelines of good taste. They can tell a joke, ask a riddle, draw a cartoon, or share a funny story that happened during the week. During the other days of the week, when a child interrupts the lesson, she says, "Please save it for Giggle Recess," and keeps her class on track.

We suggest a take-a-number machine. It not only has a number, but also includes a joke or riddle for the child to enjoy while waiting. If you use index cards, you can reuse them and reinforce recycling habits.

In Tucson, Arizona, a small boy thought it was more fun to throw rocks at the garbage truck than to do math. When he returned to class, the students watched as the teacher, David Anderson, said, "There's only one way to settle this. We'll have to arm wrestle. If you win, you do your math. If I win, you can do what you like."

In Tucson, Arizona, a small boy thought it was more fun to throw rocks at the garbage truck than to do math. When he returned to class, the students watched as the teacher, David Anderson, said, "There's only one way to settle this. We'll have to arm wrestle. If you win, you do your math. If I win, you can do what you like."

At the word "Go,_ Anderson slammed his own hand backwards on the desk, pulling the student's hand on top of his. "OK," the teacher sighed resignedly. "You win. You have to do your math. Go back to your desk. But watch out. Next time I might win."

At the word "Go," Anderson slammed his own hand backwards on the desk, pulling the student's hand on top of his. "OK," the teacher sighed resignedly. "You win. You have to do your math. Go back to your desk. But watch out. Next time I might win." The silly ploy worked even though the student knew it was a silly ploy.

HUMOR AS A CREATIVE CURRICULUM AID: WHAT'S SO FUNNY ABOUT LEARNING NEW THINGS?

Stephanie Radke, from Orange, Texas, often turns the tables and allows children to see and learn through a humorous perspective. She also teaches them how to approach a problem through a different channel. For example, while studying mammals, she wanted the children to see what was so special about thumbs, so they took the animal's viewpoint. She instructed each student to tape their thumb and index fingers together, and then asked them to do simple tasks. The children laughed when they saw the humor of the situation, and they also discovered the uniqueness of thumbs.

Stephanie Radke, from Orange, Texas, often turns the tables and allows children to see and learn through a humorous perspective. She also teaches them how to approach a problem through a different channel. For example, while studying mammals, she wanted the children to see what was so special about thumbs, so they took the animal's viewpoint. She instructed each student to tape their thumb and index fingers together, and then asked them to do simple tasks. The children laughed when they saw the humor of the situation, and they also discovered the uniqueness of thumbs.

We suggested to a workshop of teachers that they assign their students to count how many times the word "peace" is used on the evening news, and which countries the commentators are talking about. Those who complete the assignment get a "peace" of cake at the end of the week.

No student in one classroom in Hyannis, Massachusetts, forgets the vocabulary word "prostrate," because their teacher pretends that one of his students is a king in the Middle Ages and throws himself at the student's feet to beg a piece of land for his family.

RELIEVING TEST STRESS: GROANING WON'T HELP

Many teachers include a few humorous questions on multiple choice or matching tests to break the tension. On a science test on mollusks, Gary Engler, in Gypsum, Ohio, included: The squid's natural enemy is: a) sperm whales b) snails c) sharks d) Muhammed Ali Slug.

In another high school, students enjoy the end-of-the-year "What was funny in Senior English?" essay.

One teacher asks students to caption cartoons using proper grammar while another asks them to make up a joke about the subject matter.

Another teacher puts a short note at the bottom of his test: "Sorry the projector quit again, but I'm glad you are still working. It's over. Smile!"

Dr. Gordon Emslie, an avid parachutist, fell out of the sky at the University of Alabama at Huntsville to deliver his final exam. "I wanted my students to relax before taking their final. Everyone always gets so uptight and tense. I thought this would be a good way for students to have some fun and loosen up." Humorous, but obviously not for everyone!

SKILLS: WHO SAID GENIUSES HAVE TO SUFFER?

To familiarize students with the many machines available at the library, high school teachers can devise a reference machine treasure hunt. The team that finds the answers first is served at the end-of-the-year class party by the team that loses.

Another teacher helps students learn to use reference materials by asking them to find answers to funny questions in *The World Almanac* and *The Guinness Book of World Records.* Question: When Sarah Cross ordered two hamburgers from a Wendy's Restaurant drive-in window in Augusta, Georgia, the bag did not contain hamburgers. What did it contain? Answer: A thousand dollars in cash. The manager had been preparing a bank deposit and put the cash into the bag. The window clerk picked it up by mistake. Sarah Cross returned the money for her two hamburgers *(The World Almanac).* Question: What is the greatest distance at which a grape, thrown from level ground, has been caught in a person's mouth? Answer: 327 feet, six inches, by Paul J. Tavilla of East Boston, Massachusetts, on May 27, 1991 *(The Guinness Book of World Records).*

When Sarah Cross ordered two hamburgers from a Wendy's Restaurant drive-in window in Augusta, Georgia, the bag did not contain hamburgers. What did it contain? Answer: A thousand dollars in cash.

What is the greatest distance at which a grape, thrown from level ground, has been caught in a person's mouth? Answer: 327 feet, six inches, by Paul J. Tavilla of East Boston, Massachusetts.

A teacher in Missouri creates an archaeological dig in a large sandbox, where students unearth and reconstruct a broken pot. When they decipher the funny message written on the pot, they have to make up a story about the pot's origin, age, and significant place in history.

NEATNESS: "MOM USED MY PAPER TO KILL A ROACH"

Students who hand in papers without messy mistakes, smudges, wrinkles, fingerprints, peanut butter, or dog drool get certificates of neatness.

David Hegner, in Newton, New Jersey, has a pair of Groucho glasses in his desk that he puts on when someone turns in a paper he can't read.

TARDINESS: SCHOOL STARTS WHEN?

In a workshop at Warner Robins, Georgia, teachers offered the following solutions that helped them prevent tardiness:

- Hold the class outside, and leave a note on the blackboard. "No school today. Gone to the beach. Hope you'll make it to our next outing."
- Give worm awards for early birds.
- Play the paper-pencil game of "Hangman" with the chronically tardy student. If he hangs the teacher, no homework for the child for that day. If the teacher hangs him, the class chooses his homework for that day.

In a workshop at Warner Robins, Georgia, teachers offered the following solution that helped them prevent tardiness:

Hold the class outside, and leave a note on the blackboard. "No school today. Gone to the beach. Hope you'll make it to our next outing."

MEMORY AID: INDELIBLE ETCHING WITH HUMOR

Rick Owens in Carnegie, Oklahoma, was discussing a unique biological characteristic of camels. They have two eyelids on each eye, one transparent so they can see in sandstorms. He told the class that if students had two eyelids, at least half of them would fall asleep during social studies. Among the answers on the multiple choice test he included, "The camel's extra eyelid is for the purpose of sleeping without anyone knowing it."
No one missed the question!

In teaching volume, Ronald Lee Rubin asks his students if the correct terminology for the unit of measurement is "hippopotamus toes, elephant trunks, or cubic grasshoppers?" The funny association with humor helps students remember facts.

Experienced teachers know that humor brings the people in a classroom closer together. The students come to realize that the teacher is not just a "creature with a red pen that bleeds on their compositions."

Ronald Lee Rubin, headmaster of The Equinox School, said it well: "Through it all, I believe with laughter we learn a bit more about everything, especially our own humanity. Humor builds esprit de corps, enabling learning to be a process that is fun, interesting, and highly valued."

Humor and Health: The Salt-Free, Low-Calorie, Polyunsaturated, All-Natural Guide to Feeling Good

The stroke victim, unable to talk, lay in his hospital bed while his nurse carried on a one-sided conversation. Knowing he too lived on a tobacco farm, she reminisced about her childhood. The patient, alert, responded with his eyes. Eventually she even told him about her secret trip behind the barn to learn to chew and spit tobacco like her father.

The patient burst out laughing, his first physical response since the stroke. When she returned the next day, he smiled and spoke his first word—"Tobacco."

Although in the past a few physicians have recognized the value of humor in health care—thirteenth-century surgeon Henri de Mondeville told jokes to his patients coming out of surgery because he felt laughter would aid their recovery—until recent years the therapeutic uses of humor have largely been overlooked by the mainstream of health professionals.

> The stroke victim, unable to talk, lay in his hospital bed while his nurse carried on a one-sided conversation. Knowing he too lived on a tobacco farm, she reminisced about her childhood. The patient, alert, responded with his eyes. Eventually she even told him about her secret trip behind the barn to learn to chew and spit tobacco like her father.
>
> The patient burst out laughing, his first physical response since the stroke. When she returned the next day, he smiled and spoke his first word—"Tobacco."

Norman Cousins, former editor of *Saturday Review,* changed this with the publication of *Anatomy of an Illness,* recounting his battle with ankylosing spondylitis, a progressive disease of the joints of the spine.

Refusing to accept the specialist's pessimistic prognosis of permanent disability, Cousins devised his own therapy in partnership with his doctor, experimenting with large doses of vitamin C combined with regularly scheduled doses of laughter. He discovered that ten minutes of genuine belly laughs had an anesthetic effect that gave him at least two hours of pain-free sleep. It also lowered his rate of sedimentation, a blood test measurement that increases with infection.

Cousins recovered and eventually became an adjunct professor at U.C.L.A. School of Medicine, bringing medical students an awareness of the potential of positive emotions. Cousins always emphasized that humor is not a cure-all, and you should not substitute it for competent medical treatment. Rather, a patient's own inner resources enhance the effectiveness of medical treatment.

"Laughter has therapeutic value," said Cousins, "because it serves as a bulletproof vest that protects you against the ravages of negative emotions. Laughter interrupts the 'panic cycle' of an illness. In blocking panic, it prevents constriction of blood vessels and negative biochemical changes." Thousands of physicians wrote him with their own experiences corroborating the importance of positive emotions in healing. In 1988 Lee S. Berk, D.H.Sc., of Loma Linda (CA) University School of Medicine, and his associates reported at the annual meeting of the Endocrine Society that laughter may act as an antagonist to the classic stress response by reducing plasma levels of certain neuroendocrine components.

We still have much to learn about the physical components of humor, but even after Cousins's death in 1990 (of a heart attack) scientific studies continue to reinforce his theories of the linkage between humor and health. William F. Fry, Jr., M.D., a psychiatrist formerly at Stanford University, has for thirty years studied the positive physiological effects of laughter.

Fry concludes that laughter is good exercise, similar to stationary jogging. Your blood pressure rises, your pulse may double from sixty to

120 beats a minute, extra adrenaline enters your bloodstream, and the muscles in your chest, abdomen, and shoulders contract.

Subsequently these measurements return to normal or below normal, indicating a decrease in stress. The reduction of muscle tension may also explain laughter's role in relieving some kinds of headaches. Dr. Fry's continuing study on laughter and the stimulation of endorphins—hormones that create a feeling of well-being—may reveal how laughter alters the brain's perception of pain.

Try this exercise the next time you experience a tension headache: Lie down and listen to one side of a funny comedy album by someone like Steven Wright, Lily Tomlin, or Billy Crystal. Then evaluate your headache again to see if laughing has made an appreciable difference.

Even the act of smiling can alter muscle tension. An advertising executive called us from New York to relate that when he has trouble falling asleep, he intentionally lies in bed with a smile on his face. Just the physical act of smiling helps him relax enough to fall asleep. (Of course, it may also incite wifely questions about what prompted the smile, but that's another book.)

The act of smiling can alter muscle tension. An advertising executive called us from New York to relate that when he has trouble falling asleep, he intentionally lies in bed with a smile on his face. Just the physical act of smiling helps him relax enough to fall asleep. (Of course, it may also incite wifely questions about what prompted the smile, but that's another book.)

HUMOR AND THE CARE OF THE ELDERLY: SMILE AT YOURSELF IN THE MIRROR AT LEAST ONCE A DAY. WHO DESERVES IT BETTER THAN YOU?

What is your conception of a typical nursing home? Do the residents sit in the lobby staring vacantly, buried in memories of the past with no hope for the present? Or is it a place energized by opportunities for creativity, expression, and purpose?

Dr. Fry's humor project in a convalescent home also has implications for future treatment programs for the elderly. In this three-month study, the experimental group met fifteen minutes daily, five times a week. Each session was led by a different patient responsible for selecting material for the day's humor session—tapes of old Jack Benny radio shows, for example. Each day the leader also led each participant in a round of joke-telling.

By the end of the study, Dr. Fry observed much more mirth, more interaction, less complaining, more sociability, more alertness, and a greater degree of interest in personal appearance. "The group effect of humor is important. Humor enhances the healing process particularly for the aged, who face the possibility of deterioration, regression, withdrawal. Humor has a counteractive effect on these negative processes."

The Ethel Percy Andrus Gerontology Center at the University of Southern California has experimented with a humor program for its residents and published a handbook on using humor in long-term care, *Humor: The Tonic You Can Afford.* Among the activities are sing-alongs of familiar songs, showings of old movies, play-readings by residents, puppet shows, and parties of all kinds (April Fools' Day, Thanksgiving, National Smile Week).

> "The group effect of humor is important. Humor enhances the healing process particularly for the aged, who face the possibility of deterioration, regression, withdrawal. Humor has a counteractive effect on these negative processes."
>
> William F. Fry, Jr., M.D.,

And whether you're a physician, nurse, aide, or concerned family member, your awareness of humor's value and your support of humor programs for the elderly can improve the quality of life not only for the cared-for, but also for you, the care-giver.

Humor has value even in dealing with Alzheimer's patients for as long as they have periods of lucidity. In several years' teaching an adult education course on writing a cookbook for fun or profit ("The Celery Stalks at Midnight"), we have encouraged participants who care for a relative with Alzheimer's to compile a family cookbook or memoirs.

Little by little, during the patient's lucid moments, you can gently ask questions prompting memories of special occasions, holidays, recipes, and family history. Tape record or write down the responses, and collect them in file folders. This exercise has several benefits:

1. The patient feels useful, with her memories of long-ago times valued as a family treasure, and, she doesn't get upset that the past is the only part of her life she remembers well.

2. It provides the patient with a positive topic of discussion, and shared laughter can relieve stress temporarily for the care-giver.

3. It provides other family members and visitors with a positive topic of discussion: "Which recipe of Mom's do you remember most? Remember that Thanksgiving when . . ." These stories can also enhance your collection.

4. It provides the care-giver, whose energies can be consumed by unrelenting demands on his time, with a chance to focus on something upbeat and fun.
5. Ultimately the patient (and you) will have something *concrete* to show for your efforts which she can proudly show to visitors or, in a nursing home setting, to other patients.

When we say "cookbook," we mean a photo album with the recipes, related anecdotes and pictures grouped together; typed pages reproduced at a copy shop; or something as simple as a handmade calendar (with pages made by children in the family) with twelve favorite recipes and memories taped on, one for each month. What counts is not the elaborateness of the finished product, but the process of doing it together.

An ever-growing book of recipes and funny memories could also be an effective framework for a group project at a nursing home, convalescent center, or hospital for patients requiring long-term stays. For people who never cooked (or never liked to cook) questions concerning hobbies or funny home remedies can also elicit colorful recollections.

An ever-growing book of recipes and funny memories could also be an effective framework for a group project at a nursing home, convalescent center, or hospital for patients requiring long-term stays.

HUMOR IN HOSPITALS

SUPPORT STAFF

Typically, the intake staff who handle the paperwork are the first people who meet patients entering the hospital. As representatives of the hospital, they set the tone for the patients' first impression, good or bad, of the health care they are about to receive. The hospital's employee training program should remind the staff that even small gestures of reassurance and good humor can relieve some anxiety and put the incoming patient in a better frame of mind. This is certainly not the time for insensitive jokes about being sick, or jokes about doctors operating on the wrong person. If you are on the intake staff, look up from your work a moment for eye contact, a smile, and a lighthearted comment about the joys of paperwork, and put the patients a little more at ease as they face the uncertainty of their stay.

Even better, print up some "coupons" entitling the bearer to a chocolate good-bye "kiss" or a sugarless candy when they leave. Considering the power of suggestion in many people, this token can help them focus on the ultimate goal of their stay—getting well and going home—and reinforce their expectation of recovery.

HOSPITAL HUMOR ROOMS

Health professionals are beginning to recognize that humor can reduce patient anxiety, open up communication, give support, and serve as a safety valve for patient frustration and anger. Many hospitals, in fact, have formally introduced humor into the healing process by establishing humor therapy rooms, which provide humorous books, records, movies, games, song fests, and entertainment for patients and families. The prototype is the Living Room at the William Stehlin Foundation for Cancer Research at St. Joseph's Hospital in Houston, Texas.

Two elderly women visiting their mother began laughing with delight over items in the 1927 Sears Catalog—items they had wanted or owned as children. Wiping a tear from her eye, one lady said, "That's the first time I've laughed in so long. It feels good."

Several nights a week musicians stop by the Living Room, and sometimes such celebrities as David Hartman and Marvin Hamlisch come in to entertain or just to chat. The room also serves as a place for group therapy for patients and families, new patient orientation, and staff meetings.

The staff sees positive results—treatment rate is better, recovery is quicker. Humor provides perspective and, according to staff, can inaugurate a recuperative atmosphere once the patient has gone through the anger, recognition, and acceptance stages of illness.

The Lively Room at DeKalb General Hospital in Atlanta, Georgia, serves cancer patients. Although it is mainly geared to patients, seventy-five percent of its twenty users each day are family members who are frightened and drained. Renewed by humor, the family can then take those positive feelings back to the patient.

Two elderly women visiting their mother began laughing with delight over items in the 1927 Sears Catalog—items they had wanted or owned as children. Wiping a tear from her eye, one lady said, "That's the first time I've laughed in so long. It feels good."

The staff nurses think the atmosphere and available activities improve a patient's outlook as well as provide informal support for patients to get strength from each other. Although there's no scientific documentation, the head nurse found that some patients, after laughing and enjoying themselves in the Lively Room, could decrease to some degree their pain and nausea medications.

The room has also been the site of celebrations—a champagne party for a couple's tenth anniversary, a daughter's wedding where a terminally ill father had a day of joy.

Other hospitals—in cities across the country from Mesa, Arizona, to Schenectady, New York, and Clearwater, Florida—are opening similar rooms where patients and their families can find healing through laughter. Humor as therapy is only an adjunct to other forms of medical treatment, but in periods of crisis a laugh can sometimes be as effective as a pill.

HUMOR TRAINING FOR HEALTH CARE PROFESSIONALS

Even health professionals may need guidance to use humor appropriately. The "gallows humor" used between doctors gives them a much needed, stress-reducing laugh ("That's the third gall bladder I've removed today. At least I *think* it was a gall bladder . . .") but it will surely offend or frighten a patient. Many health professionals have found training in the use of humor through seminars sponsored by hospitals, all-day workshops, and adult education courses at nearby universities.

Even health professionals may need guidance to use humor appropriately. The "gallows humor" used between doctors gives them a much needed, stress-reducing laugh ("That's the third gall bladder I've removed today. At least I *think* it was a gall bladder . . .") but it will surely offend or frighten a patient. Many health professionals have found training in the use of humor through seminars sponsored by hospitals, all-day workshops, and adult education courses at nearby universities.

Dr. Joel Goodman, an educator and the director of the Humor Project at Sagamore Institute in Saratoga Springs, New York, first realized the importance of humor while taking his father to Houston for emergency surgery, which led to the discovery of an aortic aneurysm. Shuttling back and forth between hotel and hospital, he found that the van driver had won the Bellman of the Year Award.

"It soon became obvious why," observed Goodman. "He had a wonderfully contagious sense of humor that had us in stitches. I marveled at his ability to take families, rigid with fear, and have them melt in just the short five-minute ride to the hospital." Goodman realized that as a result of the driver's good humor, he and his mother could give his father support rather than dragging him down with their own fear and tension.

Patients and their families may be tense, but the doctors and nurses who carry the responsibility of their patients' well-being are also vulnerable to stress. In a short seminar in humor, health care professionals can find specific techniques for using humor to reduce their own stress and deal more effectively with office staff and patients.

They can also find creative and adaptable ideas in a problem-solving group with colleagues.

At one of our convention workshops, a group of dentists were discussing ways to make waiting in reception rooms more pleasant and less stressful for patients. Here are some of their brainstorming suggestions:

- Display a chalkboard with a topic, several ideas to get patients started, and chalk for patients to add to the list. Erase for the next day.

  EXAMPLE: "Other Uses of Dental Floss": a fishing line, a pull for a lawn mower, tie around finger to remember to floss., etc.

- Start a scrapbook of relevant cartoons, with an invitation for patients to bring more.
- Use a hand puppet for hygienist to teach children proper brushing.
- Provide books of short humor (anecdotes, vignettes) that can be checked out from the receptionist.

And because anxious patients and their families often forget or confuse spoken instructions, several physicians at another meeting suggested creating and photocopying whimsically illustrated instructions on subjects they often discuss: doses of medicine, instructions for new mothers, or aftercare for dental procedures. This will not require artistic talent—photocopy shops and bookstores sell books of drawings that are in the public domain.

NURSES (AND THE AIDES AND VOLUNTEERS WHO MAKE THEIR WORK EASIER) AND HUMOR

If you are a health professional, you might also turn to Dr. Vera Robinson, author of *Humor and the Health Professions,* for knowledgeable advice. Former chairwoman of the Nursing Department at California State University in Fullerton, Dr. Robinson began studying humor twenty-five years ago.

As a nurse, Dr. Robinson sees humor as a tool for reducing patient stress. "Almost everything in the hospital builds intense fear and anxiety. The patients are prodded and poked all over the place, and they are being told every other minute to take off their clothes for some procedure. But it is amazing how a little bit of humor can get rid of a lot of tension.

When you help patients laugh, they let go of anger, frustration, anxiety, and hostility."

An attractive woman broke her neck in a freak accident and was facing months of rehabilitation and medical treatment. One day a nurse handed her a line drawing of a beautiful woman. "If you don't behave and do everything you're supposed to, you'll end up looking like this." As he turned the drawing upside down, it magically became the drawing of an old hag.

An attractive woman broke her neck in a freak accident and was facing months of rehabilitation and medical treatment. One day a nurse handed her a line drawing of a beautiful woman. "If you don't behave and do everything you're supposed to, you'll end up looking like this." As he turned the drawing upside down, it magically became the drawing of an old hag. The woman laughed, felt better, and the visual image strengthened her resolve.

The humor should never poke fun at the patient or express frustration or anger. Using humor requires respect, compassion, and concern for the patient, and it requires consideration for the variables of age, education, culture, and level of physical pain.

Because the skill of conveying information through humor does not necessarily come naturally, Dr. Robinson offers nurses a continuing education course devoted exclusively to humor and health care. The nursing department at Fullerton is also one of the few in the country to incorporate discussions of humor in undergraduate courses.

Dr. Robinson predicts that five years from now, "humor will become an acceptable part of communication skills, recognized for its therapeutic use rather than just something spontaneous and incidental. Humor is one of the most important coping mechanisms humans have, a biological phenomenon. Laughter is there just as well as tears."

If you're a nurse, you may want to join others who want to increase their awareness of humor's role in healing by subscribing to the *Journal of Nursing Jocularity*. Editor and publisher Douglas Fletcher says, "In the highly stressful field of nursing, we see an overwhelming amount of burnout and stress-related disease. We hope to relieve some of that stress by allowing nurses to laugh at themselves." Fletcher, a registered nurse at Mesa Lutheran Hospital in Mesa, Arizona, wants to make nurses aware of available resources for therapeutic humor, not only for their patients but for the entire hospital staff. Wisely used, it can reduce stress on both sides of the scalpel.

At Christmas someone at Sunnyview Rehabilitation Center in Schenectady, New York, pulled out a reindeer decoration and discovered it had a broken leg. He then sent it to a staff physician who started a chart,

At Christmas someone at Sunnyview Rehabilitation Center in Schenectady, New York, pulled out a reindeer decoration and discovered it had a broken leg. He then sent it to a staff physician who started a chart, wrote a prescription, and sent it to therapy. After making the rounds, the reindeer finally returned, all patched up, with a diagnosis—"slightly impaired to pull sleighs."

wrote a prescription, and sent it to therapy. After making the rounds, the reindeer finally returned, all patched up, with a diagnosis—"slightly impaired to pull sleighs."

And if you're a volunteer working directly with patients, you're in a unique position to bring a moment of light-hearted relief as you deliver flowers or wheel patients to X-ray. One volunteer keeps a bedpan full of jokes and witty quotes (each typed on a separate slip of paper) on her book cart as she makes her patient rounds, and she always gets a smile when she asks, "Need the bedpan today?"

HOW TO GET STARTED

If you are interested in initiating a humor program in your community, either as a professional or as a volunteer, here are several suggestions.

1. For expert advice concerning humor in nursing homes, write the Ethel Percy Andrus Gerontology Center, University of Southern California, University Park, MC-0191, Los Angeles, California 90089-0191, for their handbook outlining their innovative humor experiment using funny materials in caring for the elderly.
2. For workshops, seminars, and guidelines from humor rooms, see Chapter 14.
3. If you are a hospital volunteer, nursing instructor Debbie Lieber suggests:

   a) Begin informally to tell humorous stories to patients as you do your volunteer activity, keeping in mind the receptivity of the patient.

   b) Continue until the patients start anticipating your return and you get positive feedback.

   c) While going over a patient's medical history, take a "funny bone history," as one Tulsa, Oklahoma, nurse does, to find out what brand of humor each patient is most likely to appreciate.

   d) Do your homework and prepare a detailed proposal for the program you envision, covering factors such as structure, participants, implementation, and cost. (For specific guidelines, learn about existing humor rooms in Chapter 14.) Then take your proposal to the administration.

e) Collect humorous cartoons, quotes, or funny headlines, and share them with patients.

f) Subscribe to *The Journal of Nursing Jocularity* for the hospital nursing staff on a particular unit of the hospital.

4. If none of these ideas is feasible, here's one last suggestion that you can pursue on your own: inaugurate informal humor programs, bringing your own talent as a clown, musician, or storyteller to hospitals as an entertainer.

A LOT OF LAUGHTER AND A LITTLE CHICKEN SOUP (WHEN *YOU'RE* THE PATIENT)

Lying on the operating table immediately before her hysterectomy, the groggy woman looked around at the equipment, the nurses, and her anesthesiologist, and exclaimed, "I can tell by the way you all are dressed that this is going to be no fun at all!"

As Norman Cousins did, you too can take an active role in the healing process by bringing humor into a hospital stay and recuperation—for you, your friends, or family. Saul Sutel, a New York insurance executive, mapped out a strategic and detailed humor plan for his scheduled aortic valve replacement.

First, he wrote a letter to his new surgeon and sent a copy to his cardiologist. It read,

As the time approaches for this momentous occasion, I promise to cooperate, and I will maintain a level head. I want to ask you to:

1. *Be calm.*
2. *Do your best.*
3. *Talk to me during the operation.*
4. *I don't want any negative talk around the operating room, even when I'm under sedation.* [This tactic is corroborated by a study at London's St. Thomas's Hospital which showed that patients under anesthesia may be affected by what they hear, even though they do not consciously recall it. The researchers played soothing suggestions—"You will not feel sick. You will not have

any pain."— to one group of randomly assigned patients during surgery. These patients left the hospital earlier and had significantly fewer complications.]

5. *If problems develop during the surgery, use highfalutin terms I won't understand.*
6. *Keep a light attitude.*
7. *Keep me abreast of what you are doing (it might be your twentieth surgery of the month, but to me it's life and death).*

Then, on the day of his catheterization, Sutel placed a sticker of a large, red kiss on his right hip. As the nurse removed his gown, the technicians noticed the kiss. He told them the floor nurses gave him that kiss for good luck, and he hoped they'd do the same. They all laughed, and it broke the tension. The anticipation of the effect of the joke defused his anxiety and took his mind off unpleasant thoughts. The technicians noticed the calming effect humor had on the patient. From time to time during the two-hour procedure they referred to "the kiss," relaxing him and breaking up the constant tension.

And on the morning of his surgery, Sutel taped a paper sporting red dashes and the words "Cut here" to his chest. As he went into the operating room, he was thinking about his sign. He felt a release of tension when his doctor chuckled and said, "This is the guy who was kissed on the hip by the nurses." The last thing he remembered before blacking out was laughter. Humor had kept his thoughts positive. "I know what you're going to do. Let's get it over with, I'm going to be OK."

On the morning of his surgery, Sutel taped a paper sporting red dashes and the words "Cut here" to his chest. As he went into the operating room, he was thinking about his sign. He felt a release of tension when his doctor chuckled and said, "This is the guy who was kissed on the hip by the nurses."

To keep his surgery in proper perspective, he listed his life goals on a poster tacked up in his room, announcing to himself and everyone else that he had every intention of recovering completely. Helping the patient look ahead to the future fosters his expectation for recovery and shores up his determination to get past the pain of the moment.

This executive's experience underlines the theory that the healing process requires not only the expertise of medical science but also the patient's inner resources of optimism, faith, humor and purpose. Under the right conditions, humor can indeed help relieve anxiety, provide emotional strength, and instill hope.

If you or someone you know anticipates a hospital stay (or a long recuperation at home), here are some ideas for filling a Humor First Aid Kit. Use your imagination and design one to suit your needs and sense of humor.

Basic Contents for Your Own Humor First Aid Kit

1. A sign to hold, to hang around your neck, or to tape to the front of a wheelchair. Aides frequently move patients from test to test in a wheelchair, so carry a sign or ready-made bumper sticker to provoke smiles along the way. Example: "I Break for Orthopedists."
2. A sign for the door: "No One Admitted Without a Joke." Then ask for them.
3. Joke books, old copies of *Reader's Digest,* and other collections of short humor you can read in small doses.
4. Humorous fiction. You may need to consult your librarian, because fiction is not subdivided according to humor.
5. A tape recorder with tapes of your favorite comics and old radio comedy shows.
6. Phone calls. If you feel up to it, ask one or two friends to call each day just long enough to tell you a different joke or amusing story. And when a visitor threatens to tell you his own hospital tale of woe, interrupt with, "Now tell me some good news."
7. Name tags to make hospital room equipment "user-friendly." For instance, for your I-V, "My Roommate Slim."
8. Humorous comments or drawings instead of signatures for your cast.
9. A funny family picture, a photo of your pet, or anything else that makes you smile.
10. A child's "Big Bird" bandage to make a neck brace less intimidating.

Collections of short humor you can read in small doses.

A tape recorder with tapes of your favorite comics and old radio comedy shows.

A child's "Big Bird" bandage to make a neck brace less intimidating.

Additional Contents for Humor Kit for a Friend

1. A homemade audio tape for a sick friend, recording good wishes and favorite jokes and anecdotes from family, friends, and co-workers.

2. A whimsical hat for the patient to wear on a morning when she's feeling pretty good. It might give the staff a smile, too.

3. A seasonal holiday decoration for the room—a large paper four-leaf clover, a small flag, or a trick-or-treat plastic pumpkin.

4. Visual jokes: a bottle of concentrated effort; tongue "anti-depressors"; Mother's advice for speedy recovery; a toy syringe for needling the doctor.

5. A cookie tin labeled "David's Feel Good Box," containing twenty-five to thirty pieces of brightly colored paper, each stating a reason—some funny, some serious—why he's a terrific friend (or uncle, husband, or boss). Example: "I love you because, although you always take my last piece of gum, you never stick it under my dining room table."

   This is a gift the patient can read over and over. It lends moral support even when you aren't there and bolsters his sense of worth at a time when he is most vulnerable to feeling dependent or non-productive.

HUMOR AND DISABILITY

It's "hat day" at the Shepherd Spinal Center in Atlanta, Georgia. Staffers and patients alike show off their favorite hats, from the pretty black straw hat with a veil to a zany alligator-shaped cap with funny slogan buttons plastered all over the tail. All day long they share stories about their hat's history or trade laughs as they pass each other in the hall.

It's "hat day" at the Shepherd Spinal Center in Atlanta, Georgia. Staffers and patients alike show off their favorite hats, from the pretty black straw hat with a veil to a zany alligator-shaped cap with funny slogan buttons plastered all over the tail. All day long they share stories about their hat's history or trade laughs as they pass each other in the hall.

Says Mark Johnson, Advocacy and Community Affairs Coordinator at the Center and a wheelchair user for twenty-one years, "Besides having fun for the patients, we also need to keep the staff loose. They are constantly bombarded with young men eighteen to thirty-three who come in with severe injuries, and humor helps the staff keep their perspective too."

Humor can be a practical, constructive aid for the disabled. They can tell us the best ways to use humor in the beginning stages of hospital care, during the recuperative stage (characterized by rehabilitation to the extent possible) and in everyday interactions as the disabled begin to rebuild their lives. It is essential for the public to recognize that being disabled is not a disease. Humor is an excellent way for the disabled to dispel misconceptions and ease social acceptance.

HUMOR IN THE HOSPITAL

When Mark Johnson was bedridden in the hospital the first thing his family did was to decorate his room. "I couldn't even look out a window," says Johnson, "so they taped a poster of a window on the ceiling over my bed." They added a butterfly mobile and other things to change the view. His dad revved up the collection of quotes he used in sales and taped a quote of the week on the wall. Johnson used humor to "keep my sanity and increase the likelihood of keeping perspective."

When Mark Johnson was bedridden in the hospital the first thing his family did was to decorate his room. "I couldn't even look out a window," says Johnson, "so they taped a poster of a window on the ceiling over my bed." They added a butterfly mobile and other things to change the view. His dad revved up the collection of quotes he used in sales and taped a quote of the week on the wall. Johnson used humor to "keep my sanity and increase the likelihood of keeping perspective."

June Ray broke her neck in a freak accident and had to go back into a hospital because of complications. Her friends, knowing that her attention span would be short and concentration difficult, read her brief portions from collections of very short humor like *Dear Wit: Letters from the World's Wit*. We were flattered when Ms. Ray gave one of our books this compliment: "Even now that I'm walking, I have to rest every afternoon, so I'll keep a copy of *Oh, Lord, I Sound Just Like Mama* next to my bed and read a few pages. It always lifts my spirits."

HUMOR IN RECUPERATION

Humor can help shape attitudes and teach social skills to the recently disabled. The Shepherd Spinal Center recognizes the value of humor by:

1. Including humor as a topic for peer support groups.
2. Sponsoring a theater group which puts on plays and shows. Johnson observes, "We're prepared to laugh at ourselves. Yes, it's sometimes sick, but it's funny. Caretakers want to protect you, but paternalism isn't healthy, the kind that says, 'Don't rock the boat, someone else knows best.'"

3. Encouraging goofy celebrations in the hospital, including costumes at Halloween, where patients, their families, and staff can all relax and have some good, old-fashioned fun together.

4. Showing a video of different scenarios that demonstrate social skills. Each scenario presents two responses: first an inappropriate one which comes from the patient's anger and frustration, and then a positive one. The negative response is always funny, exaggerating what not to do. In the scene of a woman transferring herself from her wheelchair into her car, someone approaches and demands, "Oh, let me help you," and tugs vigorously on her chair as she's trying valiantly to hold onto it.

Quadriplegic John Callahan's cartoons are another relevant source of humor. Although his sometimes bizarre drawings exploring the disabled world may offend some people: a man with no arms walks into a bar, and the bartender says, "Sorry, I can't serve you. You can't hold your liquor."

Quadriplegic John Callahan's cartoons are another relevant source of humor (his collections include *Do Not Disturb Any Further* and *Digesting the Child Within*). Although his sometimes bizarre drawings exploring the disabled world may offend some people—a man with no arms walks into a bar, and the bartender says, "Sorry, I can't serve you. You can't hold your liquor"—Johnson thinks most disabled people can appreciate Callahan's humor because they do not perceive it as vicious, malicious, or reinforcing stereotypes. "We are all part of the melting pot." And *Accent on Living Magazine* collects related cartoons by other artists in a book called *Living with Accent* (Chapter 14).

HUMOR FOR THE LONG FUN

For people with long-term but temporary injuries, the disability ends with physical and mental recovery. For others, disabilities are permanent. It takes time to accept the realities, cope with problems, and move on. And our society still doesn't expect much from disabled people. So it's up to the disabled person to motivate himself to accomplish and develop a sense of perspective that can lead to a healthy "let's get on with it" attitude.

Perhaps the biggest single problem, day in and day out, is that other people often respond to disability with pity or avoidance rather than with understanding, acceptance, and a desire to include. Changing negative into positive reactions depends on 1) the attitude of the disabled in reacting to other people—strangers as well as friends, and 2) making equipment—wheelchairs, walkers, canes, braces—function as a catalyst for understanding rather than as a hindrance.

Mark Johnson says, "It has taken years to realize that I, or my disability, is not the problem. People's attitudes are. But I am willing to be part of the solution. That perspective needs to be developed. I found myself needing to loosen up other folks. I try to convey, 'OK, I'm disabled, let's get on with it.'"

Equipment for the disabled has become more high-tech and user-friendly. Neon colors, for instance, or the space-age look of seat cushions, open avenues for positive comments from strangers and break down communication barriers.

Here are some suggestions and conversation pieces others have used to brighten their apparatus:

1. Political slogans or bumper stickers taped to wheelchair backs. "If I can't do it, it isn't worth doing."
2. Horns on the chair.
3. Reflector lights.
4. Slogan buttons stuck to wheelchair backpacks, common accessories.
5. Tourist tags of places you've been.
6. Small clip-on koala bears—especially on a child's brace or crutches—in places that won't get bumped.
7. A college pennant or favorite sports team insignia.
8. An item related to a hobby, such as a hand-tied fly for trout fishing.

These touches draw comments from a "great idea" from a stranger walking by, to an inquisitive "Does your koala have a name?" from a young child. They make comfortable connections with other people and end the isolation that many disabled people feel.

As Mark Johnson says, "Disability is not a health issue. Yes, there are medical things that people need, but in most cases they are getting on with their lives and need other people to take the same attitude."

If humor can help change attitudes, then it can help dispel the most prevalent disabilities of all: ignorance, fear, and prejudice toward a valuable segment of our society.

PART

Parenting

Parenting, Your Other Job: Bringing FUNdamentals Back Into the Family

STARTING EARLY: FUN, LIKE CHARITY, BEGINS AT HOME

On "CBS This Morning," when Harry Smith asked actress Sigourney Weaver, "What is the best thing about being a mother?" she immediately replied, "The laughter—my little girl's sense of humor—seeing that glint in her eyes."

Sometimes being a child is a nasty job, but somebody's got to do it. Too often, caught up in the complexities of an adult world, we grown-ups forget that growing up is hard to do.

The pressures on today's families are enormous. Two-career families are becoming the norm, as parents struggle to make ends meet. And many single mothers and fathers are also struggling valiantly to find balance between their work—which puts food on the table and provides shelter, financial security, and personal growth—and their other job: raising precious children in the best way possible.

On "CBS This Morning," when Harry Smith asked actress Sigourney Weaver, "What is the best thing about being a mother?" she immediately replied, "The laughter—my little girl's sense of humor—seeing that glint in her eyes."

It isn't easy, but many parents are not only working outside the home but also doing a good job raising their children. And they're having fun doing it. These are the parents who realize that they aren't perfect; that in order to survive, they must keep their equilibrium; and that humor is a finely tuned instrument to help them and their children meet life's challenges head on.

THEY'RE STILL KIDS: DON'T EXPECT MIRACLES!

While experiencing dramatic physical changes, a child is expected at the same time to develop rational, cognitive, and social skills in a complicated world that is often confusing, sometimes frightening, and frequently made too vivid by simply turning on a television set in the family living room.

A young child is a tireless bundle of energy constantly on the move—both physically and mentally. In the center of all this activity is the parent, trying to give the youngster some direction and control in the growing and learning process.

Whether your children are toddlers or teenagers, your constructive use of humor can act as a buffer between them and the complicated transition into an adult world. If you use humor with your children, they in turn will learn to adopt it as a valuable coping tool in dealing with people in an increasingly complex world.

UNDERSTANDING FORMS A BASIS FOR HUMOR

Parents are sometimes shocked, surprised, and even angered at what their children consider uproariously funny. Consequently it is helpful to understand two things before you can start using humor with your child effectively: 1) how your child uses humor is linked to the various stages of growth and personality development, and 2) your child's motives for using humor are much the same as yours—to elicit approval, to attract attention, to express aggressive feelings, to figure out his place in the scheme of things, or just purely for the fun of it.

While "feeling his oats" and anxious to be part of the grown-up world around him, a child is confronted with the persistent pressures of adult opinions and ideas. He is surrounded by "no-nos." And although he may find aggressive behavior fun, he soon hears, "no hitting, no kicking, and no spitting."

Human body functions seem quite marvelous. But your child soon learns that bathroom words, just like name calling, are not socially acceptable at the dinner table no matter how hilarious they may seem. Calling mashed potatoes "doo-doo," or calling cousin Izzy "cousin Icky" may not be as funny to others as it seems to your four-year-old.

Your child's fears and anxieties are also compounded by the added problem of shortness. It's hard to assume power and compete when you are eye level with everyone else's knees. Perhaps now is a good time to remember what it is like to be very small and scrunched up in the back of a crowded elevator or walking down a busy street holding on to your mother's skirt.

Humor helps. It can dissipate some of your child's apprehension and, by providing a common ground for child and parent, it can ease the growing-up process for everyone.

WHAT YOUR CHILD FINDS FUNNY AND WHY

You probably will not find your young child's jokes very funny, because technically they are too simple (you're unlikely to hear this joke on your next coffee break: "Why does the fireman wear red suspenders?" "To hold his pants up"). And, unless you have lived a very sheltered life, you have probably heard them all before.

A parent's scope of humor, covering all the stages of development, is much broader than the child's, whose humor does not extend beyond the present level of maturity. Occasionally you may laugh at a "younger" style of joke, but children cannot appreciate humor they don't yet comprehend. With a little patience you can gently guide your child through the different stages in his humor development, just as you do with other learning experiences.

One of our students told us of a neighbor's child who was frightened by a gentle but huge furry dog. The woman suggested the child view the dog as a friendly "Beast" (the ultimately lovable character from the movie *Beauty and the Beast*). The little girl, delighted with the humorous concept, lost her fear of the dog.

WHAT TO DO

Be sensitive to your child's concerns. Just because she is only three-feet tall doesn't mean her problems aren't ten-feet tall to her. After acknowledging the problem, use humor to put it in perspective. One of our students told us of a neighbor's child who was frightened by a gentle but huge furry dog. The woman suggested the child view the dog as a friendly

"Beast" (the ultimately lovable character from the movie *Beauty and the Beast*). The little girl, delighted with the humorous concept, lost her fear of the dog.

- *Laugh with your child—not at him—and temper your teasing with understanding.* A child can feel stupid if he doesn't understand a riddle or get the point of a funny story.

- *Be aware that children don't always understand what you say.* Imagine what a simple statement like, "I gave him his walking papers," might conjure up in a child's mind. Children sometimes laugh at seemingly inappropriate times, because they misunderstand or because they want to appear in-the-know.

- *Don't use humor when your child is visibly upset,* or you may leave your child confused, embarrassed, and unwilling to express herself. Ridicule can stifle a child's ability to gain humorous perspective on the situation.

  If a child falls down, she might appear with tears streaming down her face and a knee poking through the hole in her new jeans. If her father says, "Oh, stop crying like a baby," he will magnify the already hurt feelings. But if Dad says, "Let's paint a funny face on your knee," even a tentative smile paves the way for offering constructive solutions such as adding a patch to the jeans or cutting them off for shorts.

"What funny faces do you see in the clouds?" "Imagine what those dogs are saying to each other." "What is that lizard on the wall thinking?" "What stories can you make up about the strangers riding on this bus? What secret missions do you think they're on?"

- *Encourage constructive humorous expression.* As children discover the wonder and beauty in nature and in everyday life, you can expand their imagination and awareness of humor by pointing out the humor around them and asking questions: "What funny faces do you see in the clouds?" "Imagine what those dogs are saying to each other." "What is that lizard on the wall thinking?" "What stories can you make up about the strangers riding on this bus? What secret missions do you think they're on?"

- *Listen to the underlying message in your child's humor to understand what he is thinking or feeling.* For instance, one mother said "no" to her child's request for a puppy. So the child made up a funny story of a family who owned one hundred puppies, trained to help around the house. One was a bed-making puppy, another was a dish-washing puppy. They all had helpful jobs that made them indispensable to the mother. Through the story the youngster could express disappointment and dissipate it with laughter, without intensifying the conflict. When the mother laughed, she was letting the child know humor was an acceptable way to express angry feelings.

- *Remember that humor preferences change as your child matures.* There are good joke books and riddle books, as well as humorous fiction written for children. Your librarian can recommend those appropriate for your child's reading level.

- *Encourage your child to play with words.* For instance, give him a word he knows, like "hyphen," and ask him to make up a silly definition that fits the sound. "It's the greeting bears use when they see each other after hibernating all winter." Or give a description and ask him to make up a new word. QUESTION: "What's the word for the crusty ring that collects around the neck of a ketchup bottle?" POSSIBLE ANSWER: "klup." By being receptive to your children's experimenting, you also encourage them to explore the humor possibilities of real words and word combinations.

Give him a word he knows, like "hyphen," and ask him to make up a silly definition that fits the sound. "It's the greeting bears use when they see each other after hibernating all winter." "What's the word for the crusty ring that collects around the neck of a ketchup bottle?" Possible answer: "klup."

- *Read the funny papers together.* Climbing in bed with Mom or Dad on a Sunday morning and reading the funnies aloud can become a treasured ritual as well as a permanent association between humor and happy family memories.

React to your children's humor attempts with laughter, but respect their privacy. Perhaps they don't want their humor repeated to others. Eventually you may develop a family humor code, a secret signal. For example, one set of parents used their little boy between the two of them as the filling in a "kiss sandwich." Sometimes the parents missed his cheeks and kissed each other. Saying "I think it's time for a sandwich" would precipitate laughter wherever they were.

One set of parents used their little boy between the two of them as the filling in a "kiss sandwich." Sometimes the parents missed his cheeks and kissed each other.

Make up funny bedtime stories about things your children will enjoy and from which they will learn. Encourage them to suggest some themes so they learn that humor can be found almost anywhere. One father made up a series of adventures about "Claude Belly Bunion's Belly Button Cleaning Service." And another parent spins her tale weekly about the "Camp for Whiners."

When your children intentionally say something funny, write it down to begin a humor album. Or, if they are feeling especially creative, let them dictate to you or tape-record original humorous stories or riddles.

Gently explain to your children what isn't funny. Teach them that ridicule can hurt others, and show them how to redirect humor constructively. Mark's mother heard him teasing his friend Jeff because he wears a hearing aid. Later when ten-year-old Mark began watching television, his mother turned down the volume. He protested that he couldn't hear his favorite program, and she replied, "Now you know how Jeff used to feel. Isn't it wonderful that his hearing aid can help him? How do you think he feels when you make fun of such a beautiful invention? Maybe you should find something about yourself to joke about instead."

The next day Mark told his friend, "You're lucky you've got a hearing aid. I wish they'd come up with an aid for improving my batting average." And they both had a good laugh.

- *Help your children learn that what their peers laugh at isn't always funny to adults.* Explain to them that some humorous behavior—such as entertaining your fifth grade pals at lunch time by burping the entire alphabet—is only acceptable among friends.
- *Reward your child's appropriate use of humor with approval, encouragement, and genuine laughter.* Amy's little brother became so frustrated trying to tie his shoelaces he broke into tears. Amy, leaning over to help, intentionally tied her finger to his shoelace, replacing his tears with giggles. To reinforce Amy's helpfulness, her mom presented her a cardboard badge proclaiming her, "The Family Giggle Master."
- *Most importantly, be flexible in dealing with your children, leaving room for both of you to experiment with different humor solutions.* By dealing humorously with your own frustrations whenever possible, they will learn by example. On her one morning off from work, a woman found a puddle under the front of her car. Her children listened as she called the mechanic and repeated what he told her, "If the puddle's brown, it's oil. If it's green, it's radiator fluid. And if it's red, it's transmission fluid. Well, hang on," she said, "I'll take a look, but I hope it's yellow, because then I'll know it's from my neighbor's cat." Their laughter followed her out the door and helped prop her up for the rest of the day.

On her one morning off from work, a woman found a puddle under the front of her car. Her children listened as she called the mechanic and repeated what he told her, "If the puddle's brown, it's oil. If it's green, it's radiator fluid. And if it's red, it's transmission fluid. Well, hang on," she said, "I'll take a look, but I hope it's yellow, because then I'll know it's from my neighbor's cat."

HUMOR AND SELF-IMAGE

Used properly, humor can help your child start out with a positive image of herself and the world around her. One of the first and most common games a baby plays is "peek-a-boo." When Mother or Daddy says, "Where's Sandy?" and then laughter and hugs are the response to discovering Sandy's smiling face behind baby's hands, humor is helping develop a positive self-image.

A little brother borrows a baseball glove without asking and forgets to return it. The older brother is angry but can step back from the anger enough to make his point with humor. "If you borrow my glove again without asking, I'm going to flatten you and use you for a hockey puck."

Gently using humor with your children throughout their growing years will also enhance their self-image and coping skills as they learn to joke about their frustrations and negative feelings. If young people can laugh about some of the pressures and emotional turmoil they may be experiencing (for instance, sexual impulses or hostile or angry feelings), they'll be better equipped to resolve them.

A little brother borrows a baseball glove without asking and forgets to return it. The older brother is angry but can step back from the anger enough to make his point with humor. "If you borrow my glove again without asking, I'm going to flatten you and use you for a hockey puck." He makes his point, but they both laugh at the exaggerated visual picture it conjures up. Granted, the remark could be hostile, but a playful tone of voice makes all the difference. It is a healthier expression than physical confrontation or a personal verbal attack.

Sometimes the child's anger will be directed at *you* when he feels left out or overlooked when your job takes you out of town or causes you to miss a family activity. In one of our workshops, a group of country club managers came up with some workable humor solutions that could help soften the disappointment:

1. Suggest that the children publish a newspaper for the week, so Mom will have a special edition upon her return to catch her up on what she missed. God bless computers!
2. Take funny photos (or a videotape), "What we really do when Dad's away."
3. Place Dad's picture at the dining room table.
4. Have a dress-up-backwards party where the kids can cook a "crazy meal." They can serve whatever combination they like—popcorn and cheese and pie—whatever.
5. Have children pack a surprise card in Dad's luggage.
6. Make a "welcome home" sign or rehearse a singing welcome.
7. Plan a non-traditional holiday dinner and save the traditional one for a belated celebration when the family is together. In some families Thanksgiving is celebrated again when

the college students return home in December (in others it's celebrated again when they go back to school).

Finally, don't underestimate your children's capacity for humor. If you give them the basics, their humor range will expand as they mature, and you will have given them a valuable coping and communication tool. You will know you've succeeded when they can use humor on their own to deal with the pressures and frustrations that face everyone around the clock. One busy executive found this note penned in youthful script on her calendar: "Saturday, 10 AM — appointment with your daughter to shop until we drop!"

HOW TO GET STARTED WHEN CHILDREN ARE OLDER

If you've never experimented with humor in dealing with your children, their initial response may be a startled, "Dad's acting really weird. What's going on?" Whatever your parenting style, even if it includes yelling, criticizing, or occasionally badgering your children, they are used to it—it's the known, the expected.

As you begin to incorporate humor into your parenting, therefore, expect some initial resistance—or at least, suspicion—until they become accustomed to the new you. You can help by making it clear that you're joking with them, and more importantly by respecting them and their feelings. Parents who use confidences to tease their children will quickly erode their sense of trust.

Ten-year-old Michelle shyly confided to her mother that she had a crush on a boy in her class. Imagine her embarrassment and sense of betrayal the next day when her mother joked about it in front of visiting relatives. Even though the teasing was gentle, all Michelle heard was her mother's disregard for her feelings in mentioning it to someone—anyone—else. So the same cautions about avoiding stress-producing humor are even more vital in dealing with impressionable youngsters who have not yet gained the sense of perspective that comes (if we're lucky) with age.

Ten-year-old Michelle shyly confided to her mother that she had a crush on a boy in her class. Imagine her embarrassment and sense of betrayal the next day when her mother joked about it in front of visiting relatives. Even though the teasing was gentle, all Michelle heard was her mother's disregard for her feelings in mentioning it to someone—anyone—else.

YOUR FAMILY HUMOR POTENTIAL

Since neither you nor your child is perfect, stresses from office and school sometimes end up sending sparks around your living room. If you have found that high voltage is threatening to overload your family communication system, perhaps it's time to recharge your batteries with a few laughs.

To determine the Humor Potential in your family life, consider these questions:

1. Do you frequently have to nag your children before they will do their chores?
2. Is yelling often your first, even automatic response when they've done something wrong? Even if it was an accident?
3. Are you overly critical, expecting behavior beyond their age and level of maturity?
4. Do you make sarcastic remarks in anger?
5. Do you underestimate your children's abilities?
6. Are you teaching your children to overreact to problems by your own overreaction to daily mishaps?
7. Do you stifle your child's expressions of opinion when they differ from yours?

If you answered yes to any of these questions, here's how humor can help you tune up your family communication system, short-circuit ingrained, unproductive parenting, and put a little fun into it besides.

KEEP ROWING, WE'RE ALL IN THIS BOAT TOGETHER

Children's chores take on an added dimension when they are an essential part of your daily routine. You may have to depend on your children to help you get to work on time, to supervise a younger child after school, or to help get dinner on the table at a reasonable hour. Humor will help you keep things in perspective and avoid unpleasant confrontation.

USE HUMOR:

Before parental anger escalates. If your teenaged son has forgotten, for the fifth Monday in a row, to take out the garbage, you may have accumulated too much anger to even think about using humor. The pent-up anger explodes, and the ensuing confrontation is unpleasant, destructive to positive feelings, and probably unproductive in the long run. (You'll get him to take out the garbage today, but you're not likely to instill in him a sense of responsibility through your anger.)

By dealing with the problem earlier, you will be able to manage your anger. One father's solution: He plopped the garbage (bagged!) on his son's bed, with a ransom note compiled from cut-out magazine ads. The note read: "Dear Randy: Am holding your car keys hostage. Will ransom in exchange for prompt garbage removal. Please comply by nine PM or your car keys will be mailed to Siberia."

One father's solution: He plopped the garbage (bagged!) on his son's bed, with a ransom note compiled from cut-out magazine ads. The note read: "Dear Randy: Am holding your car keys hostage. Will ransom in exchange for prompt garbage removal. Please comply by nine PM or your car keys will be mailed to Siberia."

The next Sunday night, without bag or note, Dad tacked a picture of a cold, desolate wasteland on his son's door. Humor softened the lightly veiled threat of punishment and provoked a laugh instead of defiance. By making a humorous connection to a neutral "triggering idea" (in this case, Siberia) the father can then, like Pavlov, stimulate the association in his son's mind using the "triggering idea" alone.

Before children's anger escalates. When children hit the teen years, whatever sense of perspective they may have developed goes dormant, not to pop out again until several years later. In the meantime, they are likely to react to problems, both large and small, in extremes. Well-timed humor can often defuse their angry feelings and put the situation into perspective for them.

Todd was angry because he couldn't find his English book. Gruffly he accused his mother, "Where's my book?"

Instead of responding angrily, "It's not my responsibility," she said, "Perhaps it is buried under the pile of debris in your room. And like the swamp creature, it will come to life when you're sleeping and will slowly creep up on you and begin conjugating verbs without mercy."

"Oh, Mother, very funny, very funny." But he did cool off and found the book under the bed in his room, affectionately known thereafter as "The Swamp."

Before criticism becomes destructive. Children all too often take any criticism, gentle or otherwise, personally. Immediately on the defensive, the chastised child ceases to accept the parent's opinion, no matter how reasonable. And criticizing a teenager is a delicate exercise in diplomacy. Humor offers a marvelous path to circumvent defensiveness and to spark feelings of cohesion and unity rather than opposition.

Fourteen-year-old Bobby preferred his room messy—games everywhere, papers scattered, clothes both dirty and clean wherever they fell. Checking the mailbox one day after school, he found an official-looking letter addressed to him from the "County Health Department." It read:

Dear Bobby:

In a routine check of your neighborhood for health hazards, toxic wastes, and wild animals, we discovered in your room the worst collection of offenses of the day. We observed objects on the floor likely to cause tripping, with possible subsequent lawsuits, vintage dust balls (a health hazard in the state of Ohio), school papers contributing to a fire hazard, and violation of Ordinance 583 which forbids the sleeping of children in any room where the floor is not visible.

Therefore your property has been condemned by order of the Chief of Police. No sleeping or playing there until cleanup is completed and approved by deputy-inspector

Mom.

Across his door she had taped two criss-crossed strips of brown paper to board it up. Bobby uttered an "Oh, Mom, how silly," but he smiled as he said it and started cleaning.

It is no coincidence that each parent chose the written word. By writing a note, you can put a little extra distance between yourself, the reprimand, and your child. It gives the guilty party time to react privately to the criticism, think about it, and then respond.

To encourage independence and enhance a positive self-image. Children on the brink of adolescence are tottering at the edge of maturity, sometimes wholeheartedly reaching toward independence, at other times clinging to the fraying edge of dependence like a teddy bear. Because dependent feelings often spring from a lack of self-confidence and a fear of making the wrong decision, parents can, with quiet humor, point out the relative importance or unimportance of the situation and help children learn that mistakes happen, but so what?

Mrs. L, in times of her fifteen-year-old's wavering decisions, asks Marcy, "What's the worst thing that can happen?" They then proceed to list all the exaggerated consequences. "If you go to the party tonight where you don't know anyone, 1) no one will speak to you all night and you'll turn into a pumpkin, 2) someone will mistake you for Brooke Shields and ask for your autograph, 3) a boy will break your toe teaching you the latest dance, or 4) while you're out the local radio station will call that you could have won ten thousand dollars if you'd answered the phone."

Mrs. L, in times of her fifteen-year-old's wavering decisions, asks Marcy, "What's the worst thing that can happen?" They then proceed to list all the exaggerated consequences. "If you go to the party tonight where you don't know anyone, 1) no one will speak to you all night and you'll turn into a pumpkin, 2) someone will mistake you for Brooke Shields and ask for your autograph, 3) a boy will break your toe teaching you the latest dance, or 4) while you're out the local radio station will call that you could have won ten thousand dollars if you'd answered the phone."

Exaggerating Marcy's fears in a light-hearted way acknowledges her concerns, but enables her to laugh at herself and gain perspective without feeling Mom is ignoring or belittling her. Knowing that her mother accepts her doubts as genuine gives her more confidence to face them. In this situation, humor can also have a delayed result, the "rebound effect."

If, during the party, Marcy finds herself alone for a while with no one talking to her (as she and Mom discussed), the experience may bring to mind their earlier conversation, and she may smile to herself at the image of turning into a pumpkin. Each success in gaining confidence and good feelings through humor will encourage her to use it again to cope with problems.

 *To help children deal with rejection.* Rejection hurts us all, but it is particularly rough for children and teens to handle.

Twelve-year-old Noel cried to her mother because she wanted to ride to camp with her two friends. The friends had replied that with all their gear the car wouldn't hold another person. Nonetheless, Noel felt rejected. Mother asked, "Did they say they didn't like you?"

"No."

"Did they say they didn't want you at camp if you find a ride?"

"No."

"Did they offer to tie you and your foot locker to the hood of the car?"

Noel laughed, "No."

"Well, then, let's go. I'll take you." Humor illustrated that she wasn't being rejected for personal reasons and minimized her disappointment.

To praise skillfully. Child behavior experts frequently recommend appropriate criticism: criticize the behavior but not the child. But far fewer mention the need for caution in praising. Praising the child ("You must be the best artist in class") instead of the action ("That is a beautiful picture. It makes me smile inside") can put pressure on children to perform up to standards that they cannot meet next time or every time.

Humor is a fun way to let children know you appreciate them, without being heavy-handed. It can also make praise palatable to a teenager who shies away from demonstrative expressions of parental love. A father, for example, lets his son know he is handsome: "Well, son, it takes a little adjusting when girls open the door for me so they have an excuse to smile at you, but I'll learn to live with it."

> CHILD: I want to go. Everybody's going.
>
> DAD #1: I said no, and that's final!
>
> DAD #2: Everybody's not going, because you're not going, and you are certainly somebody.

To set limits.

CHILD: I want to go. Everybody's going.

DAD #1: I said no, and that's final!

DAD #2: Everybody's not going, because you're not going, and you are certainly somebody.

Pulling in the reins requires a deft touch. Humor can help prevent a defiant response by absorbing the shock of an abrupt "no." The second Dad's answer to his daughter's lament acknowledges the problem, and lets her know that he values her even though at the moment he overrides her opinion. (On the other hand, if your child is a "Philadelphia lawyer," after twenty-five minutes of her detailed, statistically supported objections, the proper response is, "I said no, and that's final.")

It's never too late to improve communications with your children, and these are only a few suggestions. The variations are endless and will depend on your knowledge of your child's personality, sense of humor, and maturity. As your children grow and mature, they are constantly changing. If humor can help you and them adjust to those changes, it's not only worthwhile, it's also fun!

COOPERATION, SIBLING RIVALRY, AND FAMILY HUMOR

COOPERATION

If you look closely at families where children seem naturally cooperative, you will usually find, along with mutual respect and a sense of fairness, a lot of affection and good-natured humor at work, enhancing the sense of family cohesiveness and we're-all-in-this-together attitudes.

Mrs. B. takes the *direct humor approach:* She places a candy bar on her son's bed and says, "This is a bribe. Clean up your room." Providing incentives gets results for her.

The *indirect humor approach* can be just as effective. With younger children especially, distracting them with humor while doing a tedious job will keep them working longer with a more positive attitude.

Mr. R. plays this game while doing yard work with his two children, ages eight and eleven. "If you could invent anything at all, what would it be?" Ari and Scott then conjure up gadgets like 1) a child's shirt with a pocket built inside the neckline for surreptitiously dropping in spinach during dinner, 2) a homework robot named Einstein, 3) a gerbil that changes compact discs on the CD player, 4) a calendar full of extra holidays, such as "My-Football-Needs-Inflating-Day."

Mr. R. plays this game while doing yard work with his two children, ages eight and eleven. "If you could invent anything at all, what would it be?" Ari and Scott then conjure up gadgets like 1) a child's shirt with a pocket built inside the neckline for surreptitiously dropping in spinach during dinner, 2) a homework robot named Einstein, 3) a gerbil that changes compact discs on the CD player, 4) a calendar full of extra holidays, such as "My-Football-Needs-Inflating-Day."

While making the work at hand go quicker, this amusing game also allows children to vent their frustrations harmlessly about everyday aggravations. Humor also creates positive connections between people, linking them through enjoyment. It nourishes feelings of shared experiences that are necessary to the health of a well functioning family.

Doing chores together almost always elicits better cooperation from children. If, while scrubbing the bathroom or folding laundry, you designate this as "joke time," you can take turns telling jokes, riddles, stories, and family anecdotes (children love to hear them repeated).

You could make up a story that continues each time you do that chore. One family has a running story about the adventures of Sammie, the three-toed sloth. Each Saturday during clean-up, father and daughter add another chapter. It has become a family tradition. The daughter still doesn't look forward to cleaning the house, but neither does she strenuously object, and humor makes it as fun as possible.

Humor can also create cooperation by diverting attention from an unpleasant task. Mrs. A. had to fight with young Eve every night to brush the snarls out of her long hair. Most evenings ended in yelling and tears.

One night Mrs. A. sat on her daughter's bed and began talking about Tammy and Teddy Tangle, who needed to go home so Eve could sleep. Eve smiled a bit and endured the brushing. Even when the brushing hurt, Eve and Mom could blame Tammy and Teddy instead of Mom. Humor conquered some of Eve's resistance and provided a neutral pressure valve for venting her discomfort.

Mrs. A. had to fight with young Eve every night to brush the snarls out of her long hair. Most evenings ended in yelling and tears.

One night Mrs. A. sat on her daughter's bed and began talking about Tammy and Teddy Tangle, who needed to go home so Eve could sleep. Eve smiled a bit and endured the brushing. Even when the brushing hurt, Eve and Mom could blame Tammy and Teddy instead of Mom.

SIBLING RIVALRY

Nothing in child-rearing provokes controversy like sibling rivalry. Is it normal? Is it natural? How much is too much? Why can't I stop it? When should I interfere?

There is no magic solution for eliminating sibling rivalry, but maintaining a sense of proportion and humor can help parents keep the situation in perspective. Well-timed humor can also interrupt the blossoming hostilities.

When Mrs. R's two children, ages five and ten, start squabbling and complaining, she says, "Time out while I get my striped shirt and whistle." The picture of Mom umpiring their fight like a football referee gets either a laugh or an "Oh, *Mom.*" Either way, the mounting confrontation pauses. Extending the football terminology, she may send one child to her room for five minutes for a personal foul, unprofessional conduct, or, for physical fighting, roughing the passer. You can alter the terminology to suit your own family's interests.

When Mrs. R's two children, ages five and ten, start squabbling and complaining, she says, "Time out while I get my striped shirt and whistle." The picture of Mom umpiring their fight like a football referee gets either a laugh or an "Oh, Mom."

This technique does not bring perfect results and quiet children. But it does allow you, particularly if you act quickly, to maintain a certain distance from the problem without getting pulled into the conflict.

Humor during sibling fights also shifts attention from the source of conflict, allowing room for making constructive suggestions to resolve the problem.

CHILDREN'S USE OF HUMOR

The flip side of using humor with children is their learning to use it with you. Actually, this is a positive step; for at this point you know they have internalized your example and can use humor on their own not only for fun but also as a tool for coping.

Children realize that if they make you laugh, you won't be angry—or at least, as angry.

Mother in kitchen to fourteen-year-old Ken in breakfast room: "Why haven't you emptied the dishwasher yet?"

Ken: "I'm waiting for the earth's crust to move me in there."

The son skillfully averted a confrontation by defusing her anger. (However, after laughing, she still insisted he do it.)

Another mother often puts short notes in her ten-year-old daughter's lunch box. One morning, after a harried and angry evening of mother-daughter bickering, the mother found this note taped to her purse: *"Dear Mom, Have a good morning, get all your errands done, smile a lot, and be sure to take a nap so you won't be grouchy today. Love from your wonderful daughter."* The daughter had learned the value of inspiring a little smile even when she wasn't there.

Another mother often puts short notes in her ten-year-old daughter's lunch box. One morning, after a harried and angry evening of mother-daughter bickering, the mother found this note taped to her purse: "Dear Mom, Have a good morning, get all your errands done, smile a lot, and be sure to take a nap so you won't be grouchy today. Love from your wonderful daughter."

FAMILY HUMOR

Family humor does not have to be limited to parents and children. Grandparents can add a lot to the good feelings in a family. One woman often writes funny letters to her grandchildren, and she manages to make the children feel good about themselves while they're laughing.

In a recent letter to her eleven-year-old granddaughter, she wrote,

Thank you for the beautiful Valentine you made for us. You are very talented, just like your parents. My side of the family can't boast of any talents except music! Here's a list of attributes contributed by my family to the genealogical pool:

YES	*NO*
Honesty	*Beauty*
Niceness	*Wealth*
Good health	*Athletic ability*
Capability	*Grace*
Sense of humor	

Anything else that is you, must have come from Grandpa or your daddy's family.

In a birthday letter to her teenaged grandson that included a whopping big check, she wrote, *"Here's your birthday check—spend it on something you want. The amount reflects how much we think of you. If you don't feel you deserve that much, please let us know and you can refund the difference. However, I'm sure you wouldn't want to hurt our feelings by telling us we are wrong in our estimation of you!"*

Here are a few suggestions to increase the humor volume in your home and add some lighthearted moments to your collection of family traditions and memories:

- *Set aside a weekly joke time,* either during chores or during dinner, where everyone takes a turn telling a joke or a funny thing that happened that day.
- *Let the Humor Fairy visit younger children occasionally.* While they're asleep, leave a (washable) note on their mirror. In one household, the Tooth Fairy has this job and recently left this note: "Good morning! I know you didn't lose a tooth last night, but I was in the neighborhood so I decided to drop by. Love, the Tooth Fairy. P.S. Don't forget to floss!"
- *Create funny skits for special celebrations.* On Father's Day, one family took several of Dad's made-up bedtime stories, rolled them together, and entertained him with parodies of the family's favorite Gilbert and Sullivan songs. They taped the performance and occasionally replay it.

"Good morning! I know you didn't lose a tooth last night, but I was in the neighborhood so I decided to drop by. Love, the Tooth Fairy. P.S. Don't forget to floss!"

- *Focus birthdays on humorous recollections from the past.* For her son's sixteenth birthday, Ms. B. secretly invited eight of his friends to a pizza parlor and asked each boy to write a funny anecdote he remembered involving himself and the birthday boy. After devouring the pizza, each guest eagerly shared his story. Later his mother arranged them in a scrapbook along with pictures from the party and additional anecdotes sent by grandparents and other relatives.
- *Cut out cartoons or comic strips* that seem especially relevant for your children, laminate them and give them as bookmarks.
- *Create a family humor scrapbook* with anecdotes, pictures, or stories.
- *Let younger children practice putting new captions under cartoons* where you've marked out the real caption.
- *Encourage experimenting with new forms of humor,* like playing with words—puns, funny definitions, and so forth. When children are young, they get positive feedback from peers for rudimentary humor.

But what's funny to twelve-year-olds is not necessarily funny to thirty-five-year-olds. Some people never get past that stage of humor and therefore have an arrested humor development. When adults use adolescent humor exclusively, they may elicit uncomfortable laughter and may not recognize the difference between nervous laughter and genuine laughter. Sticking green beans up your nose may provoke gales of laughter in a school lunchroom, but only embarrassed titters at a dinner party. By laughing at your child's attempts at more mature humor, you will encourage him to keep trying. If you reserve criticism for those times when he oversteps the bounds of good taste, he'll probably listen.

For her son's sixteenth birthday, Ms. B. secretly invited eight of his friends to a pizza parlor and asked each boy to write a funny anecdote he remembered involving himself and the birthday boy. After devouring the pizza, each guest eagerly shared his story.

 *Put humor in your parental bag of tricks.* Take any of the following typical frustrations you experience with older children and invent funny solutions to these very real situations. Amidst the humor you will probably find an answer worth trying.

—haircuts

—taking out garbage

—too much makeup

—curfews

—homework

—baby-sitting with siblings

—cleaning rooms

—dress style

—dating

—telephone use

—yard work

—table manners

 *Discourage sarcasm.* Nothing wounds as swiftly as sarcasm. Under a veil of humor, people attack with anger and expect you to laugh. For some, sarcasm becomes so ingrained that they can't see its negative impact. You can help your children avoid this habit by allowing them to vent their feelings more directly and by pointing out their inappropriate use of sarcasm when it happens.

A healthy, well-adjusted child needs many skills to cope with the natural ups and downs of modern life. With a little practice and forethought, a child can learn to use humor as a shield to deflect minor blows and to cushion major ones. What better gift can parents give their children than the gift of laughter?

EASING TIMES OF ILLNESS

There's never a good time for your child to get sick, but obviously the world will not come to an end if you have to miss a few days of work.

When your child says, "My tummy hurts," you or your spouse may have to put your other job on hold for a day or two. And, in all fairness, the little person with the fever should be the one with the whining franchise.

When one dad told his little girl that they would have to visit the doctor, she started crying. So he said, "Let's pretend. You be the patient, I'll be the doctor. Here's your shot, now you cry." She started giggling. "No, honey, you're confused. You're supposed to be crying, not laughing." More giggling broke the tension and eased the child's fear.

Being sick is no fun at all for either parent or child, particularly when the parent is uptight about missed work. Although the doctor can prescribe medicine for the bacteria, it's up to Mom and Dad to deal with their own worry and their child's boredom, which accentuate the child's discomfort. Humor to the rescue!

Here are a dozen ways to ease times of illness for everyone:

- *At mealtime, deliver the tray of food with a sign on it.* Use either a funny saying, or perhaps the "riddle du jour." (Save the answer for when the meal is finished.)

- *Using an ink pad or marking pens smudged directly on the thumb,* make thumb prints on pages of paper in varying combinations. Let your child draw them into stick figures and then create a comic strip story to send to grandparents or out-of-town friends.

- *Cut out cartoons from magazines.* Together, make up new captions for them, naming the characters after real people your child knows.

- *Ask your child for suggestions for a quarantine sign for the bedroom door,* such as "Beware—Caged Lion. Enter at Own Risk," or "Eight-year-old Behind Bars. Visiting Hours Are 10 AM—2 PM."

- *Try using a hand puppet to give eardrops, eyedrops, "yucky" tasting medicine, and to take temperatures.* Nothing is quite so frustrating to a parent as trying to administer needed medicine to a frightened, reluctant child. "Maurice the Medicine Man," soft and fuzzy, succeeds when parents can only struggle.

- *Once a day, deliver mail from the Humor Fairy*—a joke or word of encouragement. Children love written messages.
- *Read funny stories and joke books,* five or ten minutes at a sitting, sporadically through the day. If your child can look forward to a "fun break" in an hour, you will probably get other things done with less interruption.
- *Make up a story, taking turns with your child for each chapter of the adventure.* For children over nine or ten, add puns related to the story. One mother related the story of the Red Rock Eater, who vacationed in Boulder, Colorado, and golfed in Pebble Beach, California. Her daughter added that she was born in Rock City, Tennessee, left no stone unturned, and marched down the aisle at her wedding to "Rock Around the Clock." (The next morning the daughter said, "Thank you for nursing me back to health. Being sick was more fun this time.")

When one dad told his little girl that they would have to visit the doctor, she started crying. So he said, "Let's pretend. You be the patient, I'll be the doctor. Here's your shot, now you cry." She started giggling. "No, honey, you're confused. You're supposed to be crying, not laughing."

- *Give them extra snapshots that are lying around the house and a cheap scrapbook.* Let them either make up funny captions or create a story from the pictures. That in turn can be a fun gift for the whole family.
- *Let your child make a collage* on the Kleenex box, or any extra box around the house, for him to use bedside. Use cartoons and jokes cut out of magazines. This activity is time-consuming and can be done alone.
- *For older children, get a couple of tapes* of old radio comedy shows or let them improvise on a blank tape to create their own version of a comedy show, news broadcast, or sports event.
- *Let your child cut up magazine and newspaper advertisements,* mixing the slogan of one for the product of another.

These are just a few suggestions to get through "sick days" with a minimum of frustration, boredom, and angst. And your child will feel better, too!

PART

Getting Funny

Humor Resources: Thanks, I Needed That

CONFERENCES, ORGANIZATIONS, AND SUBSCRIPTIONS

Please include a self-addressed, stamped envelope when you write for more information.

AMERICAN ASSOCIATION FOR THERAPEUTIC HUMOR (AATH). A professional society designed to disseminate information about humor. AATH provides educational lectures, seminars and conferences, and functions as an interdisciplinary network and clearinghouse of information on humor research. Newsletter: *Laugh It Up.* Alison Crane, 1163 Shermer Road, Northbrook, IL 60062.

AMERICAN HUMOR STUDIES ASSOCIATION. An affiliate of the Modern Language Association. For academics, general readers, and professional humorists. Encourages the study and appreciation of American humor from interdisciplinary perspectives. Annual meeting held in December. Journal: *Studies in American Humor.* Jack O. Rosenbalm, English Department, Southwest Texas State University, San Marcos, TX 78666.

CAROLINA HEALTH AND HUMOR ASSOCIATION (CAHAHA). A non-profit educational foundation dedicated to establishing humor systems in business, health care and the community. For details of upcoming programs contact Ruth Hamilton, 5223 Revere Road, Durham, NC 27713. (919) 544-2370.

CARTOON ART MUSEUM OF CALIFORNIA. Founded in March, 1984, to provide a permanent repository for the preservation and display of a comprehensive collection of cartoon art. Designed to serve cartoonists, historians, artists, and scholars, as well as the general public. 665 Third Street, Fifth Floor, San Francisco, CA 94107. Hours: Wednesday–Friday 11–5, Saturday 10–5. Director: Mary Bisbee. Inquiries to: Malcolm Whyte, 333 Richardson Drive, Mill Valley, CA 94941.

CURRENT COMEDY FOR SPEAKERS. Published twenty-four times yearly, *Current Comedy* provides topical new laugh material for public speakers, entertainers, emcees, toastmasters, and business, political, and community leaders. Gary Apple, editor, 165 West 47th Street, New York, NY 10036. (212) 944-6899.

EXECUTIVE SPEECHWRITER NEWSLETTER. A bimonthly newsletter of ideas, insights, quotes, and humorous anecdotal material for the executive speechmaker. Joe Taylor Ford, editor, Emerson Falls, St. Johnsbury, VT 05819. (802) 748-4472.

FELLOWSHIP OF MERRY CHRISTIANS. A non-denominational organization including pastors, bookstore managers, seminary librarians, health professionals, church officials, military chaplains and lay people. Monthly periodical: *The Joyful Noiseletter.* Cal Samra, founder, P.O. Box 668, Kalamazoo, MI 49005-0668.

FUNNY BUSINESS. A two-project humor program. The first, paired with national non-profit organizations, provides humor carts in hospitals, convalescent homes and other medical facilities in the United States. The second is the "Dr. Lollipop" program. The clown, "Dr. Lollipop," has been working with children for eighteen years to lessen their fears in medical settings. She has appeared with the Moscow Circus and will be taking her program abroad. Judy Goldblum-Carlton (Dr. Lollipop) and Judy Young, 6281 Loveknot Place, Columbia, MD 21045. (301) 290-7845 or (301) 596-6031.

GAG RECAP. A comprehensive summary of the cartoon gag lines (no drawings included) printed in forty-five publications. General audience and X-rated. Weeklies and dailies. *Recap* offers a useful means to check the originality of gags and trends and serves as a general reference for when and where a certain cartoon was published. The editors also publish *Trade Journal Recap* which covers trade journals and house organs. Al and Jo Gottlieb, editors, P.O. Box 774, Bensalem, PA 19020.

GENE PERRET'S ROUND TABLE. A ten-page monthly newsletter for comedy writers, comedians, and humorous speakers, emphasizing the "how to" of writing and presentation. Articles by well-known comedy writer, Gene Perret, are especially helpful. Linda Perret, editor, P.O. Box 1415, South Pasadena, CA 91031.

THE HOUSE OF HUMOR AND SATIRE. Publishes *Apropos,* a magazine presenting humor and satire of different nations, in English, Bulgarian, Russian, and French. Seeks to link people through humor in the spirit of mutual understanding and peace. Sponsors annual international celebration with parades, on April first. Todor Dinov, editor, P.O. Box 104, 5300 Gabrovo, Bulgaria. Tel: 27229 27125. Telex: 67413.

HUMOR DIGEST. Monthly listing of humorous items—jokes, one-liners, and anecdotes—to use in speeches. Also available, collections of items by category, such as "Congress," "Golf," or "Insurance." Mack McGinnis, editor, 448 Mitchner Avenue, Indianapolis, IN 46219. (317) 356-4616.

THE HUMOR PROJECT. Develops, collects, and disseminates information and offers computer networking for members. Offers conferences, seminars, and college credit courses. Publishes *Laughing Matters,* edited by Joel Goodman, Ph.D., a quarterly forty-page booklet filled with specific humor suggestions, reprints of pertinent articles, and business-related ideas. Joel Goodman, Ph.D., 110 Spring Street, Saratoga Springs, NY 12866.

THE HUMOUR, COMEDY AND LAUGHTER CENTRE. A center of wide-ranging humor services including: The Humour Bookshop, the largest collection of non-fiction and fiction humor books in Australia; The Humourversity, where professional comedian, Peter Crofts, conducts humor and comedy classes and provides humor in communication workshops and seminars for corporations; Creative Management Corporation, a management training and booking agency for comedians, humorous speakers, and comedy writers; and Creative Comedy Concepts, for conferences, conventions, and trade shows. 24 Station Street, Sandringham, 3191, Melbourne, Victoria, Australia. Laugh Line: (03) 598-3671.

INSTITUTE FOR THE ADVANCEMENT OF HUMAN BEHAVIOR. Coordinates the annual conference, "The Healing Power of Laughter and Play: Uses of Humor in the Healing Arts." This three-day conference has been presented nationwide for health professionals but is open to all. IAHB also sponsors "Humor and Creativity," presented by Joel Goodman. Cassettes available for most conference presenters. P.O. Box 7226, Stanford, CA 94309. (415) 851-8411.

INTERNATIONAL CONFERENCE ON HUMOR. A biennial, interdisciplinary conference to examine and appreciate the role of humor in all areas of life, backed up by scholarly analysis and commentary in more than thirty areas of study. Conferences involve participants from fifty different countries. Location varies. Lawrence W. Sherman, Educational Psychology Department, 201 McGuffey Hall, Miami University, Oxford, OH 45056.

INTERNATIONAL GELETOLOGY INSTITUTE. Dr. William Fry consults on dissertations, questions of health and science, and helps people set up experimental studies. William F. Fry, Jr., M.D., 156 Grove Street, Nevada City, CA 95959. (916) 265-5125.

INTERNATIONAL JOURNAL OF CREATURE COMMUNICATION. A pseudo-scholarly journal published biannually, with all articles dealing with some type of creature communication using the jargon of one's field. "They must be heavily footnoted and few if any of the footnotes should be authentic, or otherwise traceable." Sample articles include "Transcendental Anglerism" and "Creative Communication of Lake Michigan Salmon: Fact, Fiction or Hallucination." Membership entitles you to the spring and fall issues, Research Affiliate status, a supply of letterhead (useful for responding to IRS). Charles Larson, editor, Communication Studies, Northern Illinois University, Watson Hall 205, DeKalb, IL 60115.

INTERNATIONAL LAUGHTER SOCIETY. Brings the latest research data and how-to information on the use of "Therapeutic Humor" and "Humor in Communication." Seminars, workshops, and information on noninvasive methods to manage stress, increase communication and maintain wellness. L. Katherine Ferrari, president, 16000 Glen Una Drive, Los Gatos, CA 95030.

INTERNATIONAL MUSEUM OF HUMOR. Multimedia displays explore humor from civilization's beginnings, including cartoons, archives, a cabaret, a hall of fame, and even an interactive wisecracking chessboard. All exhibits in English and French. 2111 Saint Laurent, Montreal H2X 2T5 Canada. (514) 845-3155. Check, mate.

INTERNATIONAL SAVE THE PUN FOUNDATION. The world's largest apocryphal society, committed to fighting alliteracy by having fun with words. Sends members a monthly compilation of the best plays on words. In January each member also receives the Annual Report on the Ten Best-stressed Puns of the Year. "A day without puns is like a day without sunshine: there is gloom for improvement." John S. Crosbie, Box 5040 Station A, Toronto, Ontario, Canada M5W 1N4.

INTERNATIONAL SOCIETY FOR HUMOR STUDIES. ISHS has joined forces with *Humor: International Journal of Humor Research,* an interdisciplinary journal in humor research. Membership entitles humor scholars to journal subscription, all mailings and information on its humor conference. Don L. F. Nilsen, English Department of Arizona State University, Tempe, AZ 85287-0302. (602) 965-7592.

International Society for Humor Studies 1995 Conference (formerly called International Humor Conference). Tentatively July or August in Birmingham, England. Chair: George E. C. Paton, Sociology Department, SMPS Division, Aston University, Birmingham, England B5 and ET. (021) 359-3611.

IRISH BULL is a subsidiary of the Workshop Library of World Humour centered on the humor collection in Cork, Ireland. Dr. Des MacHale, Department of Mathematics, University College, Cork, Ireland.

THE JOKESMITH. A comedy newsletter for business and professional people. Offers roast lines, presentation aids, meeting picker-uppers, jokes, comic remarks, and stories with a point. Published quarterly. Edward C. McManus, editor, 44 Queen's View Road, Marlborough, MA 01752.

JOURNAL OF IRREPRODUCIBLE RESULTS. Articles written by academics and scientists parodying their own methods and style. Marc Abrahams, editor, Blackwell Scientific Publications, Three Cambridge Center, Cambridge, MA 02142.

JOURNAL OF NURSING JOCULARITY. A quarterly humor magazine for nurses, written by nurses, filled with satire, parody, true stories and cartoons about the wonderful profession of nursing. It also includes regular features about ways nurses can incorporate the healing power of humor into their work. Douglas Fletcher, editor, P.O. Box 40416, Mesa, AZ 85274.

JOURNAL OF POLYMORPHOUS PERVERSITY. Now entering its ninth year of publication, this is the zany spoof of psychology, psychiatry, and the closely allied disciplines that *The Wall Street Journal* called "a social scientist's answer to *Mad* magazine." Glenn C. Ellenbogen, Ph.D., editor, c/o Wry-Bred Press, Inc., P.O. Box 1454, Madison Square Station, New York, NY 10159-1454.

JUST FOR LAUGHS. A national tabloid with fifty thousand circulation put out by Jon and Anne Fox, the producers of the Stand-up Comedy Competition. Hut Landon, managing editor, 22G Miller Avenue, Mill Valley, CA 94941.

KNUCKLEHEAD PRESS. A quarterly humor newsletter featuring fiction, parodies, adventure, horror, humorous novel excerpts, and slice-of-life vignettes. "Anything that's funny, but not morally or sexually offensive." Chris Miksanek and Jim Riley, editors, 6442 West 111th Street, Worth, IL 60482.

LATEST JOKES. Monthly newsletter of humor for television and radio personalities, comedians and professional speakers. Short jokes. "No obvious, non-funny vulgar humor." Robert Makinson, editor, Box 3304, Brooklyn, NY 11202-0066. (718) 855-5057.

THE LAUGHTER PRESCRIPTION NEWSLETTER. Published monthly. Sixteen pages of upbeat articles, topical humor, and original jokes dedicated to the healing art of humor. Produced by comedy writer Karen Silver, 17337 Septo Street, Northridge CA 91325. (818) 886-8737.

THE LAUGHTER PROJECT. This project has sponsored two research studies evaluating the effectiveness of laughter in reducing subjective and objective signs of stress. The project has designed a handbook describing how to use laughter to reduce stress and a video documenting a laughter group. Research reprints, handbook, and video available. Sabine White, project director, c/o Health Education Department, Student Health Services, University of California, Santa Barbara, CA 93106. (805) 893-2630.

LAUGHTER UNLIMITED. Tailor-made workshops, classes, and support groups to show people how to improve their "laugh life" to diffuse anger and deal with stress. Sessions focus on the positive uses of humor and laughter for physical and mental well-being and provide "hands-on" experience. Pinkie Barclay, 951 West Orange Grove #03204, Tucson, AZ 85704.

LAUGHTER WORKS. Not to be confused with Jim Pelley's *Laughter Works Warehouse* (see below). Certified holistic health specialists give workshops and seminars on the connection between laughter, positive attitudes, and good health. Workshops include "Laughter Works: An Approach to Healthful Living," "Great Expectations: Dealing with Change and Mind/Body Wellness," and "Therapeutic Juggling and Other Prescription Toys." Kay Caskey, A.C.S.W., and Laurie Young, M.A., N.C.C., 34125 CR 352, Decatur, MI 49045. (616) 624-5251 or (616) 423-8102.

LAUGHTER WORKS WAREHOUSE. Full-sized mail order catalog. Features books, audio tapes, videotapes, toys and other resources dedicated to promoting the positive and appropriate use of humor in the life place. Also available, *Laughter Works Newsletter* filled with "funformation." Seminars presented at Laughter Works Weekend Retreat, "Humor in the Hills." Jim Pelley, P.O. Box 1076, Fair Oaks, CA 95628-1076. (916) 863-1592.

LONE STAR PUBLICATIONS OF HUMOR. Humorous and humor-related publications and services. Lauren Barnett, P.O. Box 29000, #103, San Antonio, TX 78229.

THE LOONIES. A salon for funny folks. Since 1978, a networking forum for humorists, cartoonists, and performers, with no fees charged. Meets about every six to eight weeks at San Francisco locations. Events are informal, both social and business-oriented, and usually involve a book signing of a Bay Area or national author. Barry Gantt, P.O. Box 20443, Oakland, CA 94620. (415) 451-6248.

MAD MAGAZINE. Published eight times a year. One million circulation. Satire, parody, and spoofs on latest trends. Nick Meglin and John Ficarra, editors, 485 Madison Avenue, New York, NY 10022.

MALEDICTA: THE INTERNATIONAL JOURNAL OF VERBAL AGGRESSION. Sponsored by the International Maledicta Society, this journal specializes in uncensored studies and collections of "offensive" words and expressions in all languages, dealing with such subjects as swear words, insults, curses, jargon of subcultures, slurs, stereotypes, terminology, wit and humor, graffiti, satire, and sarcasm. Purchasers automatically become members of the IMS. Sample journal articles are "The Deflowering of the *American Heritage Dictionary*" and "Bavarian Terms of Abuse Derived from Common Names." Surprisingly scholarly, but not for the squeamish. Reinhold Aman, Ph.D., editor, P.O. Box 14123, Santa Rosa, CA 95402-6123. (707) 523-4761.

METACOM, INC. Free catalog of radio show reruns on cassettes. 5353 Nathan Lane, Plymouth, MN 55442. 1-800-328-0108.

MUSEUM OF AMERICAN HUMOR. Leopold Fechtner, founder. Mr. Fechtner has amassed what he believes is the largest private humor library, with more than a million humorous items. The museum has four departments and is open only to people associated with the entertainment business, but organizes occasional public exhibits. He also has on record two hundred of the best comedians and a large collection of funny recordings, and more than five thousand humor books and funny magazines. This gigantic showcase of humor was created to register, keep, file, store and preserve all materials which create laughter. 84-51 Beverly Road, Kew Gardens, NY 11415. (212) 846-2002.

MUSEUM OF BROADCASTING. Offers exhibitions, seminars, and a collection of more than twenty thousand tapes covering sixty years of radio and television broadcasting. Visitors may go through the extensively cross-indexed card catalog and check out a taped television show for viewing in a console room. 1 East 53rd Street, New York, NY 10022. (212) 752-4690.

MUSEUM OF CARTOON ART. Founded in 1974 by cartoonist Mort Walker for the collection, exhibition and preservation of all forms of cartoon art. Membership includes a yearly subscription to *Cartoonist PRO-files,* featuring informative articles on the cartoon field and museum events, plus museum store discount. Comly Avenue, Rye Brook, NY 10573.

NATIONAL LAMPOON. A bimonthly magazine of "offbeat, irreverent satire." National Lampoon, Inc., 155 Avenue of the Americas, New York, NY 10013. (212) 645-5040.

THE NEW YORK COMEDY SCHOOL. Offers a wide-ranging program of workshops and lectures taught by some of the city's top professional humorists. Each covers a different genre of comedic expression, for example: "Humor Writing Workshop" and "Stand-up Comedy Workshop." New School for Social Research, 66 West Twelfth Street, New York, NY 10011. (212) 741-5690.

9TO5. The leading membership organization for American office workers lobbies against unfair working conditions, exposes abuses, counsels workers on their legal rights and job-related problems, and operates a toll-free Survival Hotline: 1-800-522-0925. National office: 614 Superior Avenue NW, Cleveland, OH 44113. (216) 566-9308. Ellen Bravo, executive director, 9to5 Headquarters, 238 West Wisconsin #700, Milwaukee, WI 53203-2308. (414) 274-0925.

NORTHERN CALIFORNIA CARTOONIST AND HUMOR ASSOCIATION. Founded in 1953 to allow cartoonists, gag writers, and collectors to meet other professionals in the field. Members hold monthly dinner meetings in San Francisco Bay area restaurants, combining a featured speaker with business and socializing. Membership fees are modest to encourage a broad participation. Art Ness, 1766 21st Avenue, San Francisco, CA 94122. (415) 665-3903.

THE ONION. Weekly humor entertainment newspaper which satirizes college life or any subject of interest to a college audience. Scott Dikkers, editor, Suite 270, 33 University Square, Madison, WI 53715. (608) 256-1372.

PROCRASTINATOR'S CLUB OF AMERICA, INC. A club for people who like to put things off. Membership entitles you to an official membership card (someday), a "License to Procrastinate," participation in all events, *Last Month's Newsletter,* and some surprises. Les Waas, president, P.O. Box 712, Bryn Athyn, PA 19009.

THE P.U.N., PLAY ON WORDS. A bimonthly newsletter for a nonexistent organization, The Silly Club. Readers are treated to humor bordering on the intellectual as well as the silly. Puns are rare, since P.U.N. in this case is an acronym rather than indicator of content. Danno Sullivan, editor, Box 536-583, Orlando, FL 32853. (407) 648-2028.

READING UNIVERSITY. The University of Reading in England is now offering studies toward an M.A. degree in Humour—an interdisciplinary course—conducted in the Graduate School of European and International Studies. Professor Christie Davies, Department of Sociology, Faculties of Letters and Social Sciences, University of Reading, P.O. Box 218, Reading RG6, England.

SAGAMORE INSTITUTE BOOKSTORE. Over five hundred humor books and materials, including teaching aids, available. 110 Spring Street, Saratoga Springs, NY, 12866. (518) 587-8770.

TEACHERS FOR ENCOURAGING ENTHUSIASM AND HUMOR IN EVERYONE'S EDUCATION. A humor users group. Consultative services. Frieda Dietrich, president, Educational Service Unit # 2, R.F.D. #6 at 2320 North Colorado Avenue, P.O. Box 649, Fremont, NE 68025-0649.

THALIA: STUDIES IN LITERARY HUMOR. Publishes articles in either English or French on most aspects of humor in literature, film, and the arts and provides an outlet for articles on the theory of humor, whether literary, psychological, or philosophical. Published twice a year, *THALIA* is the only bilingual, international, and inter-disciplinary journal devoted to a serious study of humor. Jacqueline Tavernier-Courbin, editor, Department of English, University of Ottawa, Ottawa, Canada K1N 6N5.

WHOLE MIRTH CATALOG. A delightful guide to useful and semi-useful gadgets, toys, household items, and other smile-getters and laugh-makers. The catalog is an entertaining read. Allen Klein, editor, 1034 Page Street, San Francisco, CA 94117.

WORD WAYS, THE JOURNAL OF RECREATIONAL LINGUISTICS. Focuses on words as groups of letters (anagrams, palindromes, lipograms, pangrams, etc.) but also words as carriers of meaning. Material includes research or survey articles on recreational linguistics, fictional or poetic treatments, and word puzzles or games. Quarterly. A. Ross Eckler, Spring Valley Road, Morristown, NJ 07960.

WORKSHOP LIBRARY ON WORLD HUMOR. Founded in 1975, WLWH, a non-profit organization, explores the uses of humor and examines our humor heritage from the earliest societies to the present. Publishes *Humor Events,* a quarterly newsletter for members.

WHWH acts as a clearinghouse for research into the uses of humor as well as a forum for sharing an appreciation of humor in writing, art, music, and the performing arts, past and present. Barbara Cummings, P.O. Box 23334, Washington, DC 20026. (202) 484-4949.

HUMOR CONSULTANTS, COURSES, AND HOSPITAL HUMOR PROGRAMS

LYNNE ALPERN and ESTHER BLUMENFELD. Award-winning writers, speakers, and seminar leaders. Entertain as after-dinner speakers at conventions and meetings. Conduct upbeat and informative humor workshops for businesses and conventions tailored to the audience, related to material covered in this book, including "Adding Humor to Your Life: The Salt-free, Low-calorie, Polyunsaturated, All Natural Guide to Feeling Good," "Humor at Work? Don't Make Me Laugh," and "Women, Power, and Humor." They teach humor courses at Emory University and are the authors of seven books including one for the workplace, *Oh, Lord, It's Monday Again.* P.O. Box 421461, Atlanta, GA 30342. (404) 255-5924.

STEVE ALLEN, JR., M.D. An award-winning physician with a practice in Horseheads, New York. Allen, son of comedian Steve Allen, travels around the United States conducting participatory humor workshops for health organizations and corporations. He demonstrates the therapeutic value of laughter and play as audiences juggle brightly colored scarves and laugh their way to a more stress-free life. 8 Le Grand Court, Ithaca, NY 14850. (607) 277-1795.

ARTHUR ASA BERGER. Gives humor workshops. Broadcast Communication Arts Department, San Francisco State University, 1600 Holloway Avenue, San Francisco, CA 94132. (415) 338-1787.

JAMES "DOC" BLAKELY. Author of syndicated column, "Pokin' Fun," Blakely delivers inspirational messages filled with his own brand of good clean humor; author of *Doc Blakely's Handbook of Wit and Pungent Humor.* Tapes available. 3404 Fairway Drive, Wharton, TX 77488. (409) 532-4502.

SHEILA FEIGELSON, Ph.D. Professional speaker and workshop leader. Engages audiences in learning new ways of "Putting Humor to Work—Not Just for Laughs." Regularly conducts workshops at the University of Michigan on "Laughing Matter for Serious Communication," and "Developing Positive Staff Morale: What's a Manager to Do?" P.O. Box 7264, Ann Arbor, MI 48107. (313) 662-1996.

WILLIAM F. FRY, JR., M.D. A long-time researcher and author on laughter, including its physiological aspects, Dr. Fry is available for lectures and workshops. 156 Grove Street, Nevada City, CA 95959. (916) 265-5125.

BARRY GANTT. President of The Comedy Connection. Creates humor and copy for radio and television commercials, magazine features, promotions, and cartoon productions; writes, edits, and presents slide shows. 534-C Fairbanks Avenue, Oakland, CA 94610. (415) 451-6248. For information on Gantt's twice-yearly class, "The Art and Business of Humorous Illustration," send SASE to Cartoon Class, P.O. Box 20443, Oakland, CA 94620.

ART GLINER. Teaches courses and conducts workshops discussing the creation of original humor, how to add humor to speeches, the value and uses of humor in communication, creativity, and coping with stress and tension. Humor Communication Company, 8902 Maine Avenue, Silver Spring, MD 20910. (301) 588-3561.

ANNETTE GOODHEART, Ph.D. Laughter Therapy. Goodheart is a psychotherapist in private practice in Santa Barbara, California. She has worked with cathartic processes—particularly laughter—for over twenty years and does training for professionals, lectures, and leads workshops internationally. Some of her popular workshops are "Laughter, Therapy, Laugh Your Way to Health," "Laughter in the Workplace," and "Loss, Laughter and Healing." P.O. Box 692, Aptos, CA 95001-0682. (408) 688-6937.

JOEL GOODMAN, Ph.D. Directs The Humor Project. Provides workshops, speeches, courses, training seminars, publications, and consulting services for individuals, schools, and organizations. Presents a week-long course each summer (can be taken for three graduate credits) for teachers, managers, health care professionals, business people, and others at the Sagamore Conference Center in the Adirondack Mountains. Author of several books. 110 Spring Street, Saratoga Springs, NY 12866. (518) 587-8770.

MELVIN HELITZER. Has taught "Comedy Writing Secrets—Journalism 488" for the past ten years. Author of three books on humor writing, including *Comedy Writing Secrets*. Scripps School of Journalism, Ohio University, Athens, OH 45701.

CHARLES W. JARVIS, D.D.S. Award-winning speaker who gave up his dentistry practice for the speakers' circuit. Seminars and speeches. Speeches include "Open Wide, Please . . . and Laugh!" and "Prescription for the Happy Life—Refilled." Box 1094, San Marcos, TX 78666. (512) 392-3824.

ALLEN KLEIN. Publisher of *Whole Mirth Catalog,* Klein gives workshops, lectures, and in-services to schools, hospitals, and businesses. His programs demonstrate and document the therapeutic benefits of humor. With laughter, lecture, and playful exercises, participants learn about tools and techniques to enhance their work and life. 1034 Page Street, San Francisco, CA 94117. (415) 431-1913.

CHARLES LINDNER. Stand-up comedian, lecturer, comedy writer, and humor consultant. Lectures on the art of laugh-making on television and radio for institutions and associations. Founder of comedy workshops at Hunter College and Marymount-Manhattan College. Now on the faculty of The New School for Social Research, offering a course called "The World of Comedy and Humor." Five Tudor City Place, New York, NY 10017.

BARBARA MACKOFF. Author of *What Mona Lisa Knew: How Women Can Get Ahead in Business by Lightening Up,* Mackoff is a management psychologist who specializes in presentations about "executive balance" and about women using humor as a professional tool. 1321 Vance Building, 1402 Third Avenue, Seattle, WA 98101. (206) 628-0540.

DOYNE E. MICHIE. Retired minister who now directs a Ministry of Laughter as an outreach of the Mt. Vernon Presbyterian Church. Upon request this accomplished magician visits hospitals, nursing homes, and hospices (free). He also conducts a humor workshop, "The Therapy of Laughter," for nurses, hospice volunteers, and the general public. 616 Lorell Terrace, Atlanta, GA 30328. (404) 256-1077.

LAWRENCE E. MINTZ, Ph.D. Associate Professor of American Studies with a scholarly interest in American popular culture and humor, Dr. Mintz teaches a course, "Culture and Society in American Humor," at both the junior-senior undergraduate level and graduate level. Editor of *Humor in America.* American Studies Program, University of Maryland, College Park, MD 20742.

JOHN MORREALL. Humorworks Seminars. Conducts interactive three-hour seminars which explore humor in the workplace. Shows participants how to enhance creative thinking and problem solving, reduce stress, and improve training, morale, and teamwork. P.O. Box 152, Penfield, NY 14526. (716) 248-2690.

ROBERT ORBEN. Author of over forty books of humor and former editor of *Orben's Current Comedy.* Holds humor workshops and gives speeches on the uses of humor in speeches and in business and political communication. Established speech writer for high-ranking politicians (including President Gerald Ford) and business executives. The list of his credits, as well as of articles written about him, is extensive. 1200 North Nash Street, #1122, Arlington, VA 22209. (703) 522-3666.

GENE PERRET. Humorous speaker. A three-time Emmy-winning writer for Bob Hope, Carol Burnett, Phyllis Diller, and others. Perret's program is entertaining and sure to enliven any convention or seminar. 1485 Westhaven Road, San Marino, CA 91108. (213) 793-4716.

VERA ROBINSON, R.N., Ed.D. Professor Emeritus, Department of Nursing, California State University, Fullerton. Author of *Humor and the Healing Professions: The Therapeutic Use of Humor in Health Care.* Does consultations, presentations, workshops, and programs on humor for health care professionals. 11286 East Baltic Place, Aurora, CO 80014.

BOB ROSS. Professional speaker and humorist. Delivers humorous talks as a professional "put-on" artist. Writes and conducts comedy roasts. Author of *Laugh, Lead and Profit: Building Productive Workplaces with Humor.* Publishes quarterly newsletter, *The Laugh Connection.* 3643 Corral Canyon Road, Bonita, CA 92002. (619) 479-3331.

JOHN L. SCHIMEL, M.D. Schimel, a psychiatrist, consults as an authority on humor in adolescent therapy. 40 Gramercy Park North, New York, NY 10010. (212) 674-6268.

RALPH SLOVENKO. A professor and authority on humor and the law. Wayne State University Law School, Detroit, MI 48202.

VIRGINIA TOOPER, Ed.D. Delivers funny talks about humor. Offers courses regularly at several colleges and universities in San Francisco area for educators, nurses, and general audiences on "Using Humor in the Health Professions," "Putting Humor into Business," and "Laughter and Learning: Improving Educational Skills Through Humor." P.O. Box 1495, Pleasanton, CA 94566. (415) 462-3591.

MATT WEINSTEIN, Ph.D. Founding president of Playfair, Inc., an international consulting firm that conducts a one-day workshop, "Comic Relief: the Healing Powers of Laughter and Play," designed to foster a sense of exuberant joy, reduce stress, and increase self-esteem. Participants learn about the physiological effects of laughter, study techniques for interacting humorously with others, and experience the comical side of themselves in a completely supportive environment. Coauthor of *Education of the Self,* and *Playfair: Everybody's Guide to Noncompetitive Play.* Playfair, Inc., 2207 Oregon Street, Berkeley, CA 94705. (415) 486-1244.

LARRY WILDE. Humorist and author of forty-seven "Official" joke books. Spices up the speeches presented by politicians, corporate executives, and other personalities who appear before the public. Conducts humor seminars for executives and comedy workshops for young comedians who require special tutoring. 116 Birkdale Road, Half Moon Bay, CA 94019.

STEVE WILSON. Clinical psychologist, professional speaker, consultant, author, and publisher of quarterly Steve Wilson Report. Applying psychology and humor to life and work. "Un-organizer" of the Humor Pen Pal Club. Author of *The Art of Mixing Work and Play*. Steve Wilson, DPJ Enterprise, Inc., 3400 North High Street, #120, Columbus, OH 43202. 1-800-NOW-LAFF.

HOSPITAL HUMOR PROGRAMS

COPLEY HOSPITAL. "Humor à la Cart" award-winning volunteer program which received a citation letter from President Bush. Nance Driscoll, Director of Volunteer Services, Copley Hospital, Washington Highway, Morrisville, VT 05661. (802) 888-4231.

DEKALB GENERAL HOSPITAL. "The Lively Room." Sandra Yates, R.N., O.C.N. 2701 North Decatur Road, Decatur, GA 30033. (404) 297-2700.

ETHEL PERCY ANDRUS GERONTOLOGY CENTER. Publishes a handbook outlining its innovative experiment using humorous materials in caring for the elderly. Wendy Free, Associate Director of Development, University of Southern California. University Park/MC-0191, Los Angeles, CA 90089-0191. (213) 740-6060.

LINCOLN GENERAL HOSPITAL. Connie LaFont, 2827 Ponca NE, Lincoln, NE 68506.

MESA LUTHERAN HOSPITAL. "The Love and Laughter Room." Janet Gredler, R.N., Director of Humorous Affairs. 525 West Brown Road, Mesa, AZ 85201. (602) 834-1211, ext. 3906 or (602) 461-2906.

MORTON PLANT HOSPITAL. "The Comedy Connection." Leslie Gibson, R.N., chairman, 323 Jeffords Street, P.O. Box 210, Clearwater, FL 34617. (813) 462-7841.

ST. JOSEPH'S HOSPITAL. "The Living Room" of the William Stehlin Foundation for Cancer Research. Mary Mobley, Director of Volunteers. 1919 LaBranch, Houston, TX 77002. (713) 757-1000.

SHAWNEE MISSION KANSAS MEDICAL CENTER. "The Laughing Room." Catherine Castelli, R.N. M.N. 9100 West 74th Street, Box 2923, Shawnee Mission, KS 66201. (913) 676-2000.

SOUTH FULTON HOSPITAL. "Kidd's Corner." 1170 Cleveland Avenue, East Point, GA 30344.

SUNNYVIEW REHABILITATION HOSPITAL. Connelly Bruner-Todt, Humor Program Coordinator, 1270 Belmont Avenue, Schenectady, NY 12308. (518) 382-4576.

PRESBYTERIAN MEDICAL CENTER. Dr. and Mrs. David J. Seel, Box 77, Conju, Korea-52.

UNIVERSITY OF NEW MEXICO HOSPITAL. "HAHAHA Humor Project." Kathy Knight, R.N. Bernalillo County Medical Center, 2211 Lomas Boulevard, NE, Albuquerque, NM 87106. (505) 843-2111.

WEST LAKE HOSPITAL, "Getting Well." Deirdre Davis Brigham, M.S., M.A., M.P.H., director, 589 West State Road 434, Longwood, FL 32750. (407) 260-1900 or 1-800-221-4223.

RECOMMENDED READING

Books

The books selected for this bibliography are for the student of humor and for those who want to gather humorous material to expand their growing collection of jokes and anecdotes.

Although we are proponents of humorous fiction, because of space limitations we have concentrated on material related to the subjects covered in this book. Since libraries and some bookstores have no separate classification for humorous fiction, the quickest way to find it is to ask for recommendations from your librarian or bookstore owner.

Allen, Steve. *How to be Funny*. St. Louis: McGraw-Hill, 1987.

Apte, Mahadev L. *Humor and Laughter: An Anthropological Approach.* Ithaca, NY: Cornell University Press, 1985.

Barreca, Regina. *They Used to Call Me Snow White: Women's Strategic Use of Humor.* New York: Viking, 1991.

Baughman, M. D. *Baughman's Handbook of Humor in Education.* Englewood Cliffs, NJ: Prentice-Hall, Inc., 1974.

Bonham, Tal D. *Humor: God's Gift.* Nashville: Broadman Press, 1988.

Bresler, David E., and Richard Turbo. *Free Yourself From Pain.* New York: Simon and Schuster, 1979. A Wallaby Book (paper), 1981.

Brodnick, Max. *International Joke Book, No. 4.* Norwalk, CT: Leisure Books, 1980.

Byrne, Robert. *One Thousand Nine Hundred Eleven Best Things Anybody Ever Said.* New York: Atheneum, 1984.

Chapman, A. J., and H. C. Foote, eds. *Humor and Laughter: Theory, Research, and Applications.* London: John Wiley & Sons, 1976.

Chase, William D. and Helen M., comps. *Chase's Annual Events: Special Days, Weeks, and Months.* Chicago: Contemporary Books, Inc., annual.

Cohen, Herb. *You Can Negotiate Anything.* New York: Bantam, 1985.

Cole, Ann, Carolyn Haas, Faith Bushnell, and Betty Weinberger. *I Saw a Purple Cow and 100 Other Recipes for Learning.* Boston: Little Brown, 1972. Early learning book for parents and teachers.

——*A Pumpkin in a Pear Tree: Creative Ideas for Twelve Months of Holiday Fun.* Boston: Little Brown, 1976.

Copeland, Lewis and Faye Copeland, eds. *10,000 Jokes, Toasts, and Stories.* Garden City, NY: Doubleday & Co., 1965.

Cote, Richard G. *Holy Mirth: A Theology of Laughter.* Hopedale, MA: Affirmation, 1985.

Cousins, Norman. *Anatomy of an Illness, As Perceived by the Patient: Reflections on Healing and Regeneration.* New York: Bantam, 1983.

——*Head First: The Biology of Hope and the Healing Power of the Human Spirit.* New York: Penguin, 1990.

Cox, Harvey. *Feast of Fools.* New York: Harper & Row, 1969. Describes the tradition and history of humor and clowning in religious ceremony.

Crosbie, John S., ed. Bound copy of past year's newsletters of *The International Save the Pun Foundation.* Box 5040, Station A, Toronto, Ontario, Canada, M5W 1N4.

Dickson, Paul. *New Official Rules: The Book that Answers the Question, "Whatever Happened to Murphy's Law?"* Reading, MA: Addison Wesley, 1990.

Eckert, Allen. *Whattizit? Nature Pun Quizzes.* Dayton, OH: Landfall Press, Inc., 1981.

Esar, Evan. *Esar's Comic Dictionary,* fourth edition. Garden City, NY: Doubleday & Co., 1983.

Everly, Kathleen, and Sol Gordon. *How Can You Tell if You're Really in Love?* Ed-U-Press, Inc., Box 583, Fayetteville, NY, 13066, 1983.

Ewers, Maxine, Sarah Jacobson, Virginia Powers, and Polly McConney, eds. *Humor: The Tonic You Can Afford, a Handbook on Ways of Using Humor in Long Term Care.* Los Angeles: Golden Era Associates, 1983. Write the Ethel Percy Andrus Gerontology Center, University of Southern California, University Park/MC-0191, Los Angeles, CA, 90089-0191.

Fechtner, Leopold. *5000 One and Two Liners for Any and Every Occasion.* Englewood Cliffs, NJ: Prentice-Hall, 1986.

Fine, George. *Sex Jokes and Male Chauvinism.* New York: Citadel Press, 1981.

Fisher, Roger, and William Ury, with Bruce Patton, ed. *Getting to Yes: Negotiating Agreement Without Giving In.* New York: Penguin Books, 1983.

Fisher, Seymour and Rhoda Fisher. *Pretend the World is Funny and Forever: A Psychological Analysis of Comedians, Clowns, and Actors.* Hillsdale, NJ: Lawrence Erlbaum Assoc., 1981.

Freud, Sigmund. *Jokes and Their Relation to the Unconscious.* James Strachey, trans. W. W. Norton and Co., Inc., 1963. Routledge & Kegan Paul, PLC, London.

Fry, William F., Jr. *Sweet Madness: A Study of Humor.* Palo Alto, CA: Pacific Books, 1968.

Fry, William F., Jr., and Waleed A. Salameh, eds. *Handbook of Humor and Psychotherapy: Advances in the Clinical Uses of Humor.* Sarasota, FL: Professional Resource Exchange, Inc., 1987.

Ganz, Margaret. *Humor, Irony and the Realm of Madness: Psychological Studies in Dickens, Butler and Others.* New York: AMS Press, 1990.

Goldstein, Jeffrey H., and Paul E. McGhee. *The Psychology of Humor.* New York: Academic Press, 1972.

Green, Jonathan. *Dictionary of Jargon.* New York: Routledge Chapman and Hall, 1988.

Gruner, Charles R. *Understanding Laughter: The Workings of Wit and Humor.* Chicago: Nelson-Hall, 1978.

Hageseth, Christian, III. *A Laughing Place: The Art and Psychology of Positive Humor in Love and Adversity.* Fort Collins, CO: Berwick Publishing Co., 1988.

Kallen, Horace M. *Liberty, Laughter and Tears: Reflections on the Relations of Comedy and Tragedy to Human Freedom.* Decatur, IL: North Illinois University Press, 1968.

Kaufman, Gloria, ed. *In Stitches: A Patchwork of Feminist Humor and Satire.* Bloomington, IN: Indiana University Press, 1991.

Keller, Daniel. *Humor as Therapy.* Lincoln, NE: Pine Mountain, 1984.

Koller, Marvin R. *Humor and Society: Explorations in the Sociology of Humor.* Houston: Cap and Gown, 1987.

Kuhlman, Thomas L. *Humor and Psychotherapy.* Illinois: Dow Jones-Irwin, 1984.

Lang, H. Jack, ed. *Dear Wit: Letters from the World's Wit.* New York: Prentice-Hall, 1990.

Lefcourt, H. M. *Humor and Life Stress.* New York: Springer-Verlag, 1986.

Legman, G. *No Laughing Matter: An Analysis of Sexual Humor,* 2 vols. Bloomington, IN: Indiana University Press, 1982.

Levine, Jacob, ed. *Motivation in Humor.* New York: Atherton Press, 1969.

MacHovec, Frank J. *Humor: Theory—History—Applications.* Springfield, IL: C.C. Thomas, 1988.

McDougal, Stan, ed. *The World's Greatest Golf Jokes.* Secaucus, NJ: Citadel Press, 1980.

McGhee, Paul. *Humor and Children's Development: A Guide to Practical Applications.* Binghamton, NY: Haworth Press, 1989.

McGhee, Paul, and Jeffrey H. Goldstein, eds. *The Handbook of Humor Research,* vol. I, *Basic Issues.* New York: Springer-Verlag, 1983.

——*The Handbook of Humor Research,* vol. II, Applied Studies. New York: Springer-Verlag, 1983.

Marcuse, F. L. *Humor is no Laughing Matter: Psychology and Wit.* New York: Vantage, 1988.

McGinn, Thomas A., and Nancy Dodd McCann. *Harassed: 100 Women Define Inappropriate Behavior in the Workplace.* Homewood, IL: Business One Irwin, 1992.

Mindess, Harvey. *Laughter and Liberation.* Nash, 1971. Now out of print, but photocopies are available from the author: Antioch University, Los Angeles, 300 Rose Avenue, Venice, CA, 90291.

Mintz, Lawrence E., ed. *Humor in America: A Research Guide to Genres and Topics.* Westport, CT: Greenwood Press, 1988.

Montagu, Ashley. *Growing Young.* New York: McGraw-Hill, 1983.

Moody, Raymond A., Jr. *Laugh After Laugh: The Healing Power of Humor.* Jacksonville, FL: Headwaters Press, 1978.

Morreall, John. *Taking Laughter Seriously.* Albany, NY: State University of New York Press, 1983.

Moyers, Bill. *Healing and the Mind.* New York: Doubleday, 1993.

Nilsen, Don L. F., and Allen Pace Nilsen, eds. *Metaphors Be With You: Humor and Metaphor.* Western Humor and Irony Membership Serial Yearbook, Proceedings of the 1983 WHIM Conference. Tempe, AZ: Arizona State University English Department, 1984.

Novak, William, and Moshe Waldoks, eds. *The Big Book of Jewish Humor.* New York: Harper & Row, 1981.

Orben, Robert. *Twenty-four Hundred Jokes to Brighten Your Speeches.* Garden City, NY: Doubleday & Co., 1984.

——*2000 Sure-fire Jokes for Speakers and Writers.* Garden City, NY: Doubleday & Co., 1986.

Pasta, Elmer. *The Complete Book of Roasts, Boasts, and Toasts.* West Nyack, NY: Parker Publishing Co., 1982.

Paulos, John Allen. *Mathematics and Humor.* Chicago and London: University Of Chicago Press, 1982.

Paulos, John. *I Think, Therefore I Laugh: An Alternative Approach to Philosophy.* New York: Columbia University Press, 1985.

Pendleton, Winston K. *Complete Speaker's Galaxy of Funny Stories, Jokes, and Anecdotes.* Englewood Cliffs, NJ: Prentice Hall, 1986.

——*Handbook of Inspirational and Motivational Stories, Anecdotes and Humor.* Englewood Cliffs, NJ: Prentice Hall, 1986.

Perret, Gene. *Using Humor for Effective Business Speaking.* San Bernardino, CA: Borgo Press, 1989.

——*Comedy Writing Step by Step: How to Write And Sell (Your Sense of) Humor.* 2nd ed. Hollywood, CA: Samuel French Trade, 1990.

Perret, Gene, and Linda Perret. *Gene Perret's Funny Business: Speaker's Treasury of Business Humor for All Occasions.* New York: Prentice Hall, 1990.

Peter, Laurence J., and Bill Dana. *The Laughter Prescription.* New York: Ballantine Books, 1987.

Polhemus, Robert M. *Comic Faith: The Great Tradition from Austen to Joyce.* Chicago: University of Chicago Press, 1980.

Powell, Chris, and George E. Paton, eds. *Humor in Society: Resistance and Control.* New York: St. Martin's, 1988.

Prochnow, Herbert V. *Speakers and Toastmaster's Handbook.* Rocklin, CA: Prima Publishing and Communications, 1990.

Radner, Gilda. *It's Always Something.* New York: Simon & Schuster, 1989.

Richler, Mordecai. *The Best of Modern Humor.* New York: Alfred A. Knopf, Inc., 1983.

Robinson, Vera M. *Humor and the Healing Professions.* Thorofare, NJ: Charles B. Slack, Inc., 1977.

Schutz, Charles E. *Political Humor.* Cranbury, NJ: Fairleigh Dickinson Press, 1976.

Siegel, Bernie, M.D. *Love, Medicine and Miracles.* San Francisco: Harper and Row, 1987.

Sterling, Bryan B. *Best of Will Rogers.* New York: M. Evans & Co., 1990.

Susan, P., and Steven R. Mamchak. *Encyclopedia of School Humor: Icebreakers, Classics, Stories, Puns and Roasts for All Occasions.* Englewood Cliffs, NJ: Prentice-Hall, 1987.

U.S. Congress. Senate. Committee on the Judiciary. *Nomination of Judge Clarence Thomas to be Associate Justice of the Supreme Court of the United States: Hearings before the Committee on the Judiciary, United States Senate,* S.H. 102-1084. 102nd Congress., first session., 1991. (SUDOCS # Y 4. J 89/2—S. Hrg. 102-1084 pt. 4.)

Walker, Nancy. *A Very Serious Thing: Women's Humor and American Culture.* American Culture Series. Minneapolis, MN: University of Minnesota Press, 1988.

Weinstein, Matt, and Joel Goodman. *Playfair.* San Luis Obispo, CA: Impact Publishers, 1980. Noncompetitive games for children of all ages.

Wilde, Larry. *How the Great Comedy Writers Create Laughter.* Chicago: Nelson-Hall, 1976.

Wolfenstein, Martha. *Children's Humor, a Psychological Analysis.* Bloomington, IN: Indiana University Press, 1978.

Ziv, Avner. *Personality and Sense of Humor.* New York: Springer Publishing Company, 1984.

——, ed. *National Styles of Humor.* Contributions to the Study of Popular Culture Series, no. 18. Westport, CT: Greenwood Press, 1988.

Articles

Accent on Living. This magazine for disabled people also has a cartoon book available. Phone for details. Box 700, Bloomington, IL 61702. (309) 378-2961.

Ace, Goodman. "Humor Through Adversity." *Saturday Review,* June 1980.

Adams, W. J. "The Use of Sexual Humor in Teaching Human Sexuality at the University Level." *The Family Coordinator* 23 (1974): 365-68.

"And Now . . . Software with a Sense of Humor." *PC Week* 5, 26 September 1988, 18.

Berger, A. A., "Anatomy Of The Joke." *Journal of Communication* 26 (1976): 113-15.

Birch, Robert L. "Wit and the Emancipators: the Use of Humor to Persuade; the Example of Lincoln and Others." [speech translation] *Vital Speeches* 47 (15 June 1981): 536-8.

Borges, Marilyn A., Patricia A. Barrett, and Janet L. Fox. "Humor Ratings of Sex-stereotyped Jokes As a Function of Gender of Actor and Gender of Rater." *Psychological Reports* 47 (December 1980): 1135-8.

Bradney, P. "The Joking Relationship in Industry." *Human Relations* 10 (1957): 179-87.

Bryant, J., J. S. Crane, P. W. Comisky, and D. Zillmann. "Relationship Between College Teachers' Use of Humor in the Classroom and Students' Evaluations of Their Teachers." *Journal of Educational Psychology* 72 (1980): 511-19.

Bryant, J., J. Gula, and D. Zillman. "Humor in Communication Textbooks." *Communication Education* 29, no. 2 (May 1980).

Buxman, Karyn, R.N., M.S. "The Professional Nurse's Role in Developing a Humor Room in a Health Care Setting." A project presented to the Faculty of the Graduate School, University of Missouri–Columbia, in partial fulfillment of the requirement for the M.S. degree, December 1990.

Cantor, J. and P. Venus. "Effect of Humor on Recall of a Radio Advertisement." *Journal Of Broadcasting* 24 (Winter 1980).

Chance, Sue. "Humor in Psychiatry." *The Psychiatry Times* (September 1986): 25.

Chapman, A. J., and P. Crompton. "Humorous Presentations of Material and Presentations of Humorous Material: A Review of the Humor and Memory Literature and Two Experimental Studies," in M. M. Gruneberg, P. E. Morris, and R. N. Sykes (eds.), *Practical Aspects of Memory*. London: Academic Press, 1978.

Chenfeld, Mimi Brodsky. "My Loose is Tooth: Kidding Around with Kids." *Young Children* (November 1990).

Colwell, Clyde G., and Stanley E. Wigle. "Applicability of Humor in the Reading/ Language Arts Curriculum." *Reading World* 24, no. 2 (December 1984).

Cumming, B. "The Importance of Not Being Earnest." *MD* (May 1981): 33ff.

Damico, Sandra Bowman. "What's So Funny About a Crisis? Clowns in the Classroom." *Contemporary Education* 51, no. 3 (Spring 1980).

Dillon, K., B. Minchoff, and K. Baker. "Positive Emotional States and the Enhancement of the Immune System." *International Journal of Psychiatry in Medicine* 15 (January 1985): 13-17.

Duncan, W. Jack. "Humor in Management: Prospects for Administrative Practice and Research." *The Academy of Management Review* 7, no. 1 (January 1982): 136-42.

Dunn, Donald H., ed. "The Serious Business of Using Jokes in Public Speaking." *Business Week,* 5 September 1983, 93-4.

Erhlich, Howard J. "Observations on Ethnic and Intergroup Humor." *Ethnicity* 6, no. 4 (19 October 1979).

Feigelstein. "Boring Meetings? Put Humor to Work!" *Journal of Staff Development* 8, no. 3 (Fall 1987): 63ff.

Ferguson, S., and J. Campinha-Bacote. "Humor in Nursing." *Journal of Psychosocial Nursing* 27 (April 1989): 29-34.

Fry, William F., Jr. "The Power of Political Humor." *Journal of Popular Culture* 10 (1976): 227-31.

——"The Physiologic Effects of Humor, Mirth, and Laughter." *Journal of the American Medical Association* 267 (4 April 1992): 1857-8.

Fury, Kathleen. "Okay, Ladies, What's the Joke?" *Redbook,* June 1980, 163-66.

Gray, Charlotte. "What Makes Kids Laugh? How They Develop Their Sense of Humor." *Chatelaine* (September 1988): 236.

Green, R. "Magnolias Grow in Dirt: The Bawdy Lore of Southern Women." *Southern Exposure* 4, no. 4 (1977): 29-33.

Gutman, J., and R. F. Priest. "When Is Aggression Funny?" *Journal of Personality and Social Psychology* 12 (1969): 60-65.

Hodge-Cronin and Associates Inc. "Humor in Business" [survey] (April 1986) For details, write Richard J. Cronin, c/o Hodge-Cronin, 9575 West Higgins Road, Rosemont, IL 60018. (312) 692-2041.

"Humor Transcends National Boundaries." *Soviet Life,* December 1988, 62ff.

"Ideas That Work with Young Children: Laughing All the Way." *Young Children* 43, no. 5 (May 1988): 60-73.

"In All Seriousness, Let 'em Laugh: As We Search for Motivators, Let's Not Forget a Simple Smile." [editorial] *Industry Week* (19 February 1990): 5.

Ingrando, D. P. "Sex Differences in Response to Absurd, Aggressive, Pro-Feminist, Sexual, Sexist and Racial Jokes." *Psychological Reports* 46 (April 1980).

Klein, D. M., J. Bryant, and D. Zillmann. "Relationship Between Humor in Introductory Textbooks and Student's Evaluations of the Texts' Appeal and Effectiveness." *Psychological Reports* 50 (1982): 235-41.

Labott, S. and R. Martin. "The Stress-moderating Effects of Weeping and Humor." *Journal of Human Stress* (Winter 1987): 159-64.

Lang, Susan. "Laughing Matters—At Work: Fun Makes People Feel Good and Do Well." *American Health: Fitness of Body and Mind* (September 1988): 46.

"Laughter May Help Reduce Classic Stress Response." *Clinical Psychiatry News* (September 1988).

"The Laughter Prescription (Humor and Wellness)." *Saturday Evening Post,* October 1990, 34.

Lieber, Deborah. "Laughter and Humor in Critical Care." *Dimensions of Critical Care Nursing* 5, no. 3 (May/June 1986): 162-170.

Madden, T. J., and M. G. Weinberger. "Effects of Humor on Attention in Magazine Advertising." *Journal of Advertising* 11, no. 3 (1982): 8-14.

"Make Way for the Laugh Mobile." *Parks and Recreation* (October 1990): 64-7.

Malone, P. B. "Humor: A Double-edged Tool for Today's Managers?" *Academy of Management Review* 5 (1980): 357-60.

McHale, M. "Getting the Joke: Interpreting Humor in Group Therapy." *Journal of Psychosocial Nursing* (September 1989): 24-8.

Neitz, Mary Jo. "Humor, Hierarchy, and the Changing Status of Women." *Psychiatry* (August 1980): 211-23.

"Now, Success is a Laughing Matter." *Business Week,* 8 August 1988, 81.

Olbert, Sharon. "A Prescription for Health." *Elks Magazine,* October 1987, 18-9.

"The Other Funny Thing in the Classroom . . . Kids." *English Journal* 78 (March 1989): 52ff.

"A Pie in the Face (Humor in Environmentalism)." *Alternatives,* June-July 1989, 55ff.

Pinsker, Sanford. "Humor and The Deadly Earnest Business Major." *Business Horizons,* January/February 1982, 40-1.

"The Power of Having Fun." *Design News* (25 March 1991): 400.

Roberts, F. "When Parents Kid Children." *Parents,* June 1980, 94.

Schimel, John L. "The Function of Wit and Humor in Psychoanalysis." *Journal of the American Academy of Psychoanalysis* 6, no. 3 (July 1978).

"Should You Be Funny at Work?" *Working Woman,* March 1991, 74ff.

Simon, J.M. "The Therapeutic Value of Humor in Aging Adults." *Journal of Gerontological Nursing* (August 1988): 9-13.

Stechert, Kathryn. "Can't You Take a Joke?" *Savvy,* June 1986, 36ff.

Tamashiro, R. T. "A Developmental View Of Children's Humor." *Education Digest* 45 (February 1980): 28-31.

Thaler, Mike. "Reading, Writing and Riddling." *Learning,* April/May 1983.

The Toastmaster special issue: "Going After Laughter." (March 1983).

"Unguarded Moments: Why Being Silly is a Life Skill." *Health,* August 1989, 52ff.

Valett, Robert E. "Developing the Sense of Humor and Divergent Thinking." *Academic Therapy* (September 1981): 35-42.

"When is a Joke Not a Joke? Shouts and Swastikas Are Getting the Last Laugh." *Newsweek,* 23 May 1988, 79.

Williams, L. "Treating the Funny Bone." *Time,* 5 November 1990, 17ff.

Yoder, Sharon. "Laughter is Serious Business." *Journal of Education for Business* (April 1989): 326-8.

Zillman, Dolf, Brien R. Williams, Jennings Bryant, Kathleen R. Boynton, and Michelle A. Wolf. "Acquisition of Information from Educational Television Programs as a Function of Differently Paced Humorous Inserts." *Journal Of Educational Psychology* 72, no. 2 (April 1980): 170-80.

Ziv, Avner. "Facilitating Effects of Humor on Creativity." *Journal of Educational Psychology* 68, no. 3 (1976): 318-22.

CHAPTER 1

1 Sigmund Freud, *Jokes and Their Relation to the Unconscious,* James Strachey, trans. (New York: W. W. Norton & Company, Inc., 1960), p. 95. Reprinted by permission of W. W. Norton and Company, Inc., New York, and Routledge and Kegan Paul, PLC, London.

CHAPTER 2

2 Reprinted by permission of Dr. Michael H. Mescon, former Department of Management Chairman of the College of Business Administration, Georgia State University, Atlanta, Georgia.

3 Maxwell Droke, *The Speaker's Handbook of Humor* (New York: Harper and Row, Publishers, Inc., 1956), p. 31. Reprinted by permission of Harper and Row, Publishers, Inc.

CHAPTER 3

4 David P. Campbell, *If I'm In Charge Here Why Is Everybody Laughing?* (Allen, TX: Argus Communications, 1980), p. 41. Reprinted by permission of Argus Communications, a division of DLM, Inc.

5 W. Jack Duncan, Professor of Management, University of Alabama, Birmingham, Alabama.

CHAPTER 5

6 Reprinted by permission of Jesse L. Steinfeld, former president of the Medical College of Georgia. Commencement address to the June, 1984 graduates of Georgia State University, Atlanta, Georgia.

7 Jay S. Harris, compiler and editor, in association with editors of *TV Guide Magazine, TV Guide the First 15 Years* (Radnor, PA: Triangle Publications, 1978), pp. 26-27. Reprinted by permission from *TV Guide Magazine.*

CHAPTER 6

8 George Burns, *Living It Up or, They Still Love Me in Altoona* (New York: Putnam Publishing Group, 1976), p. 80. Copyright 1976 by George Burns. Reprinted by permission of Putnam Publishing Group.

9 *Ibid.*, p. 5

CHAPTER 11

10 Robert E. Valett, "Developing the Sense of Humor and Divergent Thinking," *Academic Therapy* (September 1981), pp. 35-42.

11 *Ibid.*, p. 40.

I

J

K-L

M

N

O

P

Q-R

ABOUT THE AUTHORS

Esther Blumenfeld and Lynne Alpern are former contributing editors to *Business Atlanta* magazine. They conduct workshops on humor at conventions and for businesses and have been featured on numerous radio and television programs in the U.S. and Canada. Their humor awareness course has been offered at Emory University in Atlanta for seven years. They also teach courses in humor writing and have been guest faculty members at several summer writers' conferences. In 1986 Blumenfeld and Alpern were named Georgia Authors of the Year in Humor by the Council of Authors and Journalists.

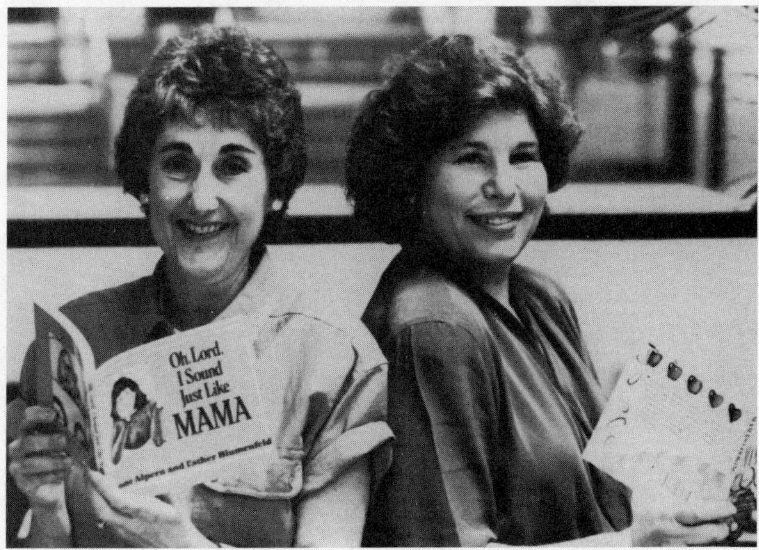

Esther Blumenfeld ***Lynne Alpern***